BREAKDOWN

BREAKDOWN

How America's
Intelligence
Failures Led to
September 11

BILL GERTZ

Since 1947
REGNERY
PUBLISHING, INC.
An Eagle Publishing Company • Washington, DC

Library of Congress Cataloging-in-Publication Data

Gertz, Bill.
    Breakdown : how America's intelligence failures led to September 11 / Bill Gertz.
       p.   cm.
Includes bibliographical references and index.
    ISBN 0-89526-148-0
    1. Intelligence service—United States—Evaluation. 2. World Trade Center Bombing, New York, N.Y., 1993. 3. Bin Laden, Osama, 1957-
4. Qaida (Organization) 5. Terrorism—United States. I. Title.
UB251.U6 G47 2002
973.931—dc21

                          2002008303

Published in the United States by
Regnery Publishing, Inc.
An Eagle Publishing Company
One Massachusetts Avenue, NW
Washington, DC 20001

Visit us at www.regnery.com

Distributed to the trade by
National Book Network
4720-A Boston Way
Lanham, MD 20706

Printed on acid-free paper
Manufactured in the United States of America

10 9 8 7 6 5 4 3 2 1

Books are available in quantity for promotional or premium use. Write to Director of Special Sales, Regnery Publishing, Inc., One Massachusetts Avenue, NW, Washington, DC 20001, for information on discounts and terms or call (202) 216-0600.

To the victims of September 11

CONTENTS

Introduction   *Breakdown* 1

Chapter One   *The Osama File* 7

Chapter Two   *The Loud Bang No One Heard* 21

Chapter Three   *The DIA: Death by Bureaucracy* 39

Chapter Four   *The PCIA—Politically
Correct Intelligence Agency* 53

Chapter Five   *The FBI: The Decline of
Domestic Intelligence* 83

Chapter Six   *Congress and
Destructive Oversight* 105

Chapter Seven   *Technical Spying* 127

Chapter Eight   *Nonsecurity* .139

Conclusion   *The Way Ahead* 157

Appendix A   *The Trace* 171

Appendix B   *The Evidence* 215

Notes 257

Acknowledgments 259

Index 261

I do not believe war the most certain means of enforcing principles. Those peaceable coercions which are in the power of every nation, if undertaken in concert and in time of peace, are more likely to produce the desired effect.

—*Thomas Jefferson, 1801*

BREAKDOWN

ABDUL HAQ WAS TAKING a big risk. He had crossed over the Pakistani border and was deep inside Afghanistan. The sound of U.S. Navy warplanes could be heard in the distance as Haq and a small band of Afghan opposition fighters made their way through eastern Afghanistan.

Days earlier, the United States had unleashed its military might against the Taliban, after President George W. Bush had demanded that the Taliban end its support of terrorism and surrender Saudi militant Osama bin Laden and his al Qaeda terrorist organization who were responsible for the September 11 attacks on the World Trade Center and the Pentagon.

Hobbled by a foot injury dating back to his days with the mujahideen freedom fighters who had defeated the Soviet military occupiers—he had in fact been wounded seventeen times—Haq was a folk hero among the Pashtun tribes in Afghanistan. He also opposed the Taliban, who were responsible for murdering his first wife and child. He had since remarried, and his wife was pregnant.

Haq knew that opposing the Taliban was a deadly business. On September 10, al Qaeda terrorists posing as television news reporters had assassinated the most popular of the Taliban's opponents, Ahmad Shah Masoud. Still, Haq hoped to open up a southern front against the Taliban. In the north, the Northern Alliance, an ill-equipped and poorly trained band of anti-Taliban fighters made up mostly of Tajiks and Uzbeks, was being supplied by the Russians with tanks and armored vehicles. Haq's plan was to defeat the Taliban on the battlefield and then restore Afghanistan's freedom and unity by restoring Afghanistan's king—who was in exile in Italy—to his throne.

In the United States, Haq's representative, Joseph Ritchie, had made the rounds in Washington talking to anyone in the U.S. government who would listen. With minimum investment, Haq could rally the Pashtuns in southern Afghanistan and oust the Taliban, he said. He appealed to Richard Armitage, the new deputy secretary of state. "We have a strategic asset in terms of opening up a southern front. All we need is some help." Ritchie succeeded in getting the support of Robert McFarlane, who had been the national security advisor to former president Ronald Reagan.

McFarlane knew Haq from the Soviet occupation days and valued him as one of the most successful resistance commanders. McFarlane took the initiative in helping connect Haq to the U.S. government.

"We received attentive hearings and encouragement at the departments of State and Defense, as well as the White House," McFarlane recalled. "In each case, however, we were told that the CIA had responsibility for this mission. Unfortunately, the CIA made it clear that it was reluctant to take on the assignment."

The CIA rebuffed appeals from McFarlane and Haq. "We received only dismissive comments and indifference," McFarlane said. "In one astonishing exchange we were told, to paraphrase, 'We don't yet have our marching orders concerning U.S. policy;

it may be that we will end up dealing with the Taliban.' Such an attitude obviously turns the mission of intelligence gathering—to inform policymakers—on its head."

McFarlane was unaware that the CIA had cast its lot with Pakistan's Directorate for Inter-Services Intelligence, known as ISI. The ISI, or elements within the ISI, backed the Taliban and had been backing them for years.

Haq finally gave up trying to get American support and decided to launch operations on his own. On October 21, Haq headed for Jalalabad in eastern Afghanistan. He knew he was under surveillance from Taliban operatives in Peshawar, but he believed he could successfully evade capture and rally the Pashtuns. Four days later the Taliban ambushed him. A call came in from Ritchie's brother in Peshawar. "We need help."

McFarlane called the CIA's operations center, and a Predator unmanned aerial vehicle was dispatched. The drone plane carried Hellfire antitank missiles and attacked a convoy near the ambush site.

Inside Central Command's headquarters, located at McDill Air Force Base outside of Tampa, Florida, an aide to U.S. army general Tommy Franks, commander in chief of the U.S. Central Command, received direct appeals from Haq supporters, including former U.S. special forces, to help the Afghan commander. Central Command refused. "We don't know who he is," came the response. And when that didn't appease the former special forces personnel who pointed out how easy it would be to help Haq, Central Command replied, "We're worried about civilian casualties." The only concession made was to provide U.S. air cover if the Taliban attackers used armored personnel carriers (APCs). But the Taliban didn't use APCs, preferring sport utility vehicles and pickup trucks.

Though Haq was moving quickly over steep mountain trails near Asara and then Sorodi, his Taliban pursuers eventually closed in. On horseback, Haq, with just a handful of guards, was trapped and captured, and, on October 26, he was executed.

Haq was one of the few Pashtuns who could have united the Afghans, and he was gone. Any real hope of a stable Afghanistan died with him.

McFarlane blames the CIA for failing to help Haq and other anti-Taliban fighters in Afghanistan *before* September 11—help that might have prevented Osama bin Laden and his terrorists from carrying out their attacks. Bin Laden had long had American targets in his sights, and Haq was a long-standing, significant opponent of the pro–bin Laden Taliban. But the CIA appeared oblivious to bin Laden's threat and to the opportunity Haq offered to combat it. "The tragedy here is not just the loss of a man of courage and excellence to whom the U.S. owed a great deal, but the dysfunction within the CIA that his loss underscores," McFarlane said. "The calamity is the CIA's failure to engage with him—or with any of the dozens of other capable Afghan commanders—a year earlier and to put in place the coordination that could have avoided his loss. Such planning would also have put us in a position today to work with Haq's fellow Pashtun commanders."

Military operations require good intelligence about the enemy. "Even the best force in the world will fail without solid intelligence," McFarlane said.[1] "The CIA cannot provide it; it has utterly failed to do its job."

America's failure to support Abdul Haq was part of a succession of missed opportunities, undetected—until too late—attacks, and unfortunate surprises that have been a hallmark of U.S. intelligence agencies over the last five decades.

By far the most damaging intelligence failure was the September 11 terrorist strikes on the World Trade Center and the Pentagon. The attacks succeeded despite the most formidable intelligence-gathering system in the world. How the U.S. intelligence community—the Central Intelligence Agency, the Federal Bureau of Investigation, the Defense Intelligence Agency, the National Security Agency, and other agencies known by their three-letter acronyms—missed the September 11 attacks is a story of a system hamstrung by bad politics, poor leadership, and bureaucratic ineptitude. But the most important problem facing U.S. intelligence agencies today is the lack of accountability—the failure to hold people and institutions responsible for the billions of dollars in taxpayer money spent each year on the stated goal of protecting America against just the type of horror that was witnessed so vividly on that fateful day.

The core problem of the CIA was identified by Angelo Codevilla, a longtime intelligence specialist who said the essence of the agency's misguided approach to itself and its mission is captured in the following statement: "We may not always be right. But we are never wrong." Such is the culture that has infused the CIA.

But the fact is, during the days leading up to September 11, the CIA *was* wrong. There were numerous intelligence reports reaching CIA headquarters in Langley, Virginia, that al Qaeda was planning an attack, as they had attacked American targets at least five times in the past five years.

During a hearing in February 2002, Director of Central Intelligence George Tenet ducked responsibility for his agency's failure to respond to these reports. Not only was there no fault in U.S. intelligence for failing to prevent the worst terrorist attack in American history—an attack that claimed more than three thousand victims—but Tenet arrogantly declared that the intelligence system in place was sound. Tenet said he welcomed a review of "our record on terrorism."[2]

But the record, examined apart from the spin and politics, will present a different story. This is a book about how U.S. intelligence failed to detect and prevent the September 11 terrorist attacks, and why. It is a story of how American intelligence has resisted all efforts to reform. The established bureaucracies that make up the U.S. intelligence community have lost sight of their purpose and function. Instead of working to support U.S. defense and national security objectives, they have become wedded to the idea that the institution—not its intended function—is what matters. This book will examine the events of September 11, what was known and what was not known. It is a story of an intelligence bureaucracy that is broken and urgently in need of repair.

THE OSAMA FILE

OSAMA BIN LADEN SAT IN his private office on a farm twenty miles from Khartoum, Sudan. It was November 12, 1995. The thin Saudi millionaire listened intently to the radio near his desk for world news reports. He was preoccupied, nervous, intense. The next day, a senior official of the Sudanese security service paid a visit to the Saudi terrorist leader. Bin Laden appeared tired. At 11:00 A.M. bin Laden and the official left the office, and bin Laden's mood had changed. He was now happy and relaxed. Around noon, on November 13, a telephone call reached the farm. The caller asked to speak to bin Laden and was told he was asleep. The caller insisted he be waked. After taking the call, bin Laden expressed pleasure at the good news. He asked for God's blessing on the caller and remarked: "This is not the first nor the last. The rains starts with one drop, and it soon becomes a downpour. Things will be ready."

Thirty-five minutes later a van exploded outside a three-story building housing the Office of the Program Manager, Saudi Arabia National Guard, in Riyadh, Saudi Arabia. The U.S. Army used the building as its headquarters for training Saudi military personnel. The van had been packed with some 250 pounds of

C-4 plastic explosive. The blast ripped through the building, causing heavy damage and killing seven people, including five Americans. Thirty-five others were injured. The explosion would shake not only the oil-rich kingdom—which, until then, had been immune to terrorism—but also the entire world. It was bin Laden's first deadly attack.

"I think this is just the beginning of a very serious opposition movement to the Saudi royal family," Vincent Cannistraro, the former deputy director of the CIA's Counterterrorism Center, said at the time. "This is not an isolated incident."

President Bill Clinton responded to the attack by saying, "We owe it to them [those killed in the attack] and to all of our citizens to increase our efforts to deter terrorism, to make sure that those responsible for this hideous act are brought to justice, to intensify and pressure the isolation of countries that support terrorism—and we must spare no effort to make sure our own law enforcement officers have what they need to protect our citizens."

After nearly half a century of U.S.-Saudi military cooperation, this was the first terrorist attack on a U.S. military base in the kingdom. It happened on Clinton's watch, and it was the beginning of a string of terrorist attacks by bin Laden and related terrorist groups that left the Clinton administration confused and unable to respond.

Within months, bin Laden struck again. The Khobar Towers barracks in Dhahran housed hundreds of U.S. airmen who took part in flight operations against Iraq. Just before 10:00 P.M. on the night of June 25, 1996, three guards posted on the roof of building 131 at Khobar Towers spotted two men parking a large fuel truck at the edge of a parking lot, eighty feet from the base of the building. The driver and his passenger jumped into a waiting car and sped away.

One of the sentries immediately radioed a warning to the U.S. Air Force's Central Security Control. The guards shouted for people to evacuate the building. In four minutes they were able to alert the top three floors before there was an explosion so loud it could be heard in the neighboring country of Bahrain, twenty miles away. The blast killed nineteen Americans, and hundreds of other American and Saudi military personnel were injured. The bomb inside the truck was estimated by the Pentagon to have been the equivalent of twenty thousand pounds of TNT. It left an eighty-foot crater.

Again, bin Laden was ecstatic about the attack, according to intelligence sources. Bin Laden ordered an assistant to telephone Mohammed al-Masari, a Saudi dissident based in London, who ran the Committee for the Defense of Legitimate Rights. "You remember when the first 'accident' occurred. Now the second has occurred. More is coming." Bin Laden then told Masari, "Let them keep our friend Safar al-Hawali in prison as he will hear good news very soon. We are working on getting him out."

Their friend Safar al-Hawali, a Saudi cleric, had been arrested and jailed by the Saudi government in 1994 for antigovernment activities. He is considered a spiritual godfather to bin Laden and his cohorts. Hawali is part of the extremist Salafi branch of the already extreme sect of Wahhabi Islam. Hawali would be released, and by October 2001, he had become a university lecturer living in Islam's holy city of Mecca and a public critic of President George W. Bush's war on terrorism.

But that was for the future. On the day of the Dhahran bombing, bin Laden received another telephone call. This call was from one of his closest associates in terror, the leader of the Egyptian Islamic Jihad, Ayman al-Zawahiri, who asked about the bombing. Al-Zawahiri offered his congratulations to bin Laden for the successful attack. Then another phone call from bin Laden's terrorist network came in. This time it was from a member of the Palestinian Islamic Jihad, Ashra al-Hadi.

On June 29, four days after the Khobar Towers bombing, bin Laden left Port Sudan on the Red Sea aboard an unmarked jet that was operated by a Sudanese aircrew. He arrived at Khartoum

International Airport and was greeted by Nafi Ali Nafi, an official of the ruling Sudanese National Islamic Front. The greeting was clearly a sign that National Islamic Front leader Hassan Turabi knew that bin Laden was in the country. The aircraft, identified as a G-8, was parked on the military side of the airport. Bin Laden's entourage included several armed bodyguards. There were three Toyota Land Cruisers waiting for them. The vehicles departed the airport and turned west, away from Khartoum to bin Laden's special farm located near Soba, about twenty miles southeast of Khartoum. The compound includes a mosque, a corral for horses and cows, space for administrative officers, and a warehouse.

The information on bin Laden's connection to the terrorist attacks in Saudi Arabia was obtained by the CIA's Counterterrorism Center. The center had been set up in the mid-1980s following several high-profile terrorists attacks. The center's stated objective was to "preempt, disrupt, and defeat terrorists." In reality, the center was created because the CIA had failed to deal effectively with terrorism. As one official put it: "You set up 'centers' when other parts of agencies fail."

By July 1996, the CIA had no one close to bin Laden, even though bin Laden had formed al Qaeda, Arabic for "the base," in 1989, dedicating the group to attacking the United States, its friends, and its interests around the world. The only information the CIA had came from a foreign intelligence service that had been able to penetrate the al Qaeda organization.

"We have no unilateral sources close to bin Laden, nor any reliable way of intercepting his communications," CIA analysts stated in a report on July 1, 1996, that is labeled "TOP SECRET UMBRA." "We must rely on foreign intelligence services to confirm his movements and activities. We have no sources who have supplied reporting on Saudi opposition cells inside Saudi Arabia, and little information about those cells' location, size, composition, or activities."

The statement was a startling admission that U.S. intelligence agencies, despite spending more than $30 billion annually, were totally helpless in tracking down the world's most ruthless terrorist leader and his organization.

The CIA, FBI, and other intelligence agencies had adopted the high-technology approach to gathering information; but these agencies significantly lacked "human intelligence" from people in a position to know the plans and activities of al Qaeda.

By 1996, when bin Laden began launching spectacular and deadly attacks, the U.S. intelligence community was effectively blind, deaf, and dumb. Even the first terrorist attack on the World Trade Center, in 1993, which would later be linked to bin Laden, did not prompt a major intelligence effort to find out what was going on among Islamic terrorist groups.

It is important to look at what U.S. intelligence agencies knew about bin Laden in the mid-1990s, when the first attacks were carried out in Riyadh and Dhahran. In 1996, as the CIA report shows, the CIA had no one even close to bin Laden, and it would be years before the National Security Agency could zero in on his Inmarsat satellite communications. Still, the foreign intelligence service had provided valuable information to the CIA. But the CIA viewed the information as unverified. "Based on a preliminary assessment of the . . . reporting, we can neither confirm nor deny most of the . . . reports," the CIA stated, adding that most of the reporting "fits well" with what is known about bin Laden's operations in the Persian Gulf.[1]

What the CIA did know was that bin Laden was working hard to build up a network of Islamic extremists of many nationalities and was "using his longtime relationship with Iraqi and Sudanese officials," the report said. In December 1995, bin Laden told his supporters not to worry about an arms cache that was found by Kuwaiti Interior Ministry officials in Al Wafrah. "There are others," he told his supporters. The weapons had been stolen from Kuwaiti military stockpiles during the Iraqi occupation. Some of the stolen weapons were later sold in Bosnia by a Kuwaiti businessman. The connection to Iraqi-occupied Kuwait pointed to support for the group from Saddam Hussein. But the CIA would play down these connections to Iraq after September 11, 2001, when the agency insisted it could not confirm links to Baghdad.

But the 1996 CIA report stated plainly: "In August [1995] bin Laden held a meeting at his farm near Khartoum with a probable Iraqi intelligence service official from the Iraqi Embassy in Khartoum, a Sudanese Army officer, an Egyptian extremist, a Palestinian believed to be an explosives expert with experience in car bombs and a man with a Bahraini passport whose family is from the Eastern Province of Saudi Arabia."

There is, moreover, evidence Iran is linked to bin Laden. A CIA report in 1996 stated that bin Laden set up a meeting with Iranian Ministry of Intelligence and Security (MOIS) officials at his residence in Jalalabad, Afghanistan. The meeting showed that the Iranians were considering a relationship with him even though bin Laden's brand of Sunni Muslim extremism differs from Tehran's radical Shiism.

Bin Laden had also traveled to Qatar, on the Persian Gulf, in January 1995 and discussed plans to attack targets in eastern Saudi Arabia during the Muslim rite of Haj. He had shipped twenty tons of the plastic explosive C-4 from Poland. Two tons of it were sent to Saudi Arabia, the rest to Qatar. In addition, he was known to be giving money to Egyptian Islamic Jihad for terrorism against the Egyptian government and would later be linked to attacks on tourists in Egypt.

Beginning in January 1996, the CIA set up a special "station" within the Counterterrorist Center at CIA headquarters, devoted solely to bin Laden. The station was allowed to operate as though it were a CIA field office and was set up because of the growing volume of intelligence reports indicating bin Laden was more than a paymaster of terror—that in fact he had set up worldwide terrorist operations with clandestine cells and linkages to foreign governments.

According to CIA officials, almost all of the analysts who worked at the bin Laden station had never served abroad and did not speak Arabic. Some were Directorate of Operations officers with foreign experience, but most were not. Deskbound and language handicapped as they were, the evidence was unmistakable that bin Laden was a major supporter of terrorism. An intelligence official told me information coming in often pointed to bin Laden. At the time, however, the CIA still wrongly assumed that bin Laden was *primarily* a financier of terrorism rather than a major organizer.

Nevertheless, the links between bin Laden and terrorism proved so serious that in 1998 President Clinton issued a secret executive order known as a "finding" that authorized covert action operations against bin Laden. Unfortunately, the CIA's efforts to track, find, and stop bin Laden—either through military action or arrest and prosecution—were a dismal failure. The problem was that the CIA remained largely ignorant about bin Laden's operations outside of tracing his financial support for terrorism.

In his first interview after leaving the Oval Office, Clinton told *Newsweek* that he had really wanted to get bin Laden. He said he had vacillated in bombing bin Laden when he had the opportunity because of concerns about civilian casualties. "We knew more or less where [bin Laden] would spend the night," Clinton said. "But keep in mind, we were told he was going to be at that training site [in August 1998] and he left a couple of hours before [the missiles hit]. So what did I have? A 40 percent chance of knowing we could have hit it. But there were a very large number of women and children in that compound and it's almost like he was daring me to kill them. And we know at the same time he was training people to kill me. Which was fair enough—I was trying to get him. I felt it would hurt America's interests if we killed a lot of Afghani women and children and didn't even get him."

The other option Clinton tried was sending special operations commandos to go after bin Laden in Afghanistan. "But the closest we could get was about nine hundred miles away on a boat, since we didn't have any basing rights then, and we didn't have anything like the international support that existed after September 11 for overthrowing the Taliban," Clinton said.

What was really lacking was the intelligence and covert operations capability America needed to defend itself and its interests. Spending on efforts to stop terrorism skyrocketed in the 1990s, but it failed to build an intelligence community that could stop bin Laden. Beginning in 1995, $6.7 billion was added to government agencies for counterterrorism. By 2001, federal spending on counterterrorism was $19.5 billion. After September 11, the budget nearly doubled to $37.7 billion. But throwing money into counterterrorism without providing vigorous leadership, policy, and direction will achieve nothing.

In the past, this money was usually spent on new computer systems, analysts, hardware, and, in the FBI, on Chevy Suburbans. What it did not do was prevent the September 11 terrorist attack. Nor, on a lower level, did intelligence operations improve in the years leading up to the attack.

In December 1997, the State Department's Bureau of Intelligence and Research (INR)—one of the "Big Five" intelligence agencies that include the CIA, FBI, Defense Intelligence Agency (DIA), and National Security Agency (NSA)—reported that the evidence of bin Laden's involvement in Middle Eastern terrorist bombings was inconclusive. "His followers may have been involved in at least one of the attacks in Saudi Arabia, although the information available also points in other directions." On the question of whether the bombings were an intelligence failure, the report said: "We were tracking this broader trend and warning that threat levels were increasing, but we were not able to predict the timing and magnitude of specific attacks." Like the CIA, the INR adopted the posture of infallibility on intelligence matters.

"Given that [terrorist] surveillance and activities designed to test our defenses continue, and militants such as Osama bin Laden continue to call for the expulsion of U.S. troops, more attacks in the region are likely," INR stated. The terrorist operations in Saudi Arabia were not capable of fomenting widespread activism or internal disorder, the INR concluded, "nor do they appear able to disrupt the economy or the flow of oil."

In early May 1997, the NSA picked up an important intelligence intercept. A top secret report by NSA's W Group was sent to senior Clinton administration officials on May 7, 1997. It stated that authorities in "an unspecified country" had arrested a senior official of bin Laden's organization. He was the head of the financial committee of bin Laden's "Islamic Army." "The committee manages the Islamic Army's finances and audits members of the Islamic Army," the report stated. The al Qaeda paymaster would prove to be a valuable intelligence source.

Bin Laden, however, soon struck again. On August 7, 1998, at approximately 10:30 A.M. local time, truck bombs exploded in front of American embassies in Nairobi, Kenya, and Dar es Salaam, Tanzania. The bombings killed 220 people and wounded more than four thousand others. Twelve American government employees and family members, and thirty-two Kenyan and eight Tanzanian nationals employed by the government were among the dead. "The bombings were carried out by members and associates of Osama bin Laden's organization, known by the Arabic word 'al-Qaeda'," the FBI stated in an internal summary of the attack.

A State Department report released in January 1999 on the bombings found that there was "no credible intelligence" in advance of the attack that would have provided immediate or tactical warning of the blasts. "A number of earlier intelligence reports cited alleged threats against several U.S. diplomatic and other targets, including the embassies in Nairobi and Dar Es Salaam," the report by a panel of experts led by retired admiral William Crowe states. The report concluded:

> All of these reports were disseminated to the intelligence community and to appropriate posts abroad, but were largely discounted because of doubts about the sources. Other reporting—while taken seriously—was imprecise, changing and non-specific as to dates, diminishing its usefulness. Additionally, actions taken by intelligence and law enforcement authorities to confront suspect terrorist groups, including the Al-Haramayn nongovernmental organization and the Osama Bin Laden (UBL) organization in Nairobi, were believed to have dissipated the alleged threats. Indeed, for eight months prior to the August 7 bombings, no further intelligence was produced to warn the embassies in Nairobi and Dar Es Salaam.

It was more no-fault intelligence. The FBI was let off the hook by the State Department panel for the failure to stop the bombing. It said that the FBI "uncovered no information indicating that the earlier intelligence reporting could have predicted the time or place of the attacks." The panel report revealed that the State Department did not have a representative at what was supposed to be an interagency Counterterrorism Center, a center that since 1997 had known about terrorists operating in Kenya. "The FBI and the Department of State should consult on ways to improve information sharing on international terrorism to ensure that all relevant information that might have some bearing on threats against or security for U.S. missions or personnel abroad is made available," the report said.

The FBI had in hand at least two intelligence warnings in 1997 about terrorist attacks in Africa. One was based on an FBI intelligence breakthrough in August 1997—a year before the embassy bombings. Working with local authorities in Nairobi, FBI agents raided the home of Wadih el-Hage, a Lebanese-born Islamic militant who was a U.S. citizen. On a computer found in the residence, the FBI discovered a letter from an Islamic militant named Haroun Fazul, who was part of a clandestine "cell" of al Qaeda terrorists operating in East Africa who were in the process of planning the bombings that would be carried out a year later.

Fazul had written to "Brother Sharif," another terrorist who was part of the East Africa cell, to warn that the security of their operation had been endangered by the arrest of the al Qaeda paymaster. "We can now state that the security position on the cell is at 100 percent danger," Fazul wrote. He spoke of communicating by the Internet and of going "underground" because of efforts by U.S., Kenyan, and Egyptian intelligence and security services pursuing them. Fazul indicated that "the sheikh," an alias used by bin Laden, had declared war on the United States and they were part of a cell that was preparing to carry out a terrorist attack. "We, the East Africa cell members, do not want to know about the operations plans since we are just implementers," he said. "We trust our command and appreciate their work and know that they have a lot of problems," he wrote.

Incredibly, this invaluable intelligence was never put to use. The failure cost hundreds of lives.

President Clinton's response to the African bombings was anemic. The administration's primary goal here, as always, was to identify terrorists, capture them, and return them for prosecution in a court of law. It was a reactive strategy that did nothing to deter attacks. Even the administration's extremely limited military counterstrikes were designed to send political signals rather than do actual damage to terrorists, their supporters, and the infrastructure they used.

The Clinton approach was illustrated in 1996 when the Justice Department convened a grand jury in New York to investigate bin Laden. The investigation would actually hinder FBI intelligence-gathering efforts because, if information was deemed grand jury material, intelligence people couldn't use it.

When military action was finally taken against bin Laden, it proved to be ineffective and even counterproductive. On August 20, 1998, U.S. warships in the Indian Ocean and Persian Gulf fired a series of cruise missiles at four terrorist training camps located about ninety-four miles south of Kabul, the Afghan capital. As a supposed exclamation point, the military was also ordered to bomb a factory in the Sudan that U.S. intelligence claimed was making a precursor chemical unique to the VX nerve agent.

The bombing of the terrorist training camps was carried out even though bin Laden was known to have left the area. Worse, Defense Secretary William Cohen stated that bin Laden was *not* a target. Instead, the strikes "were targeting these facilities and his infrastructure." General Hugh Shelton, then chairman of the Joint Chiefs of Staff, said, "We were not going directly after Osama bin Laden. It was an attack on his network of terrorist groups, as I think you can see from the targets. We will continue to go after that if we feel like it's appropriate and if the threats to Americans or American interests continue." A senior intelligence official who briefed reporters at the Pentagon on background also said that although there was intelligence indicating more terrorists would be in the camps during the attack than on other days, bin Laden was not targeted. "We targeted these facilities not to go after an individual; we went after his infrastructure. We don't know where bin Laden is. I have no information in that regard." Failing to go after bin Laden—preferring to blow up buildings instead— betrayed a lack of seriousness by the administration.

So did the attack on the Sudanese pharmaceutical factory that was supposedly making nerve gas for bin Laden. A day before the attacks, George Tenet, director of Central Intelligence, took part in a video conference that included Rear Admiral Thomas Wilson, the Joint Staff senior intelligence official known as the J-2.

"We don't have the evidence that that factory is involved in producing nerve agent," Wilson said during the secret video meeting.

"You will make it a target," ordered Tenet.

The CIA later claimed that the factory was targeted by demand of White House National Security Council staff, specifically Richard Clarke, its specialist on terrorism. This rash action embarrassed the State Department, which ended up paying damages to the Sudanese owner of the factory.

All this was a diversion from the fact that the U.S. government had failed to target a man known to be a leader of global terrorism, who was implicated in strikes on American personnel and property, and who, in February 1998, had publicly declared that "To kill Americans and their allies, both civil and military, is an individual duty of every Muslim who is able, [in] any country where this is possible, until the Aqsa Mosque [in Jerusalem] and the Haram Mosque [in Mecca] are freed from their grip and until their armies, shattered and broken-winged, depart from all the lands of Islam, [and are] incapable of threatening any Muslim. . . . By God's leave we call on every Muslim who believes in God and hopes for reward to obey God's command to kill the Americans and plunder their possessions where he finds them and whenever he can."

Rather than target bin Laden militarily, the Clinton legalistic approach worked its way forward. On November 4, 1998, a federal grand jury indicted bin Laden, charging him with conspiring to kill Americans abroad. The indictment is still pending.

2

THE LOUD BANG NO ONE HEARD

AT ABOUT 10:30 ON THE NIGHT of January 6, 1995, a security guard at the Dona Josefa apartment building on Manila's Quirino Avenue was told that black smoke was billowing from the building. He ran upstairs and saw two men trying to wave the smoke out of the sixth floor hallway.

"Don't worry," one of them told the security guard, "it was just some firecrackers."

The guard entered Apartment 603 and saw the fire expiring. When he went outside, both men were gone.

A team of firemen soon arrived, followed by officers from the Philippine National Police. Leading the police was Aida Farsical, police block commander responsible for that part of Manila. The police found pipe bombs and components—including chemicals and laboratory equipment—for making explosives.

While the police were looking through the apartment, one of the tenants returned. He was Abdul Hakim Murad, a Pakistani national, member of a secret cell of terrorists belonging to al Qaeda, and the mixer of the chemicals. Murad offered the police $2,000 in cash not to take him to police headquarters, but the police turned him down.

By 2:30 A.M. senior Philippine police officials were on the scene. Chief Inspector Nap Taas, who was in charge of intelligence for the police, confiscated a Toshiba computer. It held an amazing series of documents. One document revealed that the International Relations and Information Center, a nongovernmental organization operating in the Philippines, was a front to fund al Qaeda activities. Its leader was Mohammed Jamal Khalifa, a Filipino Muslim and brother-in-law of Osama bin Laden.

More shocking was a document that outlined a plot to assassinate Pope John Paul II during his visit to the Philippines, a visit that was only a week away. Murad's apartment was two hundred yards from the residence of the Vatican's ambassador to the Philippines, which was where the pope would be staying. The terrorists planned a suicide mission, dressing one of their number as a priest and getting close enough to the pope to set off a homemade chemical bomb that would kill the disguised terrorist and the pope.

More information: Murad's roommate turned out to have been Ramzi Yousef, the mastermind behind the 1993 terrorist bombing of the World Trade Center. Yousef walked away from the apartment before police could arrest him, but was apprehended in Pakistan on February 7, 1995, and a day later shipped to the United States to stand trial on charges related to the 1993 bombing.

The police used Rafael Garcia, a Philippine computer expert, to crack the coded information found on Yousef's computer hard drives. "This is where we found most of the evidence of the projects that were being funded by Osama bin Laden in the Philippines," Garcia said.

Another plot revealed on the computer was a major terrorist campaign against U.S. airliners. It was called Project Bojinka, which means "loud bang" in Serbo-Croatian. The plans called for planting small explosive devices on eleven American jetliners flying from Asia to the United States.

Yousef had designed small bombs operated by nine-volt batteries. The batteries would be concealed in the hollowed-out
heels of a terrorist's shoes. The bomb itself was designed to pass
undetected through airport screening machines. The plan was
for eleven airliners to explode simultaneously after the terrorists
changed shoes during stopovers and left the bomb shoes
beneath their seats. It was to have been Ramzi Yousef's terrorist
spectacular.

Yousef carried out several attacks in 1994. The deadliest was a
bomb planted on a Philippine Airlines flight to Japan on December 11, 1994, which killed a Japanese passenger. The bombing
was a test mission to see if the small explosive had enough power
to bring down the aircraft. It did not. The jet managed to land on
Okinawa.

The Philippine authorities also learned that the terrorists were
planning to fly explosives-laden aircraft into CIA headquarters.

And Murad was a pilot. He had taken flying lessons.

According to a report by the Special Investigative Group-Intelligence Command, known as SIG-IC, the documents found on
the laptop were analyzed on January 8, 1995, and in them it was
found that: "A future bombing target to be executed by [Murad]
is principally directed on CIA headquarters in Langley, Virginia."
The report said that Murad's plot involved an explosives-packed
commercial plane. "The document specifically cited the charter
service of a commercial-type aircraft loaded with powerful
bombs to be dive-crashed by [Murad]. This is apparently
intended to demonstrate to the whole world that a Muslim martyr is ready and determined to die for the glorification of Islam.
There are no other details on this specific suicide plan."

The Philippine police interrogated Murad again on April 10,
1995. He said he had discussed the suicide airline bombing with
Yousef, and he disclosed that the plan also called for bombing a
U.S. nuclear power station. "The plan to attack a U.S. nuclear

station was discussed in Qetta [Pakistan] in October 1994," the debriefing report states, "while the idea of attacking the CIA headquarters was discussed in the Philippines in December 1994 as conceptualized by Murad."

Another Filipino intelligence report, bearing the title "Significant Revelation of Abdul Hakim Al Hashim Murad," lays out in stark detail the scope of the terrorist conspiracy between Yousef and Murad. The report states that Murad "is a member of the 'Liberation Army' which is committed to fight against the United States and Israel governments." Yousef and Murad, the report continues, planned, as part of their extensive campaign of terror, "to plant a bomb on a United Airlines plane with a bomb set to explode during its route from Los Angeles to Singapore."

By September 11, 2001, the plan had become even more grandiose. "Obviously, the original Project Bojinka was modified to give it a more significant impact on the U.S.A.," Garcia said. "By hijacking planes that originated from within the United States instead of Asia, they made sure that *Americans* would be killed in the hijacking instead of Asians, which obviously would elicit a stronger reaction from the Americans."

Murad told investigators that his terrorist cell had been taking flying lessons in the Philippines for Project Bojinka. "Obviously, after they were caught and convicted, a new set of terrorists were trained in the United States for the modified Bojinka," Garcia said.

"Murad admitted when he was being questioned that he was being trained for a suicide mission," former Manila police chief Avelino Razon said in a statement I obtained. "We were able to find out that they had some targets already." Razon said U.S. intelligence and law enforcement authorities knew about Project Bojinka. He also said the terrorists had vowed to try attacking the Trade Center towers again. "I remember that after the first World Trade Center bombing Osama bin Laden made a statement that on the second attempt they would be successful," Razon said.

According to U.S. officials, the information from Murad was sent to CIA headquarters. But the CIA failed to share the information with the FBI. Instead, Filipino officials, recognizing the importance of their information, alerted the FBI. "We shared that with the FBI," said Robert Delfin, chief of intelligence command for the Philippine National Police. But the American authorities might not have realized the value of the information provided by the police, he added.

Somehow it did not set off alarm bells among American authorities when Murad disclosed that he had attended several flight schools in the United States—in New York, Texas, California, and North Carolina—as part of an effort to obtain a commercial pilot's license.

U.S. law enforcement officials said their investigators focused mostly on the Bojinka plot and not on other leads provided by Murad. Why? One reason might be that the FBI was not well enough equipped to deal with the international nature of the conspirators. The 1993 World Trade Center bombing highlighted this weakness.

Former FBI special agent Bob Blitzer was assistant section chief of the Counterterrorism and Middle East Section of the FBI from 1991 to 1995. "During the investigation [of the 1993 World Trade Center bombing and the subsequently foiled plot to bomb landmarks and tunnels in New York], a significant amount of new information came to our attention," Blitzer told me. "Much of it made sense during these criminal investigations. We conducted searches, secured evidence, made arrests, and obtained convictions. Other pieces of information made no sense to us, and we tried to figure out what was the meaning with the people we had.

"In the aftermath of the bombing, we were seeing people that we had never seen before," Blitzer recalled. "So many, many new people came on our radar screen. Several countries such as Pakistan, the Republic of the Philippines, and Malaysia also became important because some of our fugitives went there in the aftermath of the first World Trade Center bombing and the new plots to attack U.S. interests developed post-1993. So we're literally seeing snippets of terrorist activities and movements of individual terrorists all over the world. But we did not have the depth of information, or intelligence base, to understand what these activities and movements were all about.

"We worked extremely hard here at home using the FBI resources at our disposal, and with the Central Intelligence Agency and friendly foreign police and intelligence services to find answers," Blitzer said. "However, as a general statement these other agencies were, for the most part, in the same mode we were in. They were all trying to retool and collect, analyze and understand, critical intelligence information."

Blitzer told me the results of interviews of Murad and others in the Philippines were shared within law enforcement and intelligence communities. "However, nothing we had then indicated either an imminent attack or defined the long-term threat picture," he said.

The FBI's World Trade Center investigations led them to focus on mosques in the New York area. "With the exception of, I believe, one guy in the cell, they had all been recruited in mosques in the greater New York area that were under the control of the sheikh Rahman and his associates. They were trained; they did their jihad against the Russians in Afghanistan; and then came back into the United States, prior to the 1993 World Trade Center bombing," Blitzer said.

"Ramzi Yousef was clearly the leader of the group that bombed the World Trade Center in 1993," Blitzer told me. "But who was he working for? Was he working for some terrorist organization? I really felt deep down that somebody was pulling the strings. Somebody was doing the preoperational planning. Some organization was out there working against the United

States both here and abroad. It was difficult for me to believe that Yousef could come to the United States, put a group together in a short period of time, hold it together, plan a major attack in the heart of New York, and then escape, without some kind of organization behind him," he said. Bin Laden's name had come up, but only as a possible source of financial support.

Blitzer said he did not recall hearing about a major plot, part of Project Bojinka, to use commercial aircraft as missiles against U.S. buildings. "Here's what I recall," Blitzer said. "One of the guys, I think Murad during debriefings, indicated that he had it in his head to personally fly a small plane loaded with fuel or explosives into CIA headquarters in Langley. I remember that. I don't ever remember seeing anything about Yousef talking about that, or any other members of his cell saying, 'We're working on trying to put plans together to use passenger aircraft as bombs.' I remember this one guy talking about the small plane attack, but that was it."

But the information was there. It had been given to the United States by the Philippine government.

■ ■ ■

Even before the Bojinka intelligence break, intelligence information on al Qaeda terrorists was missed. One example is the case of El Sayyid Nosair, an Egyptian-American Islamicist, who was arrested in 1992 for the 1990 assassination of Rabbi Mehir Kahane.

"It was thought to be an isolated incident," said Michael Cherkasky, head of the Kahane investigation for the Manhattan district attorney's office. "There was a man, you have a gun, and that's how it was prosecuted."

The FBI, however, uncovered a bigger plot than the assassination of Kahane. FBI investigators discovered that Nosair had bomb-making instructions and photographs of New York City landmarks, including the World Trade Center. Much of the material, handwritten in Arabic, was left sitting in boxes, untranslated for years, dismissed as unnecessary to the prosecution. One reason for this was that the FBI, as late as 1998, had only two Arabic speakers who could translate documents written in Arabic. This left stacks of telephone intercepts of Islamic terror suspects sitting useless, and it was obviously one of the most serious intelligence shortcomings of the FBI.

"Obviously, both the FBI and the CIA would have been very well advised much earlier to have trained, or retrained, or hired a much larger group of people who spoke Arabic, Farsi, and some of these languages of the Mideast," said R. James Woolsey, who was director of Central Intelligence during the Clinton administration.

And there were other missed opportunities. In 1996, Mansour Ijaz, an American-Muslim businessman, traveled to Sudan and met with senior Sudanese intelligence officials who were anxious to make a friendly overture to the United States. The Sudanese wanted to turn over intelligence files on Osama bin Laden so that their country would no longer be listed by the United States as a state sponsor of terrorism—a status that comes with stiff economic sanctions, including sanctions that prohibit U.S. companies from doing business in those countries.

Ijaz said he advised the Sudanese to make a direct appeal to the United States government. A letter was sent to President Clinton from a powerful Sudanese political leader, Hassan Turabi. The letter offered to allow a team of FBI agents to come to Khartoum and examine Sudan's intelligence files on bin Laden.

"There was no response," Ijaz says.

Ijaz told the Clinton administration that Sudan's president also offered to arrest bin Laden and supply intelligence about the operations of other terrorist groups. Ijaz says the terrorist networks included two of the hijackers who flew airliners into the World Trade Center on September 11.

"The silence of the Clinton administration in responding to these offers was deafening," Ijaz says.

Clinton officials, including National Security Advisor Samuel Berger and Susan Rice, an aide responsible for national security policy on Africa, dismissed Ijaz's claim. They said the Sudanese government did not offer real intelligence on bin Laden's networks. "We wanted names. We wanted bank accounts. We wanted paper. We wanted the bodies themselves, the individuals to interview," Rice said. "And none of that was forthcoming."

The offer of Sudanese assistance evaporated in August 1998 when President Clinton ordered U.S. military forces to destroy the pharmaceutical plant in Sudan that was suspected of being a chemical arms factory. The only problem was that later evidence showed that the plant was probably *not* an arms factory. So the Clinton administration turned down an official government offer of cooperation against terrorism in favor of bombing an apparently harmless pharmaceutical plant. Intelligence assessment was not a Clinton administration strong point.

And neither was intelligence gathering, because in the early 1990s, the Clinton administration, through Attorney General Janet Reno, made it harder for law enforcement and intelligence agencies to get access to information.

John L. Martin, a career Justice Department official who spent decades prosecuting spies, believes the Clinton administration is partly to blame for the FBI failures related to September 11. In 1994, the Justice Department adopted new rules that prohibited the FBI, or the CIA, from contacting prosecutors in the Internal Security Section of the Justice Department. "It was all about turf," Martin told me. Richard Scruggs, the head of the Justice Department's Office of Intelligence Policy Review, wanted to control what the FBI was doing in the intelligence arena. As part of the administration's politicization of the Justice Department, Reno and Scruggs had tried—but failed, because of congressional opposition—to shut down Martin and the Internal Security Division. "It was based on a liberal philosophical outlook and an anti-intelligence bias," Martin recalled.

In a critical report on Reno's and FBI director Louis Freeh's handling of the botched espionage investigation of Los Alamos scientist Wen Ho Lee, prosecutor Randy Bellows severely criticized Justice Department practices on intelligence. He wrote that the self-imposed restrictions were a misreading of the law and unnecessary. According to Bellows, the Foreign Intelligence Surveillance Act (FISA), the legal underpinning of electronic surveillance of spies and terrorists, did not prohibit the use of FISA-gathered material for law enforcement purposes. Bellows found that Reno and Freeh had consistently and conveniently overlooked those provisions of the FISA that allowed using electronic intercepts for law enforcement activities. Janet Reno's rules—which remained in place after George W. Bush was sworn in as president—would have a devastating impact, including on what happened on September 11, 2001.

■■■

On August 15, 2001, an employee of the Pan Am Flight Academy in Eagan, Minnesota, called the FBI in Minneapolis with suspicions about one of the school's foreign students, Zacarias Moussaoui. Suspicions were raised because Moussaoui would not talk about his background, had paid in cash for the $8,000 training fee, and was learning to graduate from flying single-engine Cessnas to a Boeing 747 commercial airliner—a system which far exceeded his training as a small aircraft pilot. Moussaoui also showed an unusual interest in an instructor's comment that airplane cabin doors could not be opened during flight. Most alarming, Moussaoui was only interested in learning how to take off and land a 747. FBI assistant director Dale Watson told a Senate hearing that Moussaoui had "expressed strong interest in 'piloting' a simulated flight from London's Heathrow Airport to John F. Kennedy Airport in New York." The program manager suspected that Moussaoui was a potential hijacker. Later on August 15, FBI special agent Dave Rapp and an agent from the Immigration and Naturalization Service stopped Moussaoui as he was leaving the Residence Inn. Rapp, a trained fighter pilot, questioned Moussaoui as the Middle Easterner was heading to take his first ride in a 747 flight simulator.

Moussaoui claimed he had been granted an extension of his visa beyond its May 23, 2001, deadline. He accused the agents of harassment, singling him out because he was a foreigner. "You wouldn't be doing this if I was an American," Moussaoui told the agents. He was a businessman, he said. "I just want to learn how to fly a big plane."

FBI investigators wanted to get a criminal search warrant to inspect Moussaoui's laptop computer, but headquarters refused the request because there was no "probable cause" foundation that a crime had been committed.

FBI agent Coleen Rowley wrote a critical letter to FBI director Robert S. Mueller III stating that senior FBI officials put up a bureaucratic "roadblock" that hampered the investigation of Moussaoui before September 11. Rowley stated in the thirteen-page missive of May 21, 2002, that Minneapolis FBI agents were so frustrated by FBI headquarters' failure to respond to the case they tried to bypass the chain of command and notify the CIA. They were reprimanded as a result. The agents actually joked that headquarters must have been penetrated by an al Qaeda "mole" who was thwarting efforts to go after bin Laden and his cohorts.

"When, in a desperate 11th hour measure to bypass the FBIHQ roadblock, the Minneapolis Division undertook to directly notify the CIA's Counter Terrorist Center (CTC), FBIHQ personnel actually chastised the Minneapolis agents for making the direct notification without their approval," she said.

Senior officials in Washington derailed the agents' efforts to obtain a Foreign Intelligence Surveillance Act search warrant for Moussaoui's computer. The agents already had intelligence information indicating Moussaoui was tied to other terrorism suspects. "There was a great deal of frustration expressed on the part of the Minneapolis office toward what they viewed as a less than aggressive attitude from headquarters," Rowley wrote. "The bottom line is that headquarters was the problem."

Evidence obtained on Moussaoui's computer after September 11 included information that could have related to suicide attacks. Also, if the Moussaoui case had been handled differently, other hijackers involved in the September 11 plot, who did not know he had been arrested, might have contacted him by telephone, and surveillance could have led authorities to other terrorists.

Assistant FBI director David Szady, who is in charge of all FBI counterintelligence, said the passage into law in October 2001 of the USA Patriot Act, helped agents solve problems with the Justice Department, which had turned down important requests for electronic surveillance under the Foreign Intelligence Surveillance Act. The new law made it easier to obtain court permission for wiretaps or searches. It changed the standard needed for approval for wiretaps from being the "sole or main purpose" of gathering foreign intelligence information to the less strict "significant purpose."

"That helps a lot," Szady told me. The new law will make it easier for FBI criminal investigators and counterspies to work together and will prevent the Justice Department from turning down vital requests as in the past, he said.

Even without this change in the law, John L. Martin, the former Justice Department official, believes that if the FBI had gone to the career lawyers in the terrorism section, computer crimes section, or the Internal Security Section of the Criminal Division in the Justice Department, they would have been advised to go after the laptop, on any number of legal grounds. "They could have sat down with all the agents and pulled together all the relevant facts—not excluding the possibility that they could have gotten Moussaoui's consent" to search the laptop, Martin said.

Janet Reno's new rules precluded that kind of cooperation.

By August 23, less than three weeks before the World Trade Center and Pentagon attacks, the FBI was told by French intelligence that Moussaoui was linked to Islamic rebels in Chechnya. And these rebels were linked to Osama bin Laden and the Taliban militia in Afghanistan. But the connection was not enough for the FBI to pursue the investigation of Moussaoui as a foreign counterintelligence probe. Such a probe would have given them the warrant needed to do a detailed search and surveillance.

Instead, the FBI planned to deport Moussaoui to his native France, where the domestic intelligence service, DST, would have the authority to search the laptop. September 11 scrapped that plan. After the tragedy had occurred, the search warrant for the computer was finally obtained.

The computer held, among other information, a commercially available flight simulation program, data on wind currents, and information about jetliners and crop-dusting airplanes. The crop-dusting information was alarming—and led to the grounding of all crop-dusting aircraft for a time after September 11, to forestall the possible spread of chemical or biological weapons.

Moussaoui eventually would be charged with conspiracy in the September 11 attacks, the only person to face such charges. The FBI defended its handling of the case. "There was nothing in that computer that we would have been able to use to link him to terrorists, or to predict what happened on 9-11," one U.S. official told the *Washington Post* anonymously. "We just didn't have it."

One reason they "didn't have it" is because the FBI is a law enforcement agency with a domestic security mission, and law enforcement and intelligence are two very different functions.

The role of gathering intelligence on terrorism is the job of the CIA Counterterrorism Center, a special interagency group set up in the 1980s.

The center, according to a CIA statement, collects and analyzes strategic intelligence on terrorist groups and state sponsors of terrorism. But the CIA center is not really an intelligence center, because by its own definition the CIA views terrorism as "a crime" and thus acts to "apprehend and punish perpetrators worldwide."

As part of the center's responsibility it "endeavors to know all there is to know about the capabilities of terrorist elements and their sources of support and likely targets." It also provides "detailed" intelligence to policymakers and has a "warning function"—to immediately disseminate information warning of a coming terrorist attack.

In reality, the Counterterrorism Center has become a cumbersome bureaucratic tool whose effectiveness was questioned after September 11, when the CIA added personnel to the unit.

The center was the brainchild of CIA officer Duane "Dewey" Clarridge, who once said penetrating terrorist groups was nearly impossible because the groups were too tightly knit and did not allow people to join who were not trusted. Clarridge, according to former CIA officer Reuel Marc Gerecht, converted a three-man operation—sitting in a single room at CIA headquarters with a television set that monitored CNN—into a center with hundreds of analysts and action officers.

Gerecht said the center failed to make the CIA aggressive in pursuing terrorists overseas. Instead it spent most of its time in bureaucratic fights with the Directorate of Operations, the espionage branch, and particularly the Near East Division. "In my years inside the CIA, I never once heard case officers overseas or back at headquarters discuss the ABCs of a recruitment operation against any Middle Eastern target that took a case officer far off the diplomatic and business-conference circuits," Gerecht said. "Long-term seeding operations simply didn't occur."

The center is not a serious effort. It has even produced a logo called "Terrorist Busters" modeled on the Hollywood film *Ghostbusters*. It shows a black-clad terrorist holding an AK-47 rifle inside a red circle with a line through it.

The CIA noted in its statement on the Counterterrorism Center that relations between the center and the FBI "evolved" until 1996 when senior officers were exchanged between the two agencies "to help manage the counterterrorist offices at both agencies."

Despite rivalries and divided responsibilities, both the CIA and the FBI insist they share all relevant information on international terrorism.

J. T. Caruso, deputy assistant director of the FBI's counterterrorism division, told the House Intelligence Committee on October 3, 2001, that "media reports" that the FBI had advance warnings, dating back to 1995, of a plot to hijack U.S. airliners were untrue. "The FBI had no warnings about any hijack plots," Caruso said. "There was a widely publicized 1995 conspiracy in the Philippines to remotely blow up eleven U.S. airliners over the Pacific Ocean, but that plot was disrupted. As is the practice, information obtained during that investigation was widely disseminated, even internationally, and thoroughly analyzed by multiple agencies. It does not connect to the current case."

Several months after Caruso testified, the FBI was playing a different tune. FBI Director Robert Mueller testified before the Senate Judiciary Committee that there was other information in addition to the 1995 information from Murad. An FBI pilot in 1998 reported that he had seen several people from Middle Eastern countries "who appeared to be either using planes or obtaining flight training...that could be used for terrorist purposes," Mueller said. The information never left the FBI's Oklahoma City field office, where the pilot was working.

"There are things that we could have done better beforehand," Mueller said. "And, I think on each occasion that I have appeared before this committee I've indicated there are things that we should have done differently to assure that pieces of information were followed up on in ways that they should have been followed up on, and ways that we are now following up on them." Still, Mueller testified that he did not believe the FBI could have stopped the attacks. If these pieces of information had been shared and disseminated properly, could September 11 have been disrupted? "Well, I do not believe that it is likely that it would have," Mueller said.

The origins of September 11 were traced to the Manila cell by Mueller, who identified Kuwaiti-born Khalid Shaikh Mohammed as a terrorist leader. "I think we're confident that he was one of the key figures" in the September 11 attacks, Mueller told the *Washington Post*. Mohammed is related to Ramzi Yousef, the key figure in the 1993 World Trade Center attack.

Even with this history and linking threads, the FBI and the CIA say that no one could have predicted September 11. But Paul Monk, a former Australian defense intelligence specialist, views the attacks as an intelligence failure with remarkable parallels to the United States' failure to anticipate the Japanese attack on Pearl Harbor on December 7, 1941. Monk, who is senior fellow at the Australian Thinking Skills Institute (www.austhink.org) wrote in early November 2001 that the six decades between Pearl Harbor and September 11 were "littered with intelligence failures" of a less spectacular kind.

After expenditures of hundreds of billions of dollars spent since 1945 expressly to avoid future Pearl Harbors, the United States intelligence system remains prone to fundamental errors. The September 11 attacks, like the Pearl Harbor attack, were foreseeable, had intelligence analysts put together the information that was available in the public domain as early as 1996, Monk argues. The failure of U.S. intelligence agencies to do so shows the need for sustained review of analytical practices in the intelligence and policy system, he told me in a recent interview. Unfortunately, he added, the signs are not promising that such a review will take place.

Bottom line: There was a failure within the American intelligence community to think the unthinkable; there was a failure to think that a major terrorist strike against the United States was possible.

One government report that tried to highlight the danger was actually dampened. In 1995, the Pentagon released a report called "Terror 2000: The Future Face of Terrorism," which warned that "superterrorists" could target the United States.

"Tomorrow's most dangerous terrorists will be motivated not by political ideology but by fierce ethnic and religious hatreds. Their goal will not be political control but utter destruction of their chosen enemies. Nuclear, biological and chemical weapons are ideal for their purpose," the report concluded. The report was one of many studies done on future threats. This one was especially important. Marvin J. Cetron, a defense consultant, produced the report for the Pentagon's Office of Special Operations and Low Intensity Conflict. The 1995 report said weapons of mass destruction were "the most ominous trend in terrorism." It also warned that Muslim extremists could be planning a "terrorist jihad."

In light of the first World Trade Center attack, the report sought to highlight U.S. vulnerabilities, focusing on Washington, D.C. But these details were omitted in the 1995 report, Cetron told me. "We were told by the Department of Defense not to put it in. And I said, 'It's unclassified, everything is available.' And they said, 'We don't want it released, because you can't handle a crisis before it becomes a crisis. And no one is going to believe you.' "

September 11 suddenly made believers out of the very people who should have known beforehand.

3

THE DIA: DEATH
BY BUREAUCRACY

KIE FALLIS ARRIVED AT THE Defense Intelligence Agency's main offices at Bolling Air Force Base on October 12, 2000. As in the days before, he was determined to push forward an investigation into what he recognized as a coming terrorist attack. A former army interrogator fluent in Farsi, Fallis was one of the agency's top specialists on Iran, and he had recently finished a year at the FBI investigating the Khobar Towers and East Africa bombings. Using commercial computer software known as Analyst's Notebook, he had pieced together the methodology and connections of Osama bin Laden's al Qaeda terrorist network. The results were alarming. Many of the people involved in previous attacks against U.S. interests appeared to be planning others. In addition, bin Laden had released his latest videotape message three weeks earlier and called for more attacks against the United States. Similar videotapes had been released in the weeks prior to other terrorist attacks adding to the other indicators of a near-term attack.

Fallis met Jay Saunders, the chief of the DIA's Persian Gulf Division on his way into the agency's Bolling AFB offices, known to insiders as the "Death Star" because of its resemblance to the *Star Wars* space station.

Fallis had previously told Saunders about his research into another possible bin Laden strike: "I'm going to keep pushing this issue today until something is done or until I get my ass kicked."

Hours earlier and half a world away, two men left an apartment in a two-story concrete-block apartment building high above a harbor in Aden, Yemen, a desert port on the southern end of the Arabian peninsula. The apartment provided the two radical Muslims with a panoramic view of the entire harbor, including the floating refueling dock a mile away known as the Dolphin. U.S. Navy warships used the Dolphin to refuel as a security precaution, allowing them to keep their distance from the pier.

It was a few hours before dawn.

The two radical Muslims got into a red Nissan SUV and drove down the hill to a nearby house where they had stashed a small fiberglass boat on a trailer. Their thick accents identified them to neighbors as men from Hadhramaut, a remote province 500 miles northeast of Aden that is a haven for Islamic terrorists. It is also the ancestral homeland of Osama bin Laden. The two men were part of a terrorist cell that had spent months plotting to blow up a U.S. warship.

The boat was heavy and the Nissan strained to pull it. Inside the boat the two men had fashioned a bomb made up of several hundred pounds of C-4, a U.S. military explosive. The bomb was wrapped in a metal case that would intensify its impact on its target: the USS *Cole*, one of the U.S. Navy's most advanced guided-missile destroyers.

Nearby, the *Cole* was slowly making its way around the Cape of Aden to the Dolphin.

The terrorists launched their boat around 10:45 A.M. on October 12, 2000, and motored slowly toward the refueling dock. Other skiffs had been around the USS *Cole*, helping take off garbage and sending in equipment and supplies of food.

Sailors on security duty saw the white fiberglass boat approach and thought it was part of the resupply company. As the terrorists approached the side of the ship, they smiled and waved to the crew members, who waved back. The *Cole* expected nothing but a friendly reception. Only two months earlier, a Yemeni national had been invited on board one of two U.S. Navy destroyers that docked in Aden. The Yemeni was invited to dine in the officers' stateroom, but he insisted on eating in the mess deck, in the middle of the ship.

The sailors on watch noted that on previous navy ship visits to Aden, the shoreline by the port was deserted. This time the docks were lined with people, as though they were eager to see the USS *Cole*.

When the men waving from the boat reached the middle of the ship—directly in line with the mess deck—they detonated the bomb. The blast killed the two terrorists and seventeen American crew members. It tore a hole in the side of the ship forty feet wide by forty feet high.

"It was lunchtime and we were refueling," one *Cole* sailor remembers. "Thank God we didn't have fire. It was devastation, smoke, and flooding. To give you an idea of how quick it happened, there were people standing in line for their food and part of the ship wall flew back and pinned them against an inner wall, and they never knew what hit them. Three people were in the oil lab, one was blown to pieces, two were blown out of the ship, and one of them is covered with second-degree burns all over her body. All of the deceased left in the ship were blown apart. They called them missing because they couldn't get through the wreckage until certain teams came and did their investigations and so on, first."

Back at the DIA, Fallis's heart sank as the first report was delivered to him and Saunders by a member of the DIA's terrorism division. Terrorists using a small boat packed with explosives had blown themselves up next to the USS *Cole* as it tried to refuel in Aden Harbor, Yemen. The blast caused the ship to list to one side. The heroic efforts of the crew saved it from sinking.

Fallis was disgusted. For the past year he had been tracking the al Qaeda terrorist network and found that the group was intimately linked to the government of Iran—namely to agents of Iran's intelligence and security services. The alliance vastly increased the lethality of bin Laden's terrorist capabilities.

Fallis was angry that his repeated warnings to his DIA superiors that a terrorist attack was imminent in Turkey or the Persian Gulf had been dismissed. Fallis quit in protest that day. His resignation letter was sent to Vice Admiral Thomas R. Wilson, director of the Defense Intelligence Agency, the Pentagon's intelligence arm. It cited "significant analytical differences" with his supervisors in the Terrorism Analysis Division, including the fact that his warning about a terrorist attack had been ignored. Worse, he said, other terrorist attacks were coming, at least two or three more. They could take place in Bosnia or in Malaysia. But that was only part of the story. It was a heroic act by a career intelligence officer who felt compelled to bring attention to the Defense Intelligence Agency's failure to heed his warnings.

"This was a huge intelligence failure," Fallis said.

As soon as Fallis resigned he was treated like an enemy. Immediately, his computer access was cut off and his E-mail account was deleted. When he was late for work the day after he submitted his resignation, DIA security officials considered sending police after him, fearing he had defected. When he did arrive, his supervisors in the terrorism division refused to speak to him; they never asked why he was leaving.

A DIA security official told Fallis during his exit interview that the terrorism division's leadership was trying to discredit him. Fallis's performance appraisal of July 2000 rated his previous year's service as "distinguished performance," the highest possible. All of his previous appraisals had rated his analytical performance as "distinguished" as well. There was even an intelligence medal in the pipeline for him. It was a medal he would never receive—but one he certainly deserves.

The DIA tried to play down Fallis's resignation. An agency spokesman, Captain Mike Stainbrook of the U.S. Navy, acknowledged that an analyst quit on October 12, but said, "People resign from the DIA every month for personal reasons and we won't comment on those personnel actions." As for suppressing Fallis's intelligence-threat assessment of Yemen, Stainbrook would not say whether the assessment was mishandled. But, he said, "We categorically deny that any threat information has been suppressed in the case of the USS *Cole*, Yemen, or Aden, nor would we ever suppress such information." Fallis, however, had never claimed to anyone that threat information was suppressed; he correctly stated that an appropriate warning related to threat information was never produced.

Fallis's story is one of many that demonstrate the problems within the Defense Intelligence Agency, and other U.S. intelligence agencies. It highlights systemic problems in tracking and preventing terrorist attacks. It is a problem of poor leadership, mismanagement, and incredibly bad judgment.

Fallis recounted to several investigators how he had made it clear to at least five DIA intelligence officials that al Qaeda and Iranian-backed terrorists were planning deadly attacks. He had pressed the issue as hard as he could.

Fallis felt the problem with U.S. intelligence analysis on terrorism was that it was too compartmentalized. Analysts working the bin Laden account were simply not reading the intelligence reporting on Iran or other Middle Eastern terrorist groups. Likewise, specialists focusing on Iranian terrorist activities were not reading intelligence on bin Laden. As a result, each "problem set," as the analysts call them, was being analyzed in a vacuum.

Fallis, however, decided to experiment. He was allowed to research both sides of the problem—the bin Laden intelligence and the intelligence on Iranian terrorism. New and irrefutable links began to show up.

"I began finding all these relationships," he said, "between al Qaeda terrorists and the Iranians, specifically those organizations directly controlled by Iran's Supreme Leader, Ali Khamenei. Al Qaeda and Iran were also connected to terrorists who belong to the Egyptian Islamic Jihad and the Egyptian Islamic Group."

By May 2000, Fallis had written a highly classified report on his findings. The bulk of the report was based on information obtained several months earlier. "I obtained information in January of 2000 that indicated terrorists were planning two or three major attacks against the United States," he said. "The only gaps were where and when." As more information flowed into the intelligence community, it became clearer that something major was about to happen.

Around the middle of September 2000 a pivotal event took place that was a key indicator to the *Cole* bombing—and a signature of future attacks orchestrated by al Qaeda. Osama bin Laden issued a videotape broadcast on Qatari satellite television, an Arabic language version of CNN. "Every time he put out one of these videotapes it was a signal that action was coming," Fallis said.

As September ended, the DIA and the intelligence community received extremely solid intelligence information, supported by several different intelligence sources, that an attack was imminent. "I went to my supervisor and he told me there wasn't going to be a warning issued," Fallis said. It was astounding. The reason the DIA refused to put out a warning had nothing to do with intelligence. It had everything to do with office politics. Fallis had dated a woman coworker in the terrorism division who was an analyst. Less than a month before the *Cole* bombing, the woman, whom Fallis did not identify by name, produced an intelligence report stating that a small boat attack by terrorists on U.S. warships was impossible. According to Fallis, some of his supervisors falsely believed he was trying to spite the woman he had dated by arguing otherwise and predicting a terrorist attack in the Persian Gulf. "My methodology was right," Fallis said. "And it didn't have anything to do with who I dated."

■ ■ ■

One of the pieces to the puzzle that Fallis uncovered was an intelligence report about a secret meeting of al Qaeda terrorists in Malaysia in January 2000. Information after September 11 showed that of the several people attending this meeting, two of them, Khalid al-Midhar and Nawaf al-Hazmi, belonged to bin Laden's al Qaeda network. At a condominium complex, the two men met another al Qaeda terrorist who would later be linked to the bombing of the *Cole*. Khalid al-Midhar and Nawaf al-Hazmi would themselves be aboard the American Airlines Flight 77 that crashed into the Pentagon on September 11, 2001, killing 188 people and injuring hundreds more.

What alarmed U.S. intelligence was that Malaysian security officials had traced the men to the Iranian Embassy, where they spent the night. "There are definite connections between al Qaeda and Iran, namely, the MOIS [Ministry of Intelligence and Security] and the IRGC," one official said. The IRGC is the Iranian

Revolutionary Guards Corps, the Islamic shock troops that are key supporters and trainers of international terrorism.

The men had met a former Malaysian army captain named Yazi Sufaat, who was identified by Malaysian authorities as a key link in Southeast Asia for al Qaeda. Sufaat would later meet with Zacarias Moussaoui, the thirty-three-year-old French citizen who is the only person charged so far with involvement in the September 11 attacks. Authorities said Sufaat paid Moussaoui $35,000 during a visit to Malaysia. The money is believed to have partly funded the September 11 attacks.

In a classified chronology submitted to Congress in early 2002, the CIA stated that it had tracked Khalid al-Midhar and Nawaf al-Hazmi to the United States in early 2001, but failed to notify the FBI and other government agencies about the connections of the two men to al Qaeda. Months earlier, the CIA had said it did not know about al-Midhar or his several visits to the United States until August 2001, a month before the attacks, based on electronic intercepts indicating terrorists were threatening an action.

The failure to notify other agencies meant the two men were not placed on a watch list of potential terrorists and thus an opportunity to unravel the September 11 plots was missed. U.S. government officials said it was a major intelligence failure. Also, if other security agencies had known the information, it could have led to the discovery that al-Midhar and al-Hazmi had attended flight schools in the United States. An FBI agent in Phoenix warned FBI headquarters in July 2001 that Osama bin Laden's terrorists might be studying at flight schools in the United States in preparation for terrorist attacks. The CIA, however, was never notified of the warning and thus did not know that the two men had taken flight training.

For Fallis, the "eureka point" in determining the impending terrorist attack came from a still classified intelligence report in

September, which he would not discuss. But after the bin Laden video came out, Fallis said he "knew then it would be within a month or two." In the video, bin Laden, wearing a dagger in his belt, tells his supporters to free the imprisoned Egyptian Islamic Jihad leader Sheikh Omar Abdel Rahman. Rahman had been sent to prison on a life sentence for his role in the World Trade Center bombing and a subsequent plot to bomb bridges and tunnels in New York City. All other Muslim prisoners in the United States, Egypt, and Saudi Arabia also must be freed, bin Laden said. Sheikh Rahman's son, Assadullah, chanted slogans urging Muslims "forward to shed blood." Bin Laden told his followers to remember El Sayyid Nosair, who was arrested in 1992 for the 1990 assassination of Rabbi Mehir Kahane. He also said to remember Muhammed Hassen al-Owhali, who was involved in the 1998 East Africa bombings.

Why was he talking about these guys? Fallis thought. Al-Owhali was the guy who ran away from the scene of the Nairobi bombing and failed to do what he was supposed to do—blow himself up in the embassy blast. Nosair too was a relative nobody within the al Qaeda hierarchy. After the comments, Ayman al-Zawahiri, one of bin Laden's top assistants, ended the videotape with this admonition: "Enough of words, it is time to take action against this iniquitous and faithless force [the United States], which has spread troops through Egypt, Yemen, and Saudi Arabia."

Fallis felt strongly that the very least U.S. intelligence agencies could do was issue a warning. After all, isn't that what intelligence is supposed to do, provide government officials with advance word of something that affects the lives of Americans? For the United States intelligence community to issue a warning, the procedure calls for holding a meeting of the "Big Five" intelligence agencies—CIA, DIA, FBI, NSA, and the State Department's Bureau of Intelligence and Research (INR). The meetings are formed under a committee known as the Interagency Intelligence Committee on Terrorism. For a warning to be sent, four of the five agencies must agree to issue a terrorist warning. For an advisory, which is less specific than a warning, three of the five are needed.

Fallis's immediate DIA supervisor finally relented to the point of letting Fallis write a draft warning. Warning notices are semi-public and have to be "sanitized." The top secret intelligence that is used to determine a threat has to be stripped out or modified so that only less-sensitive information is released. In the third week of September 2000, Fallis wrote a hurried draft stating that Islamic terrorists were planning an attack, with likely targets being in Turkey and the Middle East. Fallis remembered thinking at the time, "What's the use, this warning will never be sent." Fallis told congressional investigators he lamented the hurried draft warning. "My legacy [in intelligence] is a poorly worded and incomplete draft warning," he recalled.

Fallis's warning was never issued. Intelligence officials worried that too many warnings could lead to "overwarning" and "warning fatigue"—a kind of letting down the guard of security forces. In the case of the USS *Cole* bombing, a warning would have put all U.S. military forces deployed around the world, especially those in hot spots like Yemen, on higher alert. And it might even have led to canceling the refueling stop in Aden.

At the DIA, the terrorism division's senior Middle East analyst, Randy MacRobbie, refused to even read the information Fallis had put together. The same was true for Gary Greco, the terrorism warning chief. Neither MacRobbie nor Greco ever offered any explanation for their failure to consider a possible warning. Randy Blake, the chief for current intelligence in the terrorism division, stated flatly that the previous assessment that a small boat attack against a U.S. warship was impossible, would stand without change and no warning would be issued. At the top of this heap, Gregg Prewitt, the senior analyst and supposed adjudicator for these types of disputes, simply remained silent and did nothing.

"Garry, we've got to put something out," Fallis said. The reply? "No."

"If this doesn't meet the threshold for putting out a warning, what does?" Fallis pleaded.

"I pushed and I pushed and I pushed," Fallis said. "I was a pain in the ass."

At the top of the DIA pecking order was the chief of the Office for Counterterrorism Analysis, Bob Pecha. But he never got word of Fallis's troubles until it was too late.

As for DIA director Vice Admiral Thomas Wilson, he tried to appear sympathetic. In a meeting with Fallis after his resignation, Wilson said, "Why didn't you come to me?" The statement was disingenuous because the highly bureaucratic structure at the DIA made that impossible.

"Yeah, I could do that one time," Fallis said. "And then I'd be out."

What is truly amazing is that a man like Fallis who had immersed himself in studying al Qaeda, Iran, and terrorism could be given such short shrift by his superiors. Fallis understood al Qaeda was a very sophisticated terrorist group. Its members, surprisingly, did not always demonstrate religious fanaticism. Many of them drank alcoholic beverages, something strictly prohibited by Islamic law. Some were into pornography. The fact that these terrorists were permitted such transgressions showed the pragmatism of al Qaeda's leaders. The foot soldiers, Fallis believed, were viewed by al Qaeda's radical Islamic leaders as "throwaways," people who could be used for terrorist operations to benefit the larger goals of the organization. And the organization was big.

"They couldn't do this without help," Fallis said. And in Fallis's view, it was the Iranians who were providing it. "Safe haven, documentation, training, explosives," he said, in all these matters al Qaeda received assistance from Iran. When Iranian government operatives referred to "friends" and members of al Qaeda referred to "brothers," they were often talking about each other. "It was only when you examined both 'streams' of intelligence reporting on these issues and groups that the complete picture became apparent," Fallis said, adding that these "anomalies" were things that other analysts would dismiss as insignificant. But for Fallis, "It was these anomalies that led to the connections."

After the *Cole* bombing and Fallis's resignation, assistant secretary of defense for public affairs and chief spokesman Kenneth Bacon admitted in a statement that a DIA analyst had resigned in protest. The analyst had informed the DIA director, the statement said, that he "had some concerns about how the agency used his analytical views." But Bacon's statement defended the DIA, saying that Fallis had no information that would have provided "tactical warning"—meaning the specific time and place—of an attack on the U.S. warship.

However, issuing a terrorism warning or advisory in the past had never required information specific enough for tactical warning. And only a few months before October 2000, the DIA's terrorism division had published an advisory about possible terrorist attacks against a G-8 economic summit meeting. The DIA later conceded to congressional investigators they had no information, specific or otherwise, of a possible attack.

Admiral Wilson, the DIA director, put out a notice labeled "FOUO"—an unclassified tag meaning For Official Use Only—on February 28, 2001. The notice was sent to all DIA civilians and military personnel. The subject of the e-mail message was "DR Statement to the DIA workforce." Wilson stated that "numerous media reports" after the *Cole* bombing said a DIA analyst had quit because "he believed his repeated warnings of a terrorist threat to

U.S. interests were ignored." Since the reports "implied" that intelligence was suppressed or ignored, "I felt it was essential to investigate the matter," Wilson said. The Department of Defense Inspector General Office then investigated and "found no evidence to support the public perception that information warning of an attack on *Cole* was suppressed, ignored, or even available in DIA," Wilson concluded. Wilson went on to say he had confidence in the DIA's "analytical process and in our people."

As always seems to be the case, a failure of U.S. intelligence to stop a terrorist attack is *not* considered a failure. The bureaucracies look out for each other.

But there was yet another intelligence failure related to the bombing of the USS *Cole*. This time it was a dissemination failure—a failure to get sensitive intelligence out to the ship in time to take action. The National Security Agency, which conducts electronic eavesdropping around the world, received an intelligence intercept about terrorists planning for an attack against the United States. On the day the *Cole* bombing was carried out, NSA produced a top secret intelligence report warning that terrorists were planning an attack on an American target in the Middle East. But the NSA report was not dispatched until several hours after the bombing. The report, according to officials who were familiar with the top secret intelligence, stated that unidentified terrorists were involved in "operational planning" for an attack on U.S. or Israeli personnel or property in the Middle East. One official said the warning was specific as to an attack in Yemen. Congressman Curt Weldon, a Pennsylvania Republican and a senior member of the House Armed Services Committee, agreed that the NSA report was specific. He investigated the NSA warning and told me that the warning "related specifically to Yemen." But other officials claimed the NSA's intercept was more general and referred to the Persian Gulf region. Either way, it was accurate. The intercept stated that a member of a terrorist group had been tracked to Dubai and Beirut and was planning terrorist operations.

One channel for reporting such urgent intelligence is the U.S. intelligence community's network known as Intelink, a kind of classified Internet for sending intelligence reports from various agencies. The NSA did not put out the intelligence on the link. The dissemination problem was the result of the NSA's strict guidelines for use of its information. It is a fine line in the intelligence business between protecting a source of intelligence or means of intelligence and ensuring that intelligence is made available to those who need it. Intelligence officials have said the mind-set at the NSA is such that once intelligence about its electronic spying is disclosed, whether in the press or through references in diplomatic exchanges, the agency considers the link compromised. "If the link doesn't disappear, then we suspect that it's being used to send disinformation," one electronic intelligence officer said. Nevertheless, NSA reports are sent to the CIA, the Defense Intelligence Agency, State Department intelligence, and the intelligence arms of the military services for inclusion in their reporting for policymakers and military commanders. In this case the NSA was cautious and slow.

And in its bureaucratic groupthink, as exemplified in the Fallis case, it is clear as well that the DIA has lost sight of its purpose and function—to provide war fighters with intelligence. As we shall see, the CIA is in equally bad shape.

4

THE PCIA—POLITICALLY CORRECT
INTELLIGENCE AGENCY

THE NATIONAL SECURITY AGENCY flagged the intercepted electronic communication from Iran as an urgent message. The next day, March 1, 1995, it was on the desk of White House national security advisor Anthony Lake bearing the code words, "Top Secret Umbra Gamma," indicating it was sensitive intelligence derived from electronic communications. The intercept had been snatched from the air by the NSA's worldwide network of electronic eavesdropping stations. It had been sent from the Iranian Ministry of Intelligence and Security in Tehran to one of its foreign stations. It stated that the Central Intelligence Agency, using the White House National Security Council as cover, was planning to conduct an assassination of Iraq's dictator, Saddam Hussein. The plot was being hatched by a CIA officer working in northern Iraq using the codename "Robert Pope."

Lake read the NSA report and was furious. Lake assumed the intercepted information was accurate and that the CIA was conducting operations on its own. Covert operations of every kind were supposed to be authorized and coordinated by the president, and that meant by Lake himself. Lake called President

Clinton and said he needed to see him right away. Inside the Oval Office, Lake waved the NSA report and shouted: "How can I run foreign policy with the CIA running rogue coups?" Clinton advised Lake to request the FBI to launch an investigation. Lake telephoned FBI director Louis Freeh, who obediently pursued the request.

Several weeks later, CIA Clandestine Service officer Robert Baer, one of the agency's few Arabic-speaking case officers, was recalled to CIA headquarters in Langley, Virginia. Baer had been in the middle of a CIA covert operation in northern Iraq to back opponents of Saddam Hussein. The agency hoped the covert action would lead to a coup in Baghdad.

Upon his arrival, Baer's supervisor, Fred Turco, told him that two FBI agents were waiting to talk to him.

"We're conducting an investigation of you for suspicion of attempting to assassinate Saddam Hussein," one of the agents told an astonished Baer. And the investigation was not frivolous. Assassination is prohibited by a presidential executive order going back to the 1970s. Every CIA officer sent to the field must sign a statement confirming that he understands the directive prohibiting assassination.

The Clinton administration Justice Department decided to investigate Baer for more than simply violating an executive order. He would be investigated and, if necessary, prosecuted under a federal murder-for-hire statute.

The intercept turned out to be false information from the Iranians. But the fact that a national security advisor believed the Iranian government over his own intelligence service showed the low regard for U.S. intelligence held by the president and his top advisors. Baer explained to the agents that he was not "Robert Pope" and that the Iranian claim of an assassination attempt against Saddam Hussein was a lie. It would take until April 1996, more than a year later, before the Justice Department would issue a "declination" letter stating that it did not plan to prosecute one of the CIA's best field officers. Baer was cleared only after he had agreed to take a lie detector test.

The CIA did not come to Baer's defense, an FBI official told me; it was the FBI that warned Justice Department lawyers that the impact of the investigation on morale could be devastating. The CIA, as Baer says, had come to accept such investigations as routine. CIA lawyer Rob Davis told Baer: "Look, Bob, you've been overseas for almost twenty years. Washington really has changed a lot. . . . These kinds of investigations go on all the time now." That CIA leaders could be so nonchalant about one of their field agents being investigated on federal murder-for-hire charges—on the basis of an Iranian government intercept—is damning in what it says about the agency.

Baer's case illustrates how the CIA is no longer central, or an intelligence service, but very much an agency of government in the worst sense of the term, where preservation of the agency's budget takes precedence over its performance. Of his experience as a whipping boy for Tony Lake, Baer is not bitter. "You know, it doesn't matter to me because I got a book out of it. And I was tired of the CIA and it was tired of me too."[1]

What did matter to Baer was how a vindictive CIA bureaucracy ignored his postemployment intelligence on al Qaeda terrorists. The story begins on a cold night in December 1997, somewhere near the Syrian-Lebanese border. Baer was meeting with a former chief of police of Qatar who had been exiled for antigovernment activities. The Qatari told him that his government had uncovered a cell of al Qaeda operatives working in the Persian Gulf sheikhdom and that two of the terrorists, Shawqi Islambuli and Khalid Shaikh Mohammed, were identified as experts in airplane hijackings. They were also linked to al Qaeda terrorist Ramzi Yousef, who was wanted by the FBI in connection with an airline bombing. The FBI contacted the Qatari government, which agreed to turn the terrorists over to the FBI, who duly sent a team. When the FBI agents arrived in Doha, the capital, the Qatari authorities sent them to a hotel and told them to wait, because, Baer told me, the Qataris wanted to "put the handcuffs on. The Qataris say 'We'll go get the guy.' They come back twenty-four hours later and say, 'Geesh, the house is empty.' They went in the house. It had obviously been ransacked, cleared of the documents." The Qatari related the story to Baer in the desert that night. It exposed how the Doha government was working against U.S. efforts to get Islamic terrorists.

According to the Qatari exile, the Doha government minister in charge of religious affairs had arranged for the two terrorists to flee the country. The men were provided with passports and travel expenses and sent to Prague, in the Czech Republic. The ringleader, Khalid Shaikh Mohammed, then set up shop using the name Mustaf Nasir. In effect, a member of the Qatari government protected two Islamic terrorists and then exported key members of an al Qaeda cell to Europe, where they could continue to carry out operations in secret.

Baer, who had left the CIA at the time of the meeting, recognized an important piece of intelligence that could be useful in stopping the al Qaeda network. "I'm not in the business but this is interesting because here's a local country in the Gulf, one of our allies, covering up bin Laden terrorism in '95, '96," Baer said. The CIA veteran did the right thing. He sent an E-mail to a friend at the CIA who forwarded it to the Counterterrorist Center. "Of course nobody called me back. Nobody sent me an E-mail. There was just no interest. So I'm out of the business, and I shut my mouth. I don't know what's going on."

Baer had no explanation for why the CIA failed to act on the intelligence of Qatari support for Islamic terrorists. But he figured out what happened. "I'm in Beirut; I'm the only one meeting people like this," he says. "I don't work for the CIA anymore.

I send it to my friend; they send it to the CTC, but the mentality is that, 'Well, Bob Baer is out and he left in a huff; even though he got an intelligence medal, we're not going to listen to him.' "

The source of the intelligence did not fare well. Apparently he got burned, as they say in the spy business. The man disappeared and was presumed kidnapped by the Qataris. Did the CIA turn on the source to protect its relationship with the Qatari government? The answer is probably yes.

The politics of Qatar and Washington are complex and the intelligence linking the government to bin Laden was ignored because of U.S. military concerns. The Pentagon operates a secret airbase known as Al Adid that could be used for future military operations against Iraq. The Al Adid airbase in Qatar is one of the largest secret airbases in the Gulf region. It has storage facilities for one hundred warplanes and a fifteen-thousand-foot runway that is capable of handling the largest U.S. bombers, like the B-52 and B-1. The airbase was built at a cost of $1.5 billion and was begun following an agreement reached with the Qatari government after an April 2000 visit by then defense secretary William Cohen. Qatar also is used to house U.S. military "pre-positioned" equipment, enough for a heavy brigade of several thousand troops.

Baer continued to gather extremely valuable intelligence that was ignored. In the summer of 2001, Baer and another former CIA officer obtained a gold mine of intelligence from Qatar: a list of some six hundred people who were known Islamic extremists linked to bin Laden and operating inside Saudi Arabia and Yemen. The new intelligence also revealed that Yemen was covering up information on the October 2000 bombing of the USS *Cole* in Aden harbor. According to the intelligence information, a Saudi merchant family had funded the *Cole* bombing, and al Qaeda was planning "a spectacular operation," Baer said.

Baer then met with a Saudi official in Switzerland and gave the list of names, contained on a computer printout, to the official. The

Saudi official never got back to Baer. The list contained the names of ten al Qaeda members living in Qatar who, after September 11, would be placed on the FBI's list of most wanted terrorists.

Baer also provided the list to a senior CIA officer, who passed it along to the Counterterrorist Center. In addition, Baer faxed his new information about the *Cole* bombing and the Yemeni government cover-up to the CIA—to no avail. "The CIA turned off free leads and information only because it did not like the source," Baer said, referring to himself.

Baer was another highly informed, highly trained, former U.S. intelligence officer willing to help his country fight terrorism, who was shut out by the all-powerful bureaucracy at the CIA that failed to see an intelligence opportunity.

■■■

George Tenet sat in the Hay-Adams Hotel restaurant, having breakfast with an old mentor, former Democratic senator David L. Boren, the retired chairman of the Senate Select Committee on Intelligence, who was now president of the University of Oklahoma. As a senator, Boren had appointed Tenet staff director of the Select Committee's oversight panel, giving Tenet his start in the secret world of intelligence. Tenet, who before that had been a lobbyist and a congressional staffer, held the position from 1988 to 1993. In 1995, after a stint on Clinton's White House National Security Council staff, Tenet became deputy director of Central Intelligence despite never having received training as a professional intelligence officer. In 1997, he was promoted to head of the Central Intelligence Agency, becoming director of Central Intelligence, known as DCI, the highest post in the thirteen government agencies and organizations that make up what is known as the Intelligence Community.

The date of Boren and Tenet's breakfast was September 11. One of Tenet's security guards approached him. "A plane has gone into the World Trade Center, Mr. Director," the guard said.

"Was it an attack? It sounds like an attack."

Tenet quickly left his plate of scrambled eggs and boarded his limousine for CIA headquarters. Before leaving, Tenet told Boren: "This is bin Laden. His fingerprints are all over it."

But if Tenet knew it was bin Laden immediately after the attack, why hadn't the CIA been more alert? Why hadn't it prevented the tragedy?

Appearing before the Senate Select Committee on Intelligence in February 2002, Tenet denied that the September 11 terrorist attacks represented a failure of American intelligence. Indeed, he said, "It's important we have a record. It is a record of discipline, strategy, focus, and action. We are proud of that record. We have been at war with al Qaeda for over five years. Our collective successes inside Afghanistan bear a reflection of the importance we attach to the problem, and a reflection of a demonstrated commitment to expanding our human assets, technical operations, fused intelligence, seamless cooperation with the military. These are things we have been working on very hard over the last five years."

Let's take a look at the record.

■ ■ ■

Before September 11, the CIA's weaknesses could be seen in numerous cases. One of the most famous and damaging was the discovery in 1994 that a senior CIA officer, Aldrich Ames, had been a longtime spy for the Russians. There was the shocking failure to predict the Indian government's underground nuclear tests in 1998. And there have been numerous other failures in recent years that have shown the CIA to be extremely unreliable as an intelligence service.

But most shocking for all Americans is the fact that when the first hijacked U.S. airliner slammed into the World Trade Center on September 11, the CIA's Counterterrorist Center knew no more about the attacks than what was being reported on television.

This, despite having a special Langley "station" of intelligence officers focused on bin Laden and his five thousand to ten thousand militants scattered in up to sixty countries.

As late as three months before, the CIA believed it was winning the war against bin Laden. But this merely betrayed the agency's focus on "spin" and public relations rather than hard results under Tenet's leadership. The Counterterrorist Center boasted to reporters that it had assisted foreign intelligence and law enforcement officials by arresting forty terrorists, including associates of bin Laden. There were also references to unspecified but "numerous" terrorist attacks that had been stopped by the CIA's spies. But officials with access to the classified reports said the agency would often play games with such numbers and count the apprehension of people caught entering the United States with false passports as "thwarted" terrorist attacks. Director of Central Intelligence George Tenet also bragged that the CIA had prevented at least five terrorist outrages between December 1999 and January 2000. But the reality is that both the FBI and the CIA had very little to do with stopping the so-called Millennium attacks. It was not the result of any advance intelligence of an attack. The credit instead goes to an alert agent of the U.S. Customs Service who questioned a suspicious foreign national.

Customs Service agent Diane Dean was working the evening shift at Port Angeles, Washington, a border crossing in the Pacific Northwest where the ferry from Canada arrives twice a day. The last driver off one of the ferries in December 1999 was a young man from North Africa named Ahmed Rassan, who would turn out to be a terrorist of the al Qaeda organization. Bomb-making materials found in the trunk of the car led to the unraveling of the al Qaeda plot for a series of Millennium bombings.

Instead of taking credit for what the CIA didn't do, Tenet should have been forced to explain why the CIA failed to prevent the bombing of the USS *Cole* in Aden harbor, Yemen, in October 2000.

Tenet did offer an explanation, but it only highlighted the CIA's shortcomings. He said the problem was that U.S. intelligence cannot act unilaterally but must work with "countries out there who have often deflected us, or have not recognized there was a terrorism problem, who didn't help us solve problems that we could not solve simply on our own."

The fact is, the CIA is next to useless if it doesn't penetrate terrorist organizations with its own agents instead of relying on foreign liaison services or defectors. Without having a unilateral capability to get inside a terrorist group, there can be no disrupting its activities.

The CIA's Counterterrorist Center employed more than two hundred people at the time of the September 11 attacks. That number has since increased dramatically to more than three hundred, including numerous CIA officials called out of retirement to take part in the war on terrorism. The center employs counterterrorism officials from other agencies, including the FBI, the Defense Intelligence Agency, and the National Security Agency. But it is predominantly a CIA show.

As for the clandestine service, the CIA is sending scores of new officers out to the field to continue the same failed policy that left the agency blind to and ignorant of the September 11 attacks. Case officers, those who actually conduct espionage operations, are being sent to work in classical embassy-reporting jobs.

Instead of sending spies to work the streets and befriend terrorists, or at least their friends and supporters, the new officers file embassy-based reports to Washington. "All this pads reporting volume and builds careers," said one intelligence professional in the U.S. government. "And yet we will have no new assets, we will not have penetrated the hard targets, and we will not know more about anything central to our national interest. But the political people—most of them anyway—will not understand this, or want to understand it."

"To say the least, the post–Cold War period has been one of difficult transition," says Senator Richard Shelby, who spent eight years on the Intelligence Committee, first as chairman and then as vice chairman. "Even before September 11, we had a rocky history of intelligence failures; among them, the bombing of Khobar Towers, the Indian nuclear test, the bombing of our East African embassies, the first attack on the World Trade Center buildings, and the attack upon the USS *Cole*.

"Examined individually, each of these failures, tragic in their own way, may not suggest a continuing or systemic problem," Shelby told me in an interview. "But taken as a whole and culminating with the events of September 11, they present a disturbing series of intelligence shortfalls that I believe expose some serious problems in the structure of and approaches taken by our intelligence community." Shelby was one of the few government officials with the courage to expose American intelligence failures. He told me that Tenet "should not be proud of the record" of CIA efforts to fight terrorism. "I think the record's mixed," Shelby said. "Could we have done better in retrospect? I think we could. I don't think we can continue to have the failures that we've had in the past few years. We have to do better."

Shelby is quick to point the finger at the Clinton administration for not aggressively going after terrorists the way the Bush administration has done since September 11. During the Clinton years, "What'd we do?" the Alabama Republican said. "Basically nothing. We 'investigated' it and they [the Islamic terrorists] became more emboldened."

After the World Trade Center bombing in 1993, and certainly before the Khobar Towers blast in 1996, American intelligence should have been alerted to the danger; "they should have been awake."

"But they didn't wake up," Shelby said. "Oh, they did some things. But nothing to sustain a fight to get to know everything about these groups as the number one priority of intelligence and military operations." Shelby was particularly upset by the CIA's performance; the CIA, he thought, merely told congressmen what they wanted to hear about the ever improving record of CIA success. The truly sad news is that things had been so bad before—going back to the congressional and presidential assaults on America's intelligence services in the 1970s—that things *had* improved. Robert Baer, the persecuted CIA field agent, said that when he first entered the CIA in 1976, the agency's espionage branch was reeling from a devastating series of firings by President Jimmy Carter's director of Central Intelligence, Admiral Stansfield Turner.

Turner, who had no professional experience with intelligence, decided to cut 820 positions within the CIA Operations Directorate. The cuts were announced in impersonal notices sent out on Halloween—October 31, 1977. "It has been decided that your services are no longer needed," the termination notes stated. For the Clandestine Service, the cuts were a blow from which it never recovered. Every director of Central Intelligence since then has tried in vain to "rebuild" the operational capability of the CIA.

Another big problem is the lack of language training for the CIA's case officers. Without the language skills, there is no way to pursue terrorists, Baer says.

And unless the CIA puts actual agents in the field, which means accepting risks—which the CIA bureaucracy is afraid to do—the CIA will never penetrate terrorist organizations. But if a twenty-year-old Islamic convert from California, John Walker Lindh, was able to join the Taliban, why is it that the CIA did not have a single agent or case officer working inside Afghanistan, let alone in the Taliban, or in al Qaeda?

"You couldn't get anybody in Islamabad to run a source into Afghanistan," Baer told me. Tenet said after the attacks that the CIA had "a huge asset base" in Afghanistan. But the reality is that if there were any CIA sources, it was more likely one or two people. Elsewhere in the region, things were just as bad. In the early 1990s, the CIA did not have a single agent inside Iraq. "I would know because I was head of Iraqi operations for a while," Baer said. "We had no agents in Iraq. We had fought in a war three years before with Iraq. We didn't have anybody on the ground. Occasionally somebody would go in from Amman. But nothing you could call a controlled, paid, vetted source in Iraq."

Instead of field agents, lawyers are the pervasive force inside the CIA, as they are in any other Washington bureaucracy. Lawyers accompany agents in the field to make sure the CIA won't be sued for their actions. Indeed, the CIA seems to fear its own people. The CIA doesn't like specialists or Arabic-speaking officers who get "too close to the Arabs," or agents who get too close to foreigners in general, Baer says. The career promotion system also was modified for the worse under John Deutch, another highly political director of Central Intelligence who served under President Clinton. The change has caused lasting damage to the Clandestine Service, Baer said. "You have to promote people depending on how many recruitments [recruiting of foreign agents] they make," he said. "In the old days if you recruited a Soviet, you were made. That recruitment became part of your corridor file forever. And that was the only standard, getting recruitments. And we just knew if we went out and recruited a Soviet we could make it to GS-15."

Deutch changed the rules so that someone with no experience in running an agent, or making an agent recruitment, could become chief of an entire operating division or even higher. Under Deutch, a CIA analyst, David Cohen, with no experience as a field agent, was put in charge of the Clandestine Service. Why? Deutch deliberately picked an outsider, as Baer put it, "to f— the place." Morale sank within the espionage branch as inexperienced bureaucrats got the upper hand.

Under Clinton appointee George Tenet, things were no better. The case against Tenet was made in a letter from a group of case officers in late April 1997, just as the Senate Intelligence Committee was examining Tenet's nomination to be promoted from deputy director to director of Central Intelligence.

According to the letter, which I obtained and which was verified by the CIA as accurate, under Tenet, "the operations directorate has been weakened more than at any time in its history.

"We are a group of officers who have served our nation in some hostile places," the letter states. "All of us have been alone on dark streets, have heard shots fired in anger, have sacrificed with great joy to serve this great nation. We deserve better. You deserve better than this."

Among the allegations contained in the letter are the following:[2]

• Tenet halted a secret operation because a U.S. ambassador "got cold feet" and backed out. "As a result, serious counterterrorism-related information is being denied to us," the letter states. "If MOIS [Iranian Ministry of Intelligence and Security] operatives kill someone in Europe, he [Tenet] will be partly to blame."

• Serious terrorism-threat information was withheld from U.S. military commanders and diplomats vulnerable to attack.

• Intelligence reports on Haiti were hidden from Republican congressional staffers trying to determine if reports were falsified, and analysis was skewed for political reasons. The hidden channel was identified as "ARCHLANE."

• CIA counterintelligence chief Paul Redmond and another senior operator were being forced out of the CIA, while David Cohen, an analyst with no espionage branch experience, was made the new deputy director of operations. Other division chiefs were "stripped of their power," the letter said. "Our field [chiefs of station] are to be either ignored or brow-beaten over the STU-III [secure telephone], or used to set up lavish entertainment when Tenant [*sic*] and the other members of the occupying forces travel abroad," the letter said.

• Three of the agency's most experienced spies, East Asian chief Sean Fitzgerald, counterterrorism expert Jim Morris, and Vince Shields, paramilitary division chief, were recently pressured to retire. (Shields denied the letter's allegation that he left on bad terms with senior CIA leaders, but said he was wrongly accused in an internal probe of operations in Latin America.)

• The investigation of CIA turncoat Harold James Nicholson, convicted as a Russian spy, was nearly botched because senior CIA leaders tried to force a "too quick closure" of the probe.

One reason for the CIA's crisis is its leadership. Preceding Tenet's appointment, the CIA had seen five directors in six years. Without question, the most damaging director was John Deutch, who was appointed to the job in 1995 and left under a cloud in 1996, after he was passed over for the job of defense secretary in the second Clinton administration.

Deutch's moment of disaster was when Senator Robert G. Torricelli, a New Jersey Democrat, alleged that the CIA was directly involved—through a Guatemalan army colonel on the CIA payroll—in the murders of an American and a leftist guerrilla in Guatemala. In response, Deutch fired two CIA officers and disciplined several others for not being candid about the case. This led to the imposition of what became known as the "Deutch Rules," which restricted the recruitment of agents by CIA case officers and led to the firing of about one thousand of its recruited agents. The fired agents included Middle Eastern sources.

"It was totally destructive," a CIA case officer told me, and effectively prevented CIA case officers from recruiting spies, because the rules blocked CIA officers from recruiting agents with criminal or questionable pasts unless such recruitment was okayed by CIA headquarters, where such approval was unlikely because of potential political embarrassment to the agency.

The rules were examined by a blue-ribbon panel of experts— known as the "Bremer Commission" from its leader, L. Paul Bremer, a former State Department counterterrorism official—who looked at U.S. counterterrorism capabilities in 2000. "Complex bureaucratic procedures now in place send an unmistakable message to the Central Intelligence Agency (CIA) officer in the field that recruiting clandestine sources of terrorism information is encouraged in theory, but discouraged in practice," the report by the National Terrorism Commission concluded.

The report is introduced with a prophetic statement, taken from a book about Pearl Harbor, that, because of its cogency, deserves to be reprinted here in its entirety:

Surprise, when it happens to a government, is likely to be a complicated, diffuse, bureaucratic thing. It includes neglect of responsibility but also responsibility so poorly defined or so ambiguously delegated that action gets lost. It includes gaps in intelligence, but also intelligence that, like a string of pearls too precious to wear, is too sensitive to give to those who need it. It includes the alarm that fails to work, but also the alarm that has gone off so often it has been disconnected. It includes the unalert watchman, but also the one who knows he'll be chewed out by his superior if he gets higher authority out of bed. It includes the contingencies that occur to no one, but also those that everyone assumes somebody else is taking care of. It includes straightforward procrastination, but also decisions protracted by internal disagreement. It includes, in addition, the inability of individual human beings to rise to the occasion until they are sure it is the occasion—which is usually too late. (Unlike movies, real life provides no musical background to tip us off to the climax.) Finally, as at Pearl Harbor, surprise may include some measure of genuine novelty introduced by the enemy, and possibly some sheer bad luck.

The results, at Pearl Harbor, were sudden, concentrated, and dramatic. The failure, however, was cumulative, widespread, and rather drearily familiar. This is why surprise, when it happens to a government, cannot be described just in terms of startled people. Whether at Pearl Harbor or at the Berlin Wall, surprise is everything involved in a government's (or in an alliance's) failure to anticipate effectively.

—Thomas C. Schelling, Foreword to Pearl Harbor: Warning and Decision, *by Roberta Wohlstetter*[3]

Another critic of the Deutch Rules was former director of Central Intelligence R. James Woolsey. Woolsey, who led the CIA from 1993 to 1995, said the rules were "dysfunctional" and may have been one cause for the CIA's failure to prevent the September 11 attacks.

"To deter CIA officers who are trying to penetrate terrorist groups from recruiting people with violence in their past is like telling FBI agents that they should penetrate the mafia, but try not to put any actual crooks on the payroll as informants. There's nobody in the mafia but crooks and there's nobody in terrorist organizations but terrorists," said Woolsey, who served on the Bremer Commission.

Bremer told me the key recommendation of the commission was for the restrictions on agent recruitment to be lifted, but the

CIA ignored the recommendation. "It's my view that the United States for twenty-five years has seen a significant run-down of its overseas intelligence capabilities, and in particular its capabilities against human targets. That progressive degeneration was accelerated by a decision in 1995 to impose restrictive guidelines on the overseas recruitment of terrorist informants."

The testimony from CIA case officers on the issue was "unambiguous, unanimous, and conclusive" that the rules had discouraged "people in the field from recruiting terrorist spies." The rules had a "chilling effect" on recruitment efforts, Bremer said. Bremer believes that the rules in effect before the 1995 restrictions, which required some consultation with CIA headquarters, should be reinstated. Bremer told Congress in January 2002 that it was "astonishing" to him that fifteen months after the commission recommended lifting the restrictions "nothing has been done on this, the most important recommendation our commission made." Lifting the curbs would be "one of the most important steps that could be taken by this country to stop terrorism, because the objective of counterterrorist policy is to prevent attacks. It's to keep Americans from getting killed in the first place. When you scrub it all down, if you are going to get good intelligence on terrorist groups, it is going to come from somebody who by definition is a terrorist. If we are not prepared as a nation to do that, then we are not going to get this intelligence. This kind of intelligence is not going to come by wandering down to the League of Women Voters and seeing what you find there."

Bremer said the guidelines are self-imposed and that Tenet could lift them easily.

Congress called on Tenet in a section of the fiscal 2002 Intelligence Authorization Act, signed into law in December 2001, to "rescind the existing 1995 CIA guidelines for handling cases involving foreign assets or sources with human rights concerns." The act also calls for new guidelines allowing "for indications and warnings of plans and intentions of hostile actions or events, and ensure that such information is shared in a broad and expeditious fashion so that, to the extent possible, actions to protect American lives can be taken."

Even with the nonbinding legislation, the CIA refused to rescind the Deutch Rules on its case officers. The 1995 rules requiring all CIA officers in the field to obtain approval from CIA headquarters before recruiting foreign agents with histories of human rights abuses were "relaxed" but not rescinded, the agency said. Following the September 11 terrorist attacks, the rules were modified in October 2001 to permit CIA officers again to recruit foreigners with questionable pasts without first checking with Langley headquarters. But they are still required to report the recruitment efforts.

"The decision to use an individual with an unsavory background, because that individual committed serious crimes or human rights abuses, can be made in the field if that individual has insights about terrorist activities and threats," a CIA spokesman told me. However, CIA headquarters must be informed within several days of the recruitment or information-collection attempt, "and a formal decision with respect to continued use rests with the deputy director for operations," the official said. The deputy director for operations is the CIA's senior official in charge of espionage operations. The spokesman said that Tenet modified the rules because of the "urgency of the situation." The message sent to field officers is simple: Why bother? If headquarters could second-guess your efforts to recruit someone who could later end up hampering your career, it is not worth the trouble.

The Deutch Rules weren't Deutch's only negative legacy to the agency. He also followed the Clinton administration tradition of playing politics, placing former Democratic congressional staffers in key CIA positions. Among these was George Tenet. Another was former House Intelligence Committee staff member Michael J. O'Neil. O'Neil worked on the notorious House Intelligence Committee panel chaired by Congressman Edward Boland, a Massachusetts Democrat, which was a major opponent of intelligence operations during the Reagan administration. As CIA general counsel, O'Neil continued his efforts to stifle U.S. intelligence capabilities.

"He's bringing the anti-intelligence mind-set of the 1970s to the current CIA," a former senior intelligence official said at the time of O'Neil's appointment. "It will politicize everything the CIA does and will prevent us from identifying the proper mission for U.S. intelligence in the post–Cold War period." The official was right.

Nora Slatkin was another former Democratic congressional staffer appointed by Deutch. She was named executive director of the agency and charged with changing the "culture" of the Operations Directorate. Changing the culture would translate into seriously undermining the CIA's capability to conduct clandestine operations.

The political cronies Deutch installed, including Tenet, were eventually accused of covering up a major security scandal involving Deutch. CIA security investigators discovered highly classified documents on Deutch's Macintosh computers in early 1997, after he had left the CIA. Deutch, it turned out later, had a habit of typing his notes into an unsecured laptop computer after secret briefings in the Pentagon. He would then e-mail copies of the notes to himself at home using his America Online account and retrieve them on a home computer. As a result, the security of the programs discussed at these secret briefings was compromised. "The only question is whether foreign intelligence services have the information or will get it," a senior Pentagon official said. "We know that foreign intelligence services routinely monitor the Internet for just such material. And AOL is a major target." By the spring of 2000, the FBI began an investigation of Deutch, though he would later be pardoned by outgoing president Bill Clinton.

The CIA in May 2000 reprimanded six current and former officials—including Slatkin and O'Neil—for mishandling the security investigation of Deutch. "The principal shortcoming in the Deutch matter was that normal agency procedures for handling and reporting a serious security incident were not followed," CIA spokesman Bill Harlow said in a statement. "Among other things, a crimes report should have been submitted sooner to the Department of Justice. The congressional oversight committees, the Intelligence Oversight Board, and other agencies such as the Department of Defense and the National Security Council should have been more promptly notified."

The reason notification was delayed was pure politics—to avoid the appointment of a special prosecutor to the case. The delay put off the inquiry, and putting off the inquiry was more important than protecting American security. The Deutch aides, an agency probe found, failed to try to control the damage from Deutch's computer compromises. The report by deputy CIA director John Gordon revealed that "concerns for Mr. Deutch's privacy at times influenced the proper handling of the security investigation." While Slatkin and O'Neil were reprimanded—O'Neil for withholding Deutch's computer disk drives from investigators—Tenet escaped punishment. But he did not escape criticism from reports issued by the President's Foreign Intelligence Advisory Board, known as PFIAB, and by the CIA inspector general. Both faulted Tenet for "not involving himself more forcefully in the Deutch matter in order to ensure a proper resolution of it," a CIA statement said.

■ ■ ■

But more important than these scandals—which were virtually standard operating procedure in the Clinton administration— was the bigger scandal that the CIA was no longer doing its job of gathering human intelligence. Reuel Marc Gerecht, a former senior CIA officer, warned months before September 11 that "Unless one of bin Laden's foot soldiers walks through the door of a U.S. consulate or embassy, the odds that a CIA counterterrorist officer will ever see one are extremely poor." Gerecht quit the CIA's Directorate of Operations out of frustration after spending nine years working on Middle East matters. He explained that the CIA was extremely "risk averse" and refused to go after bin Laden in any serious way. His overall conclusion, months before September 11: "America's counterterrorism program in the Middle East and its environs is a myth."

Intelligence analysis, which involves the lion's share of work for the thousands of officials employed by the CIA, is considered the weakest part of American intelligence. It is also the part of U.S. intelligence that has been given least scrutiny. The analysts have succeeded in dominating the institutional culture within the intelligence community. It is a culture that is dismissive of threats and arrogant over its alleged intellectual prowess.

When I wrote a column criticizing the CIA's weak analysis of China and revealing how Congress had sought to set up a special panel of outside experts to challenge the efforts within the CIA to play down the growing challenge posed by Communist China, senior CIA analysts were livid. My report quoted officials as saying key China "apologists" within the CIA had succeeded in derailing a congressionally mandated "B-Team" of outside experts to examine CIA analysis of China and that the new Bush administration was planning a housecleaning.

Winston P. Wiley, the CIA deputy director of intelligence at the time,[4] issued a memorandum to analysts on October 27, 2000:

> This morning's 'Inside the Ring' in the *Washington Times* carries a story, "Target: CIA China Shop," that I feel compelled to address. In my thirty years as an intelligence officer I consider this the most blatant and undisguised effort to intimidate and politicize intelligence that I have witnessed. Simply put there is no substantive merit to the charges. The DI's track record on China bears the hallmarks of professionalism, meeting the highest standards of objectivity, impartiality, and tradecraft. Our work reflects deep expertise, is led by officers of the highest integrity, and has benefited from long-standing contact with outside experts....
>
> I believe these baseless charges threaten to undermine not only our work on China, but all of the serious and high quality analysis done by the men and women of this directorate. I met this morning with both the [director of Central Intelligence] and [deputy director of Central Intelligence]. They share my outrage. They also share my view that the best defense against such efforts to undermine our integrity is to maintain the highest levels of tradecraft in all of our work. Each of you, from the newest recruit to our most senior office directors, needs to continue to be meticulous in your use of evidence, explicit in your reasoning, mindful of mindsets and preconceptions, and determined to call the shots like you see them—just like our China analysts have been. Meeting this high standard, which I see you do every day, is our best defense against politicization.

Another CIA analyst, Michael J. Morell, wrote a memorandum saying that senior CIA officials "all believe the Gertz charge to be baseless." Morell went on to say that the CIA's China analysis was "a model of excellence and objectivity" and among "the best work" done by the entire CIA analytical bureaucracy. "To me this article is a blatant attempt to intimidate us into seeing China a certain way," Morell said. "It is ironic that the article is trying to do to us exactly what it accuses us of doing—politicizing our analysis," he said. "It is not serious journalism."

Months later, however, the CIA's China analysis was exposed by a blue-ribbon panel of China and Asia specialists, headed by retired U.S. Army general John H. Tilelli Jr., a former commander of U.S. forces in Korea. The Tilelli commission, which included academics who were on the CIA's payroll and others who were agency critics, reviewed all CIA analyses of China and found major shortcomings. In a classified report, the commission stated that CIA China analysts were guilty of an "institutional predisposition" to play down events in China and to portray Beijing in a favorable light. The commission did not conclude that the bad analysis was the result of "politicization" by the analysts, only that it was bad for nonpolitical reasons. The embarrassing report was never made public to avoid bruising the egos of the agency China hands.

Among the findings of the China commission was that a senior CIA analyst erroneously reported that there were no divisions within the Chinese leadership, a position contradicted by intelligence reports. The CIA also failed to conduct thorough analysis of Chinese military inroads into Latin America, including increased cooperation between the Chinese and Cuban militaries. Also, sensitive intelligence reports from the Directorate of Operations were suppressed within the intelligence directorate, for political reasons.

Senator Richard Shelby, an Alabama Republican and senior member of the Senate Select Committee on Intelligence, has criticized CIA analysis of China. He told me that agency China hands "have not viewed China in a realistic way."

"They're always looking the other way to put their spin on the U.S.-China relationship, that everything is going well in the long run. It's just not very real though."

What is true with the CIA's China analysis is true across the board. Donald Rumsfeld, who headed a 1999 commission on emerging ballistic missile threats, also exposed shortcomings in intelligence analysis. In a report to Congress sent March 19, 1999, Rumsfeld, who would become secretary of defense in the administration of George W. Bush, said the problems within the intelligence community were due to "budget cuts, isolation, excessive turnover, a decline in scientific and engineering competence, a highly-charged political atmosphere, foreign penetration of the intelligence community, and stovepiping of functions and information."

"Finally," Rumsfeld wrote, "for policy makers to effectively engage analysts with respect to what they know, what they don't know, and what they think about the evidence they have gathered, analyzed and presented, the products need to routinely include alternative hypotheses as to the meaning of the intelligence presented." He identified an "erosion" of the intelligence community's ability "to provide timely and accurate estimates of the threat." Congress had formed the commission after intelligence analysis had failed to properly gauge the buildup of foreign long-range missiles.

The analyst culture with its dismissive approach to national security threats and dangers continued at the CIA after September 11. Wiley was appointed associate director of Central Intelligence for homeland security in May 2002, another bureaucratic reshuffling designed to make it look as if the CIA was improving its intelligence work.

Another glaring CIA weakness is its reluctance to engage in covert action. This was highlighted in a 1999 study carried out by Harvard University's John F. Kennedy School of Government.[5]

According to the study, even during the Reagan administration, Director of Central Intelligence William J. Casey was fed up with the CIA Directorate of Operations, which he viewed as cautious, bureaucratic, slow, timid, and unimaginative. The CIA's capability to conduct covert action, such as paramilitary operations, worsened during the Clinton administration, as all serious programs to influence events abroad were curbed. In fact, former intelligence officer Robert Steele told me the CIA is no longer able to conduct paramilitary operations.

"CIA is incompetent at paramilitary operations," Steele said. "Its only real competencies in the special operations arena are related to individual infiltrations and exfiltrations. Even in covert logistics, an area where it might excel, its mistakes are legion—including the wrong ammunition being sent to covert forces in the field." Steele believes CIA covert action should be transferred to the military's Special Operations Command. "CIA is long overdue for a major housecleaning, most especially in clandestine operations, which is a decrepit dysfunctional element of the CIA," Steele said.

Foreign policy and intelligence advisor Randy Scheunemann, who worked for Republican Senate leaders Robert Dole and Trent Lott, told me the CIA is in urgent need of reform. He believes the ban on assassinations should be reviewed. "It makes no sense to regularly target command and control nodes with precision-guided munitions, while denying highly capable sniper teams the ability to attack individual targets," Scheunemann said. "As for the 1995 Clinton-Deutch-Tenet guidelines, we would never expect Drug Enforcement Administration officers to refrain from using drug dealers as informants. It is nothing short of ludicrous to expect critically placed potential agents to pass a CIA human rights questionnaire."

CIA operations against Saddam Hussein after the Gulf War were a dismal display of ineptitude, timidity, and failure that highlighted CIA shortcomings, according to Scheunemann. "Coup plots were uncovered. Assets were killed. Sensitive equipment was lost," he said. "The most promising venture—an umbrella coalition under the Iraqi National Congress (INC)—was first supported, then undermined, and, ultimately, abandoned by the CIA. Even today, CIA personnel spend more energy criticizing the INC than they do subverting Saddam Hussein."

The effort to oust Saddam was revived by the CIA after September 11. But Scheunemann says the CIA's refusal to support a broad-based popular movement has continued to leave the INC out in the cold and has ill served America's interests.

"The CIA's Directorate of Operations contains many dedicated men and women," Scheunemann says. "But they work in a system locked in its Cold War past, unwilling and unable to adapt to fighting the forces behind [September 11's] heinous attacks. Running operations in the Soviet Union and Warsaw Pact was exceedingly difficult. But the task of implementing operations that will disrupt and destroy terrorist networks and undermine their state sponsors is far more daunting."

The current system rewards officers who play the game at headquarters and punishes those who show innovation in the field. "Today, it is little more than a semi-secret version of the State Department, relying on dinners with host country intelligence services, passing out specialized equipment, and rewarding favorites with free trips to the United States," he said. "The messy business of back-alley tradecraft has taken a back seat to the much simpler business of 'liaison' with foreign intelligence services."

Scheunemann, now a private consultant, suggests that those in charge of U.S. intelligence policy ask some hard questions and demand answers and reforms. The questions include: When is the last time a CIA officer crossed a border without a passport and an escort? How many CIA field agents have fluency in Farsi or Arabic—or Dari, Pashto, Urdu, Kurdish, or Baluchi? How does the CIA propose to penetrate cells made up of individuals who forged their ties over decades in the dust of Palestinian refugee camps, the chaos of Beirut, or the killing fields of Afghanistan?

In April 2002, the CIA's top spy defended the CIA's Directorate of Operations, saying it was all but impossible to have stopped the September 11 attacks. In a speech to a conference at the Duke University Law School, James L. Pavitt, deputy director for Operations, acknowledged that the CIA could not get someone close enough to the al Qaeda leadership to learn about the plot.

"Analysts in the intelligence world, in my field, case officers as we call them, operations officers, combine their talents and their diverse experiences to the end of getting us a fuller picture of both the terrorist threat, the terrorist mentality, and they help us to create well-informed strategies for fighting it," Pavitt said. "We've had a number of significant successes over the years, but the fact remains, and I think it's important that I cite this, that we in the government of the United States as a whole could not... prevent or precisely predict the devastating tragedy of the September 11th attacks. Why do I say that?"

Pavitt blamed the "nature of the target"—clandestine al Qaeda terrorists—for the CIA's failure to stop the attack. "We had very, very good intelligence of the general structure and strategies of the al Qaeda terrorist organization," he said. "We knew and we warned that al Qaeda was planning a major strike. There need be no question about that. What didn't we know?

"We never found the tactical intelligence, never uncovered the specifics that could have stopped those tragic strikes that we all remember so well," he said. "And as a reality of that difficult and often frustrating fight against terror, the terror cells that we're going up against are typically small and all terrorist personnel in those cells, participating in those cells, perpetrating the acts of terror, all those personnel were carefully screened. The number of personnel who know vital information, targets, timing, the exact methods to be used had to be smaller still."

Pavitt noted that bin Laden, in a videotape suspiciously uncovered by U.S. forces in Afghanistan, said that his group had kept details of the September 11 attack secret from even the most senior members of the al Qaeda inner circle. "'In my business we call that compartmentation,' he [bin Laden] said. In his business, terror, killing of innocent people, he calls that compartmentation.

"Against that degree of control, that kind of compartmentation, that depth of discipline and fanaticism, I personally doubt, and I draw again upon my thirty years of experience in this business, that anything short of one of the knowledgeable inner circle personnel or hijackers turning himself in to us would have given us sufficient foreknowledge to have prevented the horrendous slaughter that took place on the 11th."

Pavitt could not explain why, with a string of deadly al Qaeda terrorist attacks prior to September 11, the CIA could not obtain that kind of information. The CIA had years to try to penetrate al Qaeda's inner circle. It had years to try to work with other Middle Eastern intelligence services that had managed to get fairly close. But the CIA failed.

In another speech to a banquet held to commemorate the veterans of the Office of Strategic Services, the World War II predecessor of the CIA, Pavitt said intelligence officers would prove decisive in winning the war against terrorism.

"The enemy who struck from the skies on September 11 was not Hitler," Pavitt said. "Yet on the unforgettably horrible day, the forces of terrorism killed more Americans than Hitler ever could."

Pavitt recalled how as a young man he had overheard his parents talk about where they were and what they were doing on the day Pearl Harbor was attacked. "And I spoke to my officers and I said: 'You will tell your children and your grandchildren exactly where you were, exactly what you were doing, when you heard of that terrible attack in New York and here in Washington.'

"War has come to us, as it did to the generation of OSS," he said. "We, too, choose to resist and to fight. Not just for our way of life, but for life itself. We, too, fight to win. And win we will."

The sad fact is the CIA had no clue about a plot being hatched over the course of two years—in Germany and the United States, among other countries—for what would become the worst terrorist attack in U.S. history. And the FBI, meanwhile, was left distributing matchbooks in Pakistan with "Wanted" notices for bin Laden.

Such was the state of American intelligence and domestic security on September 11, 2001.

5

THE FBI: THE DECLINE OF DOMESTIC INTELLIGENCE

"PHOENIX BELIEVES THAT THE FBI should accumulate a listing of civil aviation universities/colleges around the country," FBI special agent Kenneth Williams wrote to FBI headquarters in a classified "electronic communication" sent on July 10, 2001. Williams was a forty-one-year-old former cop from San Diego who had spent time with the border crimes task force before moving on to the FBI's Phoenix office. His five-page memorandum would be a key warning that went unheeded by the FBI. If it had been acted upon, there is a chance the deadly September 11 plot might have been prevented.

More than a year before Williams sent off what congressional investigators would later call the "Phoenix memo," FBI agents in Arizona were watching Middle Eastern residents in the area. One curious connection was a group that had enrolled at Embry-Riddle Aeronautical University in Prescott, Arizona.

Williams conducted interviews with several of the men. They were Islamic radicals who expressed intense hatred for the United States. For Williams, it was clear that the men might be part of a coordinated effort by the Islamic terrorist network run by Osama bin Laden. Acting on a hunch, Williams wrote that his interviews revealed that radical Muslims might be plotting some kind of operation that would breach security within the U.S. civil aviation system.

According to the memo, one of the students at the flight school was an al Qaeda sympathizer who kept a photo of Osama bin Laden on his living room wall. Williams also stated that another student pilot had made a telephone call to Abu Zubaydah, a Palestinian terrorist who, until U.S. military forces captured him in Afghanistan in early 2002, ran bin Laden's terrorist training camps.

The memorandum warned that bin Laden might be sending terrorists to U.S. flight schools, identified two men with ties to al Qaeda, and stated that several of the men were, in FBI parlance, "of investigative interest." Several of the men were interested in aircraft construction, and one had inquired about airport security. The men had been identified by the FBI as part of a group known as al-Muhajiroun, a radical Islamic group based in London that is closely aligned with bin Laden and had called for the destruction of the United States. The memorandum stated that the group had issued religious edicts against the United States, including a "fatwah" that said U.S. commercial aviation and airports were legitimate targets of terrorist attacks.

The memorandum arrived at FBI headquarters at the National Security Division, specifically, the Radical Fundamentalist Unit and its special section in charge of tracking bin Laden. But it did not go much farther. The only place outside the division that received word was the FBI counterterrorism group in New York.

Williams provided the CIA with the names of eight al Qaeda sympathizers who were attending the flight school and asked the agency to conduct background checks on the men. The probe turned up no records.

Louis Freeh had left the FBI as director on June 30, 2001, and the acting director was Thomas J. Pickard, a veteran FBI agent. The new Bush administration had announced its replacement for

Freeh—U.S. attorney for the northern district of California, Robert Mueller—five days before the memo was sent.

At the time, the FBI was reeling from criticism over its mishandling of documents in the case of Timothy McVeigh, the convicted terrorist behind the bombing of the federal building in Oklahoma City. The FBI had failed to turn over thousands of pages of documents on McVeigh. Freeh had blamed computer and recordkeeping blunders. The document problem led to a delay in the execution of McVeigh.

But the failure to act on Williams's recommendation to investigate flight training by Islamic radicals was a blunder of monumental proportions. The information was not taken seriously by the FBI, it did not get analyzed, and it was not shared with other intelligence agencies or even other FBI field offices, except New York.

This vital information also never reached the FBI's field office in Minneapolis. Agents working there had stumbled upon the most important clue to the September 11 plot: the arrest in August of Islamic radical Zacarias Moussaoui. His arrest on immigration charges was based on a tip from an alert flight school employee. But FBI and Justice Department lawyers, as mentioned earlier, had nixed an investigation because of a lack of evidence. Thus, the twentieth September 11 hijacker remained silent, and hamstrung investigators failed to uncover the plot before it was too late.

Williams told the House Permanent Select Committee on Intelligence in May 2002 that he believed if FBI officials in Washington had acted on the recommendation to investigate flight schools, the terrorist attacks might have been thwarted.

Mueller testified before Congress in May 2002 that the threat identified by Williams was that terrorists "were looking at flight schools as well as other airline academies for a variety of positions; yes, pilots, but also perhaps as roles in security or elsewhere in airports." The FBI director said he did not believe that if the Moussaoui case had been handled differently, it would have led to the uncovering of the September 11 plot. "But should we have done more in terms of the Phoenix EC [electronic communication]? Yes," Mueller said. "I think the recommendations of the agent are something that we should have more aggressively pursued." But, he added, "I do not believe that it gave the signpost of that which would happen on September 11."

The FBI director also said in testimony before the Senate Judiciary Committee that the FBI agent in Minneapolis had told headquarters that Moussaoui, the flight student arrested in Minnesota, might be "the type of person that [flies] something into the World Trade Center."

Senator Arlen Specter, Pennsylvania Republican, believes that the U.S. intelligence community, and the FBI specifically, had more than enough information to spot the September 11 plot. "My own professional judgment is that it wasn't a matter of connecting the dots before 9/11; I think there was a virtual blueprint," Specter told Mueller during a June 2002 Judiciary Committee hearing. "I think had all of it been put together or leads followed that could have been put together, I think there was a distinct possibility of preventing 9/11."

Mueller told the Senate Judiciary Committee in June 2002 that fear of political punishment over concerns about "profiling" may have hindered the FBI's investigations of terrorism.

"I think I've seen indications of concerns about taking certain action, because that action may be perceived as profiling," Mueller said. "The bureau is against, has been and will be against any form of profiling." The FBI director preferred political correctness to the fact that al Qaeda terrorists are recruited among Islamic radicals, especially young Middle Eastern Islamic radicals.

■ ■ ■

Within a week of taking over, the new FBI director would find himself confronting the Bureau's biggest intelligence failure.

The mood was somber in the Situation Room at the White House. President George W. Bush had just convened a meeting of his top National Security Council advisors in a small, electronically sealed room in the basement of the executive mansion. It was several days after the September 11 attack. Present were National Security Advisor Condoleezza Rice, Vice President Dick Cheney, Secretary of State Colin Powell, Defense Secretary Donald Rumsfeld, Attorney General John Ashcroft, and Director of Central Intelligence George Tenet.

Robert S. Mueller, the new FBI director, was there as well. Mueller, a former U.S. attorney in San Francisco, told the secret conclave that the FBI would pursue al Qaeda terrorists to "preserve prosecutions" of the terrorists. Mueller was interrupted by Ashcroft, perhaps the most conservative of the president's cabinet secretaries.

"No, we're not going to 'preserve prosecutions,'" Ashcroft said. "We're going to use FBI intelligence to prevent further attacks."

Ashcroft spoke for the rest of the president's national security advisors by saying that no longer would terrorist attacks be treated solely as law enforcement matters, but as matters of national security. Several weeks later, the war cabinet met again at the Camp David retreat in the hills of remote western Maryland. The president called on Mueller to brief the group on the FBI's efforts against al Qaeda. Mueller was not prepared and had no information to share with the cabinet. "He just fell flat on his face," said one source familiar with the Camp David meeting. The impression left on the other cabinet members was that Mueller was completely out of his league in running what was supposed to be the world's premier law enforcement agency.

R. James Woolsey, director of Central Intelligence from 1993 to 1995, said the investigative approach to terrorism was hampered by grand jury rules that prohibited sharing information obtained on terrorists during the secretive grand jury process. Congress addressed this problem only *after* September 11, by passing the USA Patriot Act in late 2001.

As with the CIA under the Clinton administration, the Justice Department and the FBI were heavily politicized; promotions were made on the basis of politics and feel-good affirmative action rather than operations experience. As a result, the FBI had no clue that al Qaeda terrorists had been plotting secretly within the United States for perhaps as long as two years. In fact, in late 2000, the FBI reported secretly to the White House that there were no al Qaeda terrorists inside the United States. Dale Watson, the FBI's intelligence chief, stated before a Senate hearing in February 2002 that the FBI was caught off guard by the attack because most of the nineteen hijackers entered the country close to the fateful date. Asked about the presence of al Qaeda cells within the United States, Watson declined to discuss details in public. The reason was obvious: The FBI was embarrassed that its intelligence section had been so ignorant. To draw attention away from the lapse, Watson told the senators that "there are hundreds of investigations that we have open" in the search for al Qaeda cells. What he did not say was how many of these investigations were opened after September 11 and that the reason the FBI didn't know about al Qaeda cells in the United States was that the FBI had no agents within the Islamic community in the United States.

What happened to the FBI's intelligence capability? Short-sighted political leaders destroyed it, because they failed to understand that the world remains a dangerous place in which domestic and foreign intelligence is our first line of defense.

■ ■ ■

In 1988, a secret ceremony was held at FBI headquarters in Washington, D.C. FBI director William Sessions awarded the Presidential Medal of Freedom to Morris Childs, then eighty-four. It is the highest award a civilian can receive from the U.S. government. There were no newspaper reporters present, and the event would remain secret until 1996.[1]

Childs was honored for being without question the most successful intelligence agent in American history. Using his executive position in the Communist Party USA, Childs had successfully infiltrated the highest councils of the Soviet government during the Cold War. Upon Morris Childs's death in 1991, FBI special agent James Fox said in remarks at the funeral: "Most of you here today probably think you knew Morris Childs. I can tell you with certainty that outside the FBI no one here today knows of the enormous contributions Morris Childs made to the security of the United States."

Three years earlier and a short time after the Berlin Wall was torn down, Childs wrote a Christmas card to Fox. "Our dreams of half a century," he wrote, "are coming true to life—it is difficult to understand the speed and reality. We are glad we gave it a push."

Fox was among a handful of FBI special agents who took part with Childs in the most important intelligence operation of the Cold War. The operation was so secret, the CIA, supposedly the main intelligence agency of the United States government, was kept out of it. At one point, the CIA offered to pay Childs $250,000 a year if he would work jointly for both the FBI and the CIA. He turned the offer down, favoring the FBI, which he trusted, over the CIA.

One of Childs's intelligence coups was meeting with senior Soviet Politburo officials when President John F. Kennedy was assassinated in November 1963. Childs was able to report that Soviet leaders were not involved in the assassination.

The FBI's handling of Childs was extraordinary and represented the apex of the FBI's intelligence capability. Childs would become known in FBI reporting as "CG-5824S*," but he was referred to as Agent 58. The asterisk in his file designation meant he was a source who could never testify in court or otherwise be identified. To mask the identity of the agent, the FBI allowed other government officials to suspect that CG-5824S* was an electronic eavesdropping operation based on a bug planted in the Kremlin somewhere. The spy effort was known as Operation Solo and lasted from 1958 to 1977, during which time Childs made fifty-two dangerous spying missions to Moscow and was never detected. Ironically, Childs was almost exposed not by the Soviet KGB, but by the U.S. Congress.

In February 1975, the Senate Select Committee on Intelligence Activities, headed by Senator Frank Church, an Idaho Democrat, launched a hostile investigation into FBI intelligence-gathering activities. Church requested a document that, if released, would have exposed that the FBI had a spy in the Kremlin. The FBI considered shutting down the operation in order to protect Childs's life. They had a choice: Shut down the operation or "read" Senator Church into it, an extremely risky idea considering the leaks that were flowing out of Capital Hill at the time. Top FBI officials took the chance. They explained to Senator Church that if the Solo operation were exposed, the United States would lose the most important intelligence agent it ever had. The senator withdrew his request and the secret agent stayed secret.

David Szady, the FBI's chief of counterintelligence, agreed that Operation Solo represented the best of the Bureau's intelligence operations. Szady disagrees with critics who say the FBI is capable of conducting such successful counterintelligence, counterterrorism, and even intelligence operations like Solo, today.

"We drifted after the wall came down [in 1989], but there's been a lot of pockets of brilliance out there," Szady said. "If we can get recruitments, if we can get assets, if we can do the operations properly and utilize the intelligence from those operations and make conclusions and assessments, we can get back to where we were."

Gathering cold, hard facts for evidence is far different from the more nuanced work of gathering secret intelligence, which in most cases does not lead to espionage prosecutions, Szady said.

■ ■ ■

The Church Commission investigations were only the beginning of a political war waged by congressional liberals and by the Carter and Clinton administrations against the FBI and the CIA, hampering them with greater and greater restrictions, bureaucratic oversight, and politically correct directives.

Oliver B. "Buck" Revell, former associate deputy director of the FBI for investigations, lost friends in the September 11 attacks and says the strikes should have been expected. "I wish that I could tell you," Revell said in detailed testimony before the House of Representatives in October 2001, "that the attacks could not have been anticipated and that we are unlikely to face such devastation again. I cannot. For it is very clear that we have been the targets of a sustained campaign of terrorism since 1979."

Revell viewed the history leading up to September 11 as beginning with two events that happened during the Carter administration. First was the fall of the shah of Iran and the establishment of a fundamentalist Islamic regime in Iran. Second was the Soviet invasion of Afghanistan. These, he said, were the "predicates for the tragedy we suffered on September 11.

"Out of that experience the Iranian-backed Hezbollah bombed our embassies in Beirut twice, and Kuwait once, as well as killing over two hundred Marines in a suicide truck bombing," Revell said. "The Hezbollah took Americans hostage and hijacked our airliners, and yet we seemed impotent to respond. Before we even knew of Osama bin Laden, Imad Mugniyah of the Hezbollah was the leading terrorist against America. He was directly responsible for the attacks against our personnel and facilities in Lebanon, and yet he and his organization have never been punished for their crimes against our nation."

Al Qaeda learned the lessons of Hezbollah and Mugniyah and of the cadres of mujahideen—holy warriors—who fought against the Soviet occupation of Afghanistan. Osama bin Laden and al Qaeda believed guerrilla fighters, employing terrorist tactics, could beat a superpower like the United States. "He learned from Mugniyah that America was not likely to fight back," Revell said.

The laundry list of crimes committed against Americans by Islamic terrorists linked to al Qaeda was long and included attacks on American forces in Somalia in 1992, the first World Trade Center bombing in 1993, and the bombing of a U.S. military building in Riyadh, Saudi Arabia, in 1995. There was also the bombing of the U.S. military residence in Dhahran in 1996, the simultaneous bombings of U.S. embassies in Kenya and Tanzania in 1998, and the successful suicide bombing of the USS *Cole* in Yemen in October 2000. Then there were the plots that didn't hatch. These included attacks on tunnels and bridges in the New York area in 1993, assassinating Pope John Paul II—not an American, obviously, but a key Western leader—during a visit to the Philippines in 1995, and assassinating President Bill Clinton in the Philippines in 1995. Other foiled plots included bombing commercial airliners over the Pacific Ocean in 1995, bombing U.S. landmarks in December 1999 and January 2000, and bombing a U.S. warship in Yemen in January 2000. With all that history, why wasn't the FBI focused on the possibility of an Islamic terror strike on the United States?

"By September 11 we certainly should have known that we were the principal target of a terrorist campaign unlike any we had ever faced," Revell said. "And yet we totally failed to recognize the impending disaster that stalked our nation. Some of us in the counterterrorist business tried to warn of the danger, but we were generally thought of as alarmists. For the purpose of lessons learned, I am citing the concerns I, among others, expressed about our lack of preparedness for the struggle we now face as a war. Islamic extremism has spread to the point where it now has a global infrastructure, including a substantial network in the United States," Revell said.

In the past, counterterrorism officials worried about terrorists gradually increasing the scale of their attacks to include chemical, biological, and nuclear weapons strikes, but "we believed that most terrorist groups thought mass casualties were counterproductive," Revell said. "This was because mass casualties seemed to delegitimize the terrorists' cause, would certainly generate strong governmental responses, and erode terrorist group cohesion. In essence, we thought a certain logic and morality line existed beyond which terrorists dared not go."

Of all the variants of extremist violence, Islamic terrorism is the most active in terms of the sophistication, number, and scale of its attacks. "Many of these groups are considered separatists, and desire a seat at the recognition and negotiation table," Revell said. "Others, considered extreme Islamic zealots, operate as loosely affiliated groups, as in the first World Trade Center and East African bombings," he noted. "For these groups deterrence has less effect. And in fact many have stated that they wanted to maximize casualties to punish the United States, which they have demonized as the Great Satan."

Revell said that when he took charge of counterterrorism in 1980, "the United States was suffering approximately 100 to 120 terrorist incidents per year," ranging from Puerto Rican terrorists to the remnants of the leftist Weather Underground. In meeting the threats the FBI felt hampered by the restrictions forced upon the Bureau by the liberal congressional attitudes of the 1970s, which were highly critical of the military, law enforcement, and intelligence.

"In the FBI we were trying to cope with the aftermath of one of the frequent purges that goes on in our government," Revell said. "There had been no consensus in our nation in the 1960s and 1970s on how to deal with major national issues, particularly the Vietnam War and the antiwar movement, and to some degree the more radical elements of the civil rights movement."

By the mid-1970s, the U.S. intelligence community, including the FBI, came under a harsh political attack during congressional hearings headed by Senator Frank Church, an Idaho Democrat, and Congressman Otis Pike, a New York Democrat. As a result of the controversy, by the late 1970s, the FBI had almost completely shut down its entire domestic security apparatus for fear of being accused of civil rights violations. The FBI was left to deal with specific criminal acts after they had occurred and had "virtually no collection, analysis, or utilization of intelligence prior to the commission of any sort of violent action by a politically motivated organization," Revell said. By 1980, the FBI was facing hundreds of terrorist attacks and incidents and felt it could no longer stand by and investigate the attacks after the fact. As Revell put it, "We had to become proactive again" and not wait for the attacks to take place.

The FBI then began conducting very limited intelligence gathering operations, under strict guidelines set by the attorney general. "These guidelines were intended not only to tell us the limitations of our authority, but also to sanction those actions that we did take, and to make sure that people understood that this was a legitimate exercise of the legal authority of the president, the attorney general, and those charged with carrying out their responsibilities," Revell said. By 1982, the new Reagan administration made antiterrorism a national priority of the FBI, though liberal congressional opposition so undercut the administration's efforts that, according to Revell, by "1988 again we almost went down to ground zero in carrying out our counterterrorism responsibilities. And that's what led us, in my view, to what happened at the 1993 World Trade Center bombing."

Still, the Reagan administration tried. In 1983, the Justice Department issued guidelines permitting investigations of domestic groups that "are engaged in an enterprise for the purpose of furthering political or social goals wholly or in part through activities that involve force or violence" and violation of U.S. law. Prior to a full-scale investigation, federal agents can conduct a "preliminary inquiry" based on accusations or information "indicating possibility of criminal activity."

"The FBI guidelines required, and as far as I know still require, a very clear criminal predicate in order to open a full-scale investigation," former director of Central Intelligence R. James Woolsey told me. "Now they can open something short of that, but by criminal predicate, they mean planning with respect to an act at a specific place and time."

That restriction, Woolsey believes, is still far too severe, because as the law stands now, groups that believe in violence cannot be investigated unless there is evidence that they are about to commit a crime. By that time, intelligence gathering—whether by electronic surveillance or recruiting informants—could be too late.

"Buck" Revell agrees. "Under the guidelines as they are today, the FBI is in the very unusual position of being perhaps the only people in our society who cannot take official cognizance of what people say, of what people do, of what people pronounce and promulgate that they will do until they do it," Revell said. The FBI "is prohibited under the current guidelines and a provision of the Privacy Act, from collecting public information even from groups that directly espouse the use of violence to accomplish their objectives," Revell notes.

■ ■ ■

As part of the see-no-evil problem, the Clinton administration decided to bend the FBI to its own political agenda and purposes.

For instance, under the Clinton administration the Justice Department sought to refocus counterintelligence efforts onto antiabortion bombings, even though the FBI recognized that the problem was not as serious as the growing problem of Islamic terrorism.

John P. O'Neill, the chief of the FBI's counterterrorism section, said in a speech in April 1996 that the threat from Islamic radicals is "the greatest threat coming to us domestically in the United States.

"No longer is it just the fear of being attacked by international terrorist organizations—attacks against Americans and American interests overseas," O'Neill told a conference of corporate security managers. "A lot of these groups now have the capability and the support infrastructure in the United States to attack us here if they choose to." O'Neill said the FBI had observed Islamic radicals practicing in the United States with small-arms and defensive-tactics training, "and on a few rare occasions we have actually seen explosives training taking place in the United States."

O'Neill was killed in the September 11 attacks after he had become security director for the World Trade Center.

Despite FBI warnings—and despite a failed 1997 letter bomb campaign directed at American targets by associates of the World Trade Center bombers—the Clinton administration refused to recognize the threat. State Department spokesman Nicholas Burns said after the letter bombs were discovered that they were "possible acts of international terrorism." There was no "possibility"—it *was* international terrorism, but the State Department refused to recognize it. A short time after the first letter bombs were discovered, two other mail bombs went off in the offices of Al-Hayat in London, injuring two people.

But the Clinton administration simply wasn't interested in antiterrorism, though it was perfectly willing to vastly increase spending at the FBI as an adjunct of Janet Reno's Justice Department. More important to the Clinton administration was the political correctness of the FBI's reorganization under new director Louis Freeh. On October 13, 1993, Freeh, following the Clinton administration push for diversity over performance, appointed a black, a Hispanic, and a woman to top posts in the FBI. He said the appointments marked a "momentous day" for the Bureau. The reorganization that day included the first of several shifts that seriously harmed the FBI's intelligence-gathering capabilities and led indirectly to the failure to detect al Qaeda before September 11. First, Freeh abolished the position of deputy director for investigations that was held by "Buck" Revell until April 1991. At the time of the reorganization, the post was held by a Revell protégé, W. Douglas Gow. It was considered the third highest position within the FBI. Freeh also brought in three cronies who had worked with him in New York, including Robert B. Bucknam, a former assistant U.S. attorney in New York, who became Freeh's chief of staff. Bucknam was viewed as a bureaucratic gatekeeper who closely guarded access to the director and made it difficult for FBI agents to talk to him. Another crony was Howard M. Shapiro, who was named the FBI's general counsel. Both would end up as hatchet men for Freeh and were widely despised by career FBI agents as political commissars who reflected the worst excesses of the Clinton administration's efforts to politicize government.

Gow had no intelligence background, and yet he was put in charge of the intelligence division from January 1990 to June 1991, when he was promoted to the investigations post. This lack of experience severely limited the FBI's ability to go after terrorists and foreign spies. He ended up relying on the advice of David Major, a counterintelligence agent who was considered by FBI counterspy veterans to be, as one put it, "not the strongest" in understanding counterintelligence.

The Freeh shakeup of the FBI also eliminated forty-seven section chiefs and special assistants, noting that there were "unnecessary levels of review." Then he appointed a criminal-side agent, Robert B. "Bear" Bryant, to take over the newly created National Security Division, which replaced the decades-old intelligence division. Bryant had been promoted from the head of the FBI's Washington Field Office, where he had won praise for directing the investigation of CIA mole Aldrich Ames. Bryant took credit for the case, even though the real hero of the operation was the squad supervisor running the case, Leslie Wiser, who disobeyed orders in breaking the Ames case open.

Bryant, according to those who worked with him, had little use for the intelligence specialists and adopted a criminal approach to foreign counterintelligence cases. He bragged that he had taken foreign counterintelligence specialists and put them on criminal cases. As a result, the FBI's foreign counterespionage capabilities suffered. Bryant convinced Freeh that responsibility for counterterrorism, which had been within the criminal division, should be transferred to the new National Security Division. And so counterintelligence—and more important, the counterintelligence approach to terrorism—was given a lower priority.

The low esteem accorded counterintelligence was revealed most shockingly in the case of FBI agent Robert Philip Hanssen, who was found in early 2001 to have been working as a Russian "mole" within the FBI for twenty-two years. Like Aldrich Ames, Hanssen was a mediocre agent, and one with obvious personal problems. He once, for instance, assaulted a woman FBI employee. He was shunted off to a counterintelligence post at the State Department by friends in the Bureau more interested in protecting the FBI's reputation than dealing with a corrupt agent. But it also revealed just how the Bureau felt about the importance of intelligence and counterintelligence. These were places to dump mediocre agents; these functions weren't an FBI priority.

A special commission headed by former FBI and CIA director William Webster found major weaknesses in FBI security and concluded that the FBI had damaged its intelligence capabilities by fostering a law enforcement approach to crime, terrorism, and counterintelligence. "Until the terrorist attacks in September 2001, the FBI focused on detecting and prosecuting traditional crime," the commission's report stated. "That focus created a culture that emphasized the priorities and morale of criminal components within the Bureau, which offered the surest paths for career advancement. This culture extolled cooperation and the free flow of information inside the Bureau, a work ethic wholly at odds with the compartmentation characteristic of intelligence investigations involving highly sensitive, classified information."

The criminal orientation within the FBI dismissed rules aimed at protecting information as "cumbersome, inefficient, and a bar to success," the report said. "However, when a criminal investigation is compromised, usually only a discrete prosecution with a limited set of victims is at risk," the report stated. "In sharp contrast, when an intelligence program is compromised, as Hanssen's case demonstrates, our country's ability to defend itself against hostile forces can be put at risk. A law enforcement culture grounded in shared information is radically different from an intelligence culture grounded in secrecy. Whether the two can co-exist in one organization is a difficult question, but they will never do so in the FBI, unless the Bureau gives its intelligence programs the same resources and respect it gives criminal investigations, which, employing its own sensitive information and confidential sources, would also benefit from improved security."

FBI counterintelligence veteran I. C. Smith agrees with that critique. During the Clinton years, he told me, "There was a de-emphasis on the collection of intelligence. They [the leaders of the FBI] had a criminal division approach. They never really felt comfortable in handling intelligence information. They worked these cases like bank robberies." Smith recalled how, under Freeh, the FBI ceased to be a major part of the U.S. intelligence community. At one meeting with a group of outside specialists who were part of the commission on intelligence, Smith had prepared a speech for Freeh that would address the FBI's counterspy mission. Instead, Freeh talked about improving relations among law enforcement agencies. "I was watching people on the panel," Smith said. "They didn't want to hear about cop-to-cop relationships. They wanted to hear that the FBI should be the lead counterintelligence agency.... It was clear the FBI had no interest in being a player in the [intelligence] community.

"The attitude was, 'They aren't making arrests, so why are they here?'" Smith recalled.

Funds allocated for FBI intelligence-gathering activities were redirected to criminal investigations. In one case, half of a $5 million allocation for intelligence analysis was spent instead on a computer crime center. Counterterrorism funds that were spent on building a laboratory were used in part to fund criminal forensic work. A new allotment of $83 million intended for the hiring of up to one thousand new agents for counterterrorism was spent instead on regular street agents, not specialists.

Smith understood what Freeh didn't: that the FBI's antiterrorist operations needed to focus on electronic surveillance, penetrating groups, recruiting agents, and rigorous analysis of intelligence by specially trained agents who understood foreign cultures, foreign languages, and foreign threats. Such specialists were sorely lacking. At one point in the mid-1990s, the FBI did not even have a basic training course for terrorism analysts, and in 1998, there were only two Arabic-speaking FBI agents available to work on counterterrorism.

Daniel Franklin, writing in the liberal journal *The American Prospect*, pointed the finger at Freeh for mismanaging the FBI's efforts at countering terrorism:

To be fair, it can be difficult for an FBI supervisor to jus-
tify keeping his agents on the business of preventing a
threat that may never materialize while the in-boxes of
criminal investigators accumulate more and more case
files. But the ability to focus on the big threat down the
road, as opposed to the little nuisances nipping at one's
knees, is precisely what separates good leaders from bad
ones. In seeking the funds in the first place, Freeh's
expressed reasoning was, in fact, that it would "double
the 'shoe-leather' for counterterrorism investigations so
that we can address emerging domestic and international
terrorist groups." It never quite worked out that way.[2]

By November 1999, the FBI realized its counterterrorism
efforts were not working. Freeh, at the urging of Deputy Director Bryant, announced another major restructuring of FBI headquarters. Freeh said the changes were intended to "respond to
the changing threats from espionage and terrorism; the need to
enhance analytical capacities, especially across program lines;
and to make more effective use of existing resources." This reorganization created a new Counterterrorism Division, further
highlighting, at least bureaucratically, the need to do more
against terrorist attacks. Counterintelligence remained within the
National Security Division and continued to be robbed of
resources. A new Investigative Services Division was created to
coordinate FBI international activities. Freeh claimed that the
new international unit would "substantially strengthen" FBI
analysis.

But as September 11 proved, it didn't work, and in December
2001, FBI director Robert Mueller announced another restructuring. The decade-long program to homogenize the FBI had eliminated many specialty jobs, he said. "Over the years, the FBI
tended to hire generalists, operating within a culture that most
jobs were best done by agents. We need subject matter experts in

areas like computers, foreign languages, internal security, area studies, engineering, records, and the like. We have not adequately recruited and hired towards such a specialized work force, or matched very well who comes in the door with the skill sets we not only need now, but what we will need two, three, or five years out.

"Given the tragic events of September 11th, a different FBI is needed with a new focus, new tools, and new resources, and, in some instances, employees with new or different skill sets," Mueller said. "We have to do more to fix what is broken and to reshape what no longer fits after the events of September 11th."

Mueller announced that since September 11 the FBI has created a new Office of Intelligence aimed at "building a strategic analysis capability and improving our capacity to gather, analyze, and share critical national security information." As part of the reorganization of the FBI, Mueller is developing a "massive prevention effort"—something that distinguishes the Bush administration's approach from the Clinton administration's law enforcement method of fighting terrorism. "Given the gravity of the current terrorist threat to the United States, the FBI must make hard decisions to focus its available energies and resources on preventing additional terrorist acts and protecting our nation's security," Mueller said. The fiscal 2003 budget request was $4.2 billion, including $7.7 million for hiring 110 new intelligence analysts who, it is hoped, will "address tactical and strategic intelligence gaps" in the fight against terrorism.

The White House recognizes that U.S. intelligence agencies must be restructured to better deal with terrorism. A White House fact sheet states, "The President believes that an effective use of intelligence and closer coordination across all levels of government will help stop future terrorist attacks."

After September 11, the White House discovered that information about the nineteen hijackers' activities was available on a variety of computer databases at the federal, state, and local government levels, as well as in the private sector. "Looking forward, we must build a system that combines threat information and then transmits it as needed to all relevant law enforcement and public safety officials," the statement said.

And it is encouraging that Robert Mueller, in a public speech in April 2002, recognized the intelligence shortcomings of the FBI and said steps were being taken to improve intelligence analysis. "The September 11th terrorists," he noted, "spent a great deal of time and effort figuring out how America works. They knew the ins and outs of our systems. We need to have a complete grasp on how terrorists operate as well. Our analysts do some great work, but we need more of them and we need to do more of the kind of strategic thinking that helps us stay one step ahead of those who would do us harm."

But not all blame resides with the main domestic and foreign intelligence agencies, the FBI and the CIA. Congress also shares the blame, and its oversight of intelligence—or lack of it, or wrong use of it—is a prime cause of the intelligence breakdown that led to September 11.

6

CONGRESS AND
DESTRUCTIVE OVERSIGHT

ON DECEMBER 22, 1974, a *New York Times* banner headline announced: "Huge C.I.A. Operation Reported in U.S. Against Anti-War Forces." The story was written by veteran reporter Seymour Hersh. Two days before it appeared in print, Hersh found himself at the CIA's headquarters building in Langley, Virginia, sitting inside the seventh floor office of William Colby, director of Central Intelligence. The reporter had learned about secret efforts by the Central Intelligence Agency to monitor U.S. mail, something banned under the CIA's charter.

Colby represented a left-wing political faction within the CIA that was posed against the conservative, anticommunist faction led by the CIA's legendary master counterspy James Jesus Angleton. In the political struggle, Angleton would lose his job as the powerful chief of counterintelligence. With Angleton's defeat, counterintelligence and counterespionage would become so neglected as to cease to exist within the CIA.

Angleton, in retirement, told me shortly before his death in 1987 that the essence of intelligence work is having the capability to read a foreign target's communications, without the target knowing it. His philosophy of intelligence was based on experience in World War II when the ability to read, clandestinely, both German and Japanese coded military and other communications made the difference between victory and defeat.

Angleton understood the Cold War better than most intelligence officials and realized that the way to defeat the Soviet Union was through attacking its intelligence and security services. "If I had become director, I would have reoriented the CIA in the direction of counterintelligence," Angleton said. The strategy was simple: target Soviet and Soviet bloc intelligence services for penetration and use strategic disinformation ultimately to defeat their political masters. But Angleton never had the chance to put his theory into practice. The strategy was nixed by Colby and the anti–Cold War faction within the CIA who not only opposed Angleton and his methods, but also saw themselves as the last line of defense in stopping U.S. military hawks from launching World War III.[1]

Colby was director of Central Intelligence from 1973 to 1975, a time of turmoil over the activities of the Clandestine Service. His suspected role in exposing the CIA's activities to Hersh was part of a carefully crafted strategy to push Angleton aside and diminish Angleton's authority along with the authority of Angleton's supporters—hard-line CIA officers within the counterintelligence staff and the Directorate of Operations.

The CIA establishment, led by Colby, was not content to see Angleton removed and sent into retirement. There was a concerted campaign to discredit him, and thereby discredit like-minded CIA officials. Angleton was accused—falsely—of being a paranoid, a zealot, someone who saw spies under every bed. By the late 1970s, the CIA had purged itself of all serious counterintelligence. And anyone who suggested that the agency was penetrated was dismissed as a practitioner of Angletonian "sick think," as critics of counterintelligence called efforts to find and neutralize foreign spies.

Colby, after the oversight hearings, had established an axis with the liberals in Congress who shared the view that aggressive intelligence could pose a threat to democracy. Political shackles were placed on the CIA's Directorate of Operations, and by the time President Jimmy Carter came into office, the ranks of the CIA's Clandestine Service had been thoroughly slashed through a series of devastating cuts.

The purge began during the crippled administration of President Gerald Ford. Seymour Hersh's December 1974 *New York Times* article on the CIA led to an executive branch commission headed by Vice President Nelson Rockefeller to look into allegations of CIA abuses. The President's Commission on CIA Activities within the United States (known as the Rockefeller Commission) produced a final report in June 1975. The commission delved into CIA activities that included mail intercepts and the collection of information on American dissidents.

But the mood of Congress would not permit a quiet inquiry to take place. The result was the formation of two congressional committees that will forever be notorious in the annals of U.S. intelligence. Charges of domestic spying by the CIA were at the center of the controversy, and Congress reacted swiftly. The investigations expanded to include all U.S. intelligence agencies, including the world's most sophisticated technical spying agency, the supersecret National Security Agency. The U.S. Senate created the Senate Select Committee to Study Government Operations with Respect to Intelligence Activities, on January 27, 1975. The panel was headed by Senator Frank Church, an Idaho Democrat.

The House followed suit on February 19, with its own version called the House Select Intelligence Committee, headed at first by Representative Lucien N. Nedzi, a Michigan Democrat. Five months later, he would be replaced as chairman by Representative Otis Pike, a New York Democrat.

Both panels were packed with liberal Democrats who assumed that U.S. intelligence agencies posed a threat to American democracy and engaged in widespread criminal activity. "For the first time in the agency's history, CIA officials faced hostile Congressional committees bent on the exposure of abuses by intelligence agencies and on major reforms," wrote CIA historian Gerald K. Haines. "In the Congress, there was no longer a consensus to support intelligence activities blindly. The old Congressional seniority system and its leadership were giving way. With the investigations, the CIA also became a focal point in the ongoing battle between the Congress and the executive branch over foreign policy issues and the 'imperial presidency.' "

The Church Committee focused on the sensational charges of illegal activities by the CIA and other intelligence agencies. The Nedzi Committee and its successor, the Pike Committee, focused more on CIA effectiveness and its costs to taxpayers. The Nedzi panel, which tilted heavily to the left, was made up of seven Democrats and three Republicans. One of its members was Representative Ron Dellums, a radical left-wing Democrat from California. Dellums said, "I think this committee ought to come down hard and clear on the side of stopping any intelligence agency in this country from utilizing, corrupting, and prostituting the media, the church, and our educational system."

Nedzi, while liberal, was chairman of a House subcommittee on intelligence and not reflexively anti-CIA. So left-wing Democrats opposed him and tried to hold a hearing of their own, without the chairman and without Republicans. Under House rules, the hearing was canceled, and Nedzi resigned as chairman in protest. On July 17, 1975, the House abolished the Nedzi committee and set up a new select committee with Pike as the chairman.

Later that month, Director of Central Intelligence William Colby met with Pike. According to the CIA, Pike told Colby that he, like Senator Church, believed the CIA was a "rogue elephant" operating outside of government control and needed to be restrained.

Though Colby told Pike that the CIA needed to protect its sources and methods of intelligence gathering, Pike asserted that the committee would decide unilaterally to declassify what it wanted. The CIA would not be allowed to set up standards or protections for what documents might be delivered to the panel.

Predictably, open political warfare between the agency and the Pike Committee followed.

CIA officer Richard Lehman said that the Pike Committee staff was "absolutely convinced that they were dealing with the devil incarnate." Another CIA officer, Donald Gregg, who was in charge of providing information to the committee, said: "The months I spent with the Pike Committee made my tour in Vietnam seem like a picnic. I would vastly prefer to fight the Viet Cong than deal with polemical investigation by a congressional committee, which is what the Pike Committee [investigation] was."

On the Senate side, the Church Committee's final report called for creating a permanent oversight committee, and in May 1976, the Senate Select Committee on Intelligence was formed. The first panel included seventeen members and fifty staff members, including fourteen who were part of the controversial Church Committee.

But the real legacy of the Church and Pike committees was the empowerment of an entire new set of people within the intelligence community. This new group saw its primary function as providing a check on what it regarded as the militaristic and hard-line views within the U.S. government. It was this group that created a culture of intelligence that persists today—that ignores the need for counterintelligence and relies on material gathered by foreign intelligence services rather than on the CIA's own intelligence operations. Another lasting legacy was a sense among many Republicans that their role was to uncritically defend the agency, regardless of how it performed, to prevent another Democratic attack on the intelligence services.

FBI counterintelligence chief Dave Szady said one part of the problem of the FBI intelligence can be traced to the Church and Pike Committees, including the fact that the FBI had, at the time of September 11, some of the worst computer systems in government. Szady recalled how one liberal congressman, Representative Robert Drinan, Massachusetts Democrat, said during the 1970s that he would make sure the FBI never had good computer systems because Drinan believed they would use them to spy on Americans.

"Our technical systems are terrible," Szady said. "Everyone admits to that. Congress has agreed it's a disaster. If you go back to the Church Committee days, and Congressman Drinan, he was in the FBI and going through our great records systems back in the 1970s, and it was a paper system and it was very good. And we said it had to be automated. And I remember Drinan was in there and went to the indices and found his name and threw the cards up in the air and said, 'The FBI will never have an automated system and be able to collect intelligence on American citizens.' And that was what came off the Hill at that time: The FBI will not have automated computers with information on them on Americans. Well, it wasn't for that. We were going to put our cases on it. What we had there will go into computers."

When the FBI finally switched to computers in large numbers, it did so with poorly engineered systems that prevented easy sharing of intelligence and information among divisions and even within divisions. One intelligence analyst said that during the 1990s, FBI computers located on the seventh floor, where the National Security Division is based, could not communicate with computers in a separate section two floors below. E-mail and other electronic messaging, which are vital for disseminating intelligence and information, also are extremely poor.

"In all large organizations, knowledge is power," Larry Downes, an information technology specialist and business consultant told me. "The easier it is to share, the better it flows; the more of it there is, the better our chances will be of overcoming enemies who learned that lesson a long time ago." Downes, author of *The Strategy Machine*, which addresses information sharing, said the term "stovepiping"—the failure of government intelligence agencies to communicate and share information— came from business. American businesses have struggled for years to share information from one part of the company with others. In highly bureaucratized intelligence services, giving away information is giving away influence, and organizations will fight information-sharing efforts.

Businesses have sought to solve stovepiping problems with computers and software that help disseminate information, something the intelligence community has resisted.

A U.S. intelligence official involved in oversight told me the problem of stovepiping U.S. intelligence agencies that refuse to work together and share intelligence is their biggest problem. Breaking down the pipes and improving dissemination—the same problem identified as the cause of the intelligence failure that led to Pearl Harbor—is the key to solving the problems that led to September 11.

FBI Agent Coleen Rowley, who blew the whistle on the FBI's failure to pursue Zacarias Moussaoui, told a Senate hearing that computer problems hampered the search for terrorists. She said that analysts did not have the ability to log on to a computer and search for data using words like "flight" and "airline."

"When it comes to intelligence and you really have these critical snippets out there . . . I think it's necessary. It may not in other cases be all that critical, but in intelligence, I think it is."

FBI director Robert Mueller sent a memorandum to all FBI field offices on October 10, 2001, altering FBI policy regarding the Automated Case Support System, a central database used by agents to open and assign cases, set and assign leads, store documents such as investigative and interview reports, and index, search, and retrieve these documents. The system was launched in 1995 and replaced the FBI's archaic paper document system. The ACS, as it is called, also contains administrative information, such as files on personnel and memoranda.

A special review panel that investigated the ACS in the wake of the Robert Hanssen espionage case found that agents often refused to add important case information to the system and that it had hampered the investigation into the September 11 bombings, known as PENTBOM. "Apparently, agents assigned to pursue leads in PENTBOM had been frustrated by restrictions limiting access to potentially relevant case files, and FBI senior management had determined that agents' frustration was well grounded," the report said.

With the election of Ronald Reagan, a more balanced approach to congressional oversight of intelligence was enforced, at least temporarily. Reagan's first term was, with regard to intelligence, a period "essentially dominated by an axis of [Senator Daniel Patrick] Pat Moynihan and [Senator] Malcolm Wallop," said congressional intelligence veteran Angelo Codevilla. Several key staff members with a good understanding of the complexities of intelligence—Codevilla, for example, was a naval reserve intelligence officer—managed to shift the Senate away from attacking "the intelligence community," and most especially the CIA, to improving it. "We changed the purpose of oversight to improving the capacity of the agency to function as it should," Codevilla told me. "These were the performance years." During this period the purpose of intelligence oversight, at least within the Senate, was to hold the intelligence community accountable for its performance.

Performance-based oversight ended when Senator David Durenberger, Minnesota Republican, became the Senate Intelligence Committee chairman, and performance-based oversight never returned during subsequent chairmanships. "The oversight business became an oversight lapdog," Codevilla said. Recent chairmen in both the House and Senate have been dominated by members of Congress who either are unable to grasp the complexities of intelligence oversight and how to conduct oversight, or by members intent only on protecting the CIA. In many ways, congressional oversight degenerated into a mutual admiration society for secret agencies. Instead of checking the performance of agencies and how they spend upwards of $30 billion to $35 billion annually of taxpayer money, the committees of Congress charged with oversight have become cheerleaders for poorly managed, badly structured, and improperly funded intelligence agencies.

Such is the case with Representative Porter Goss, Florida Republican and chairman of the House Intelligence Committee at the time of the September 11 attacks. Goss was notorious among congressional aides for stripping out any tough legislation from the annual intelligence authorization bills that would have required the CIA to become more effective. He played a major role in making sure oversight did nothing to improve the CIA. A former CIA officer, Goss saw it as his personal mission to protect the agency from its critics. The result was that the CIA was able to manipulate the House oversight panel and neutralize any serious effort to improve its performance.

Goss helped "cover up" for the CIA's lack of performance, Codevilla told me. "Not for any [politically] partisan purpose, but quite simply because of agency partisanship, a confusion of patriotism with agency loyalty." For Goss and those like him, any criticism of the CIA is out of bounds.[2] Partly as a result of the excesses of the Church and Pike committees, too many supporters of the CIA and U.S. intelligence agencies in general confuse performance-based criticism with anti-intelligence criticism. The resulting focus on bureaucratic structures has resulted in a misguided view that protecting the institution itself from critics, of whatever variety, is more important that getting the job done. "This has always been the case with the CIA," Codevilla said. "This really has been an enormous problem for the CIA.

"It was perfectly clear that their intellectual, moral, and effective horizon was the agency," Codevilla went on. "It was really a closed thing. They didn't really care what happened outside of Washington, D.C." For example, during the Cold War, the debate over the future of the Soviet Union had very little to do with the Soviet Union. Analysts were more concerned with who won and who lost internal bureaucratic struggles, and whose prestige was advanced and whose was denigrated in Washington. "It was navel-gazing," Codevilla said.

Codevilla, by virtue of his skill at uncovering CIA shortcomings, became the bête noire of U.S. intelligence.[3] He understood how intelligence worked and served a senator, Wallop, who wanted to make it better.

But there were plenty of graduates from the Church and Pike committees who had other ideas—very different ideas from Codevilla. One of them was L. Britt Snider, a Church Committee staff member who later became a senior official at the CIA and eventually its inspector general, not to mention staff director for a joint congressional investigation into the intelligence failure of September 11, at least for a brief period of time.[4]

Another was Karl F. "Rick" Inderfurth. Inderfurth would go from the Church Committee staff to ABC News as a reporter/producer. Then during the Clinton administration, he was appointed to the post of assistant secretary of state for Near East affairs. Inderfurth was in a key policy position during one of the most important intelligence failures that occurred during the Clinton administration: the 1998 nuclear tests by India and Pakistan, for which the administration was completely unprepared. In the months before India's May 1998 underground nuclear test, the U.S. ambassador to India, Frank Wisner, showed highly classified satellite intelligence photographs to India government officials.

Inderfurth, as the assistant secretary of state for the region, almost certainly would have approved the intelligence sharing. The photographs revealed the indicators that U.S. intelligence agencies used to identify nuclear test preparations and allowed the Indians to mask their preparation and therefore fool U.S. intelligence. Wisner told me the intelligence photographs were shown for a brief period of time, and he denied that the breach had helped Indian deception efforts. But the lapse would prove to be one of the CIA's worst failures. It triggered nuclear tests by Pakistan that have made the India-Pakistan standoff one of the most volatile in the world. It was the result of the anti-intelligence bias of officials like Inderfurth whose dislike of U.S. intelligence dated back to his work for the Church Committee.

Before taking over the State Department position, Inderfurth was a special assistant to Madeleine Albright, who was the U.S. ambassador to the United Nations during President Clinton's second term. Inderfurth was a proponent of Albright's policy of "assertive multilateralism," the liberal notion that the United States should not be the leader of the free world but should let the United Nations take the lead. Inderfurth also was a major proponent of sharing classified U.S. intelligence information with the United Nations, something opposed by senior intelligence officials because of the lack of security within the world body.

By 2001, congressional oversight of intelligence had two results. First, it had left the intelligence services burdened with a combination of restrictions, constraints, and funding controls produced during the destructive period of the Church and Pike committees. Second, and in reaction to the first, it left Congress uninterested in performance-based oversight, which meant, ultimately, that millions of dollars were wasted on bureaucracy rather than intelligence achievement.

The legal restrictions are the most inhibiting. Spies operating overseas by their very nature violate the laws of other nations. Unfortunately, lawyers now proliferate throughout the intelligence community to the point where following the rules is more important than getting the job done, whether the job is tracking and stopping terrorists or gathering information on foreign weapons systems.

One example of how the rise of the lawyers inhibited performance in the CIA was in 1989, when the agency was unable to back a coup in Panama by army officers who sought to overthrow General Manuel Noriega. The CIA balked at assisting the coup because of fears that the agency would be embroiled in a controversy either by violating the ban on assassinations, if Noriega was killed in the coup, or by failure to notify Congress in advance of an operation. This hesitancy and fear of upsetting Congress have resulted in missed opportunities and a risk-averse culture within U.S. intelligence that proved deadly, as the attacks of September 11 showed.

The pervasive influence of the lawyers was also responsible for the passage of legislation in 1989 requiring the CIA to have an inspector general separate from the agency. The CIA opposed the measure because of concerns for security. The new inspector general filed annual reports to Congress on operations, and the fact that some of the agency's secret operations could be revealed led to further institutional opposition to taking risks. It was one more restriction that put the CIA and other intelligence leaders on notice that taking risks was not worth the trouble if you could be hauled up before Congress.

On the other side of the issue—on holding the intelligence community responsible for results—in the aftermath of September 11 there is very little stomach in Congress to find out why U.S. intelligence failed to do its job and stop the al Qaeda network before it could strike.

Vice President Cheney told me in an interview that there might be lessons to be learned from "reviewing what we knew and how we collected and analyzed information leading up to 9/11.

"I don't, in principle, have any quarrel with the notion of a careful, analytical, and balanced look at how the intelligence community performed prior to 9/11," Cheney said. "I would emphasize, I guess, that I think we need to avoid recriminations and a witch hunt here. The fact of the matter is we're in the midst of a major conflict, in terms of the war on terrorism. And our intelligence agencies—both foreign and domestic—have a major role to play in defending us against further attacks and in helping us prosecute the war." Cheney expressed the fear that a congressional inquiry into the intelligence failures of September 11 might "get out of hand and become some kind of a political witch hunt.

"That would be extraordinarily unfortunate, because it would clearly inhibit the ability of the agencies to do the job that they're going to have to do here and now and in the future for us," the vice president said. "So it needs to be positive and constructive, not an effort to tear down some agencies or to malign the reputations of individuals who are doing a superb job right now in the war on terrorism."

After disclosures that President Bush was briefed in August 2001 with a vague intelligence report that said al Qaeda terrorists might hijack airliners in order to free imprisoned terrorists, Democrats called for a major investigation. President Bush and top Bush administration officials rejected the calls, however, insisting that the joint review by the intelligence oversight panels would be sufficient.

But what of their failure to prevent the terrorist sneak attack of September 11?

"I guess the question is what your expectations are with respect to our ability to be able to defend against an attack," Cheney said. "And my view is that you probably cannot construct a perfect defense. You do all you can, in terms of trying to penetrate the organizations of the terrorist, in terms of trying to harden the target here at home. But the ultimate defense here, the only thing that guarantees your security is to destroy your enemy. So our capacity to avoid future attacks is partly a function of good intelligence. But it's also going to be very much related to how successful we are at going out and destroying the terrorist organization. A good offense is the best defense here."

Defense Secretary Donald Rumsfeld has been extremely unhappy with the performance of U.S. intelligence agencies, according to defense officials. Asked by reporters about plans to "streamline and improve the flow of intelligence in government," Rumsfeld reacted with caution. "I've always felt," he said, "that in intelligence gathering, as in research and development, what you need is multiple sources of information. Those types of things are the few things where you may lose more by going for efficiency, by centralization, than you gain. For example, pharmaceutical companies make a practice of having research and development activities in different countries and different states, recognizing that it may cost a little more, may be a little less efficient, but in fact, you're not looking for efficiency, you're looking for creativity, you're looking for innovation, you're looking for information, in the case of intelligence gathering. And to be dependent upon a single source or a single line or a single viewpoint is probably not a great idea. I doubt if it will happen. Don't know. We'll see."[5]

When a joint congressional committee was finally empanelled to look into the September 11 intelligence failures, it was hamstrung from the start by poor leadership. Britt Snider, the former Church Committee veteran turned CIA insider, was picked by the joint chairmen, Senator Bob Graham, a Florida Democrat, and Representative Porter Goss, a Florida Republican. Snider was viewed as someone who would do the CIA's bidding when it came to protecting the agency from its critics.

Frank Gaffney, a former Pentagon official and president of the Center for Security Policy, said the appointment of Snider meant that "The fix is in. Given the actual nature of his associations in Congress and at the agency, . . . it is no more reasonable to expect Britt Snider to be thorough, let alone truly independent, than it would be if Enron's general counsel had been tapped to run hearings into his company's meltdown.

"It would be one thing if George Tenet had said from the get-go after September 11 that there were serious problems in the way his agency, and the intelligence community more broadly, had been doing business," Gaffney said. Tenet should have acknowledged the problems such as "the political correctness of U.S. intelligence products, the diminished priority accorded to human intelligence, and serious restraints on domestic surveillance of potentially subversive elements," which were a major contribution to U.S. vulnerability to terrorist attacks.

But since Tenet has denied there was any failure, "can someone closely tied to the director, someone who shares some measure of responsibility with him for whatever went wrong, possibly be the best choice to lead this important inquiry?

"The nation desperately needs to learn—and to apply urgently—the lessons of September 11," Gaffney said. "Regrettably, the outrageousness, and the potential costs, of failing to get to the bottom of the September 11 intelligence failures demand an even greater outcry now."

In response to the joint congressional inquiry, the CIA formed a secret task force on September 11 to prepare for the hearings. A source familiar with the inquiry said it appeared to be more an exercise in protecting the agency from congressional critics than trying to deal honestly with its shortcomings.

Then on April 26, 2002, Snider quit under pressure from Congress, which thought his choices for staff unacceptable and, according to anonymous staff members, found that Snider had made an "error in judgment" that members of Congress viewed as a firing offense. Congressional sources said Snider left in a dispute with members of the panel over the misuse of classified information by someone Snider had hired.

But, in the end, Snider isn't the only one who should be fired. Congress should use its congressionally mandated oversight powers to hold the intelligence services accountable and see that the crippling bureaucracy that grew up after the Church-Pike committees is reformed. Congress needs to insist that the intelligence community spend its vast resources in winning this new war on terrorism, and to hold it responsible for its performance.

In mid-May 2002, CIA officials in charge of congressional affairs quietly informed the House and Senate intelligence committees that they might want to ask some questions of the White House. "We hear there was an interesting PDB [President's Daily Brief]," said one official. The President's Daily Brief is the CIA's most important intelligence product. It contains the most detailed summary of intelligence deemed important to the United States and is tailored for the president and his top aides.

The committees questioned the White House and were told that on August 6, 2001, the president was given a special analytical report on terrorism that said Osama bin Laden might conduct airline hijackings to force the release of some imprisoned al Qaeda terrorists around the world.

On May 15, 2002, the story leaked on CBS News that the president had been informed that bin Laden was planning airline hijackings. The next day all major newspapers reported on the August 6 briefing with the implicit implication that the president had somehow known in advance of the September 11 attack. The most egregious headline appeared as a banner in the *New York Post*: "Bush Knew."

What had happened was a carefully crafted CIA disinformation campaign to distract attention from the CIA's failures on September 11. The campaign was picked up by congressional Democrats eager for an issue to attack the president in an election year. Richard A. Gephardt, the House minority leader, told reporters, "I think what we have to do now is find out what the president, what the White House knew about the events leading up to 9/11, when they knew it and most importantly, what was done about it."

In the Senate, majority leader Tom Daschle criticized the president. "Why did it take eight months for us to receive this information?" Daschle said at a news conference the day the August 6 briefing was reported. "And secondly, what specific actions were taken by the White House in response?"

The attacks came on the heels of the disclosure about the July memorandum from the FBI's Phoenix field office warning that al Qaeda terrorists were taking flying lessons as part of a possible operation.

According to a senior U.S. government intelligence official, the timing of the CIA operation—to divert attention away from the agency and toward the White House—was impeccable. "The FBI was twisting in the wind, and the CIA was able to say, 'We told you about hijackings,'" the senior official said.

The White House went into full damage control to try and fend off the news media feeding frenzy. National Security Advisor Condoleezza Rice met with reporters at the White House to announce that the August 6 briefing report "was not a warning briefing but an analytic report." This report, she said, "did not having warning information of the kind that said they were talking about an attack and so forth and so on. It was an analytic report that talked about [Osama bin Laden's] methods of operation, talked about what he had done historically, in 1997, in 1998. It mentioned hijacking, but hijacking in the traditional sense, in a sense that the most important and most likely thing was that they would take over an airliner holding passengers and demand the release of one of their operatives. And the blind sheikh [Omar Abdel-Rahman, who was in prison for plotting terrorist attacks in

New York] was mentioned by name...even though he's not an operative of al Qaeda but as somebody who might be bargained in this way." Rice indirectly fired back at the intelligence community. As for any intelligence warnings, "I want to reiterate that during this time, the overwhelming bulk of the evidence was that this was an attack that was likely to take place overseas," she said.

The Democrats smelled political pay dirt and would not be mollified. Daschle called for a major "independent" investigation. "I have come to the conclusion that a commission is required for us to come to some final resolution," Daschle said.

House majority whip Tom DeLay, Texas Republican, said the joint intelligence panel that was already conducting a review of the events leading up to September 11 was the best vehicle for the inquiry.[6] "We must not allow the president to be undermined by those who want his job," DeLay said. "We must not be overzealous when the situation calls for thoughtfulness."

The intelligence community's strategy for stifling the joint review committee was to "bury" the panel in documents, administration intelligence officials said. The CIA alone provided over 350,000 documents, knowing that the work of sifting out relevant material was beyond the capabilities of the small staff of thirty people and its new director, former Clinton administration Defense Department inspector general Eleanor Hill.

The review bogged down also because of disputes among members over the timetable and direction of the committee's work.

A planned joint committee hearing was scrubbed and Senate members held their own session, behind closed doors, to discuss their unhappiness with the performance of the committee, which began its inquiry by hearing testimony from staff members for the first several weeks before interviewing their first witness, former National Security Council terrorism expert Richard Clarke.

"There are some people who think we're going too slow. Some people who think we're going too fast. Some people who think we have too many closed hearings. Some people who think we shouldn't have anything but closed meetings," said Senator Bob Graham, Florida Democrat and chairman of the Senate Intelligence Committee and a co-chairman of the joint panel. "I'm not going to overreact to the fact that you've got strong positions expressed and that they are conflicting."

The staff showed inexperience and an inability to ask the right questions, committee sources said.

The head of the CIA's Counterterrorist Center was to be an early witness, but his appearance was put off because the committee could not agree on the schedule.

Meanwhile, under pressure from Democrats, President George W. Bush in June 2002 announced the creation of a new cabinet agency called the Department of Homeland Security whose mission is to consolidate dozens of federal agencies under a super security agency.

"Right now, as many as a hundred different government agencies have some responsibilities for homeland security—and no one has final accountability," Bush said in a nationally televised address from the White House. The department will incorporate the Immigration and Naturalization Service, the Customs Service, the Coast Guard, the Federal Emergency Management Agency, the Border Patrol, and the Secret Service, along with dozens of other agencies.

"I ask the Congress to join me in creating a single permanent department with an overriding and urgent mission: securing the American homeland and protecting the American people," Bush said. Some 170,000 federal employees would be part of the new agency and it would be funded by $38 billion in budgets from the agencies it would absorb.

Only days before the announcement, President Bush reluctantly acknowledged that U.S. intelligence agencies did not do enough to detect and prevent the attacks. "We are now learning that before September 11, the suspicions and insights of some of our frontline agents did not get enough attention," he said. "Information must be fully shared, so we can follow every lead to find the one that may prevent tragedy."

Of the congressional review of the intelligence failures, Bush said: "We need to know when warnings were missed or signs unheeded, not to point the finger of blame, but to make sure we correct any problems, and prevent them from happening again." The president said he had seen no sign that the September 11 attacks could have been prevented, even if intelligence had been better disseminated.

The president's plan for a new Department of Homeland Security called for four divisions. A Border and Transportation Security section will replace the Immigration and Naturalization Service, now under the Justice Department. The Coast Guard would be moved from the Transportation Department, and the Customs Services would be transferred from the Treasury Department. The Animal and Plant Health Inspection Service would join from the Agriculture Department, and the Federal Protective Service would be shifted from the General Services Administration.

An Emergency Preparedness and Response section will combine the independent Federal Emergency Management Agency; the chemical, biological, radiological, and nuclear response assets from the Health and Human Services Department; the domestic emergency support team from the Justice Department; the nuclear-incident response from the Energy Department; the Office of Domestic Preparedness from the Justice Department; and the FBI's national domestic preparedness office.

A Chemical, Biological, Radiological and Nuclear Countermeasures section will oversee efforts by the Lawrence Livermore National Laboratory in Livermore, California, the Health and Human Services Department's biodefense research program, and the Agriculture Department's Plum Island Animal Disease Center.

A new Information Analysis and Infrastructure Protection section will be set up to analyze intelligence from the FBI and CIA and absorb the Secret Service, as well as the Critical Infrastructure Assurance Office at the Commerce Department; the Federal Computer Incident Response Center from GSA; the National Communications Systems division at the Defense Department; and the National Infrastructure Protection Center at the FBI.

The most obvious problem with the new bureaucracy is that both the CIA and FBI were left untouched by the plan, a major shortfall that will not resolve the problems in both agencies and other intelligence components. By leaving out the FBI and the CIA, the president is ensuring that the intelligence agencies that need reform the most will not be changed in any fundamental way.

The plan for the new agency grew out of a congressional debate about Bush's director of homeland security, former Pennsylvania governor Tom Ridge, who had refused to testify before Congress under the principle that he was a White House employee entitled to executive privilege. The new agency will have a cabinet secretary whose appointment would require Senate confirmation, which Ridge does not have. In the meantime, the war on terror goes on.

7

TECHNICAL SPYING

DURING THE EARLY 1980s, U.S. Air Force photographic intelligence analysts—men trained to study the high-resolution images produced by U.S. reconnaissance satellites—were ordered to carry out a special project. They were asked to look for anything that seemed unusual in photographic intelligence of Moscow's continuing buildup of strategic nuclear forces targeting the United States.

One day the special group made a breakthrough discovery. A top secret satellite photograph revealed a dump truck filled with dirt, exiting a building with no other signs of construction work. The truck was part of an ultrasecret Soviet strategic program. After more careful watching over a period of months, a network of Soviet strategic underground construction was revealed. It proved that Moscow's communist rulers planned to be able to fight and survive a nuclear war.

The Air Force analysts were called to the White House to brief President Reagan. After their presentation, as the group was led out of the Oval Office, a senior official of the National Security Agency, the world's premier electronic intelligence-gathering organization, commented to a colleague, "That's an interesting briefing. There's only one problem. It isn't true." The NSA official went on to say that it was impossible for the Soviet government to have carried out the massive strategic underground construction program without the NSA's electronic eavesdroppers picking it up. Unfortunately for the NSA, the construction program was real, and the NSA had missed it. The Soviets had relied on special electronic communications channels that were never intercepted by the United States.

The National Security Agency's arrogant view of itself as the only real American intelligence-gathering service is one very big reason why the American intelligence community has come to rely too much on technical intelligence gathering as opposed to human intelligence.

The technical agencies, primarily the NSA, the National Reconnaissance Office, and its analytical arm, the National Imagery and Mapping Agency, are uniquely designed to support U.S. military operations around the world, and that is the direction they should follow in pursuing the war on terrorism. They should help direct American forces to their targets. But their methods for support and direction should not dominate intelligence gathering. However, they have dominated because their information has often been superb. The NSA in particular has scored impressive successes in identifying the operations of al Qaeda, at least until 1998.

■■■

In 1998, Air Force lieutenant general Kenneth A. Minihan, as director of the National Security Agency, was the man who kept the most important secrets of the United States government. His agency's budget was estimated at $3 to $5 billion, and he could boast of an unparalleled worldwide network of satellites, ships, and ground stations gathering intelligence. But now Minihan sat in his office at the sprawling headquarters building in Fort

Meade, Maryland, and read an intelligence report with dismay. It was the NSA-NSOC Morning Summary, a compendium of the most important signals intelligence information gathered around the world.

Since at least 1995, NSA had been eavesdropping on every telephone call made by Osama bin Laden and his close circle of terrorist assistants. The calls were made on the Inmarsat Mini-M satellite telephone system, one of the first portable systems that allowed communications any place on the globe. But the report labeled "Top Secret-Umbra-Gamma" explained that the "link" that had been providing the secret intercepts from bin Laden had stopped. According to U.S. intelligence officials, the ability to intercept Osama bin Laden's Inmarsat calls was lost shortly after America's August 1998 bombing strikes on Afghan terrorist training sites. One official told me that the link went silent after a report in the *Washington Post* quoted a former U.S. intelligence official as saying that the NSA had been monitoring bin Laden's telephone. "We lost the link after that," the official said.

U.S. intelligence officials said that, despite the loss, the NSA still managed to trace bin Laden to other bombing attacks, including the attacks on September 11. These officials said a communications intercept gathered after the attacks revealed that bin Laden operatives had relayed messages by telephone that two targets had been hit. The intelligence was confirmed inadvertently by Senator Orrin G. Hatch of Utah, the ranking Republican on the Senate Judiciary Committee. Hatch stated in an interview broadcast on CNN on September 12 that an intercept had revealed the bin Laden group claim to have "hit two targets." The comments drew swift but private condemnation from senior intelligence officials, who said the senator had given the terrorists a key indication that their communications were being monitored.

The day before the September 11 attacks, NSA's electronic ears picked up two intercepts, both in Arabic, from the al Qaeda plotters. The intercepts disclosed that a major attack was set for the next day, according to intelligence officials. One of the intercepts stated cryptically, "The match begins tomorrow." A second declared, "Tomorrow is zero day." The discussions were between terrorists in the United States and al Qaeda operatives abroad. With the huge volume of intercepted and translated messages, the key intercepts were not sent to government intelligence consumers until September 12—a day after the attacks.

The intercepts were the main reason President Bush so readily pointed to Osama bin Laden and al Qaeda as the terrorists who planned and carried out the attacks.

The intelligence community, through anonymous spokesmen, said analysts were not sure the messages were related to the World Trade Center and Pentagon attacks. The intercepts were dismissed as "noise" and "unactionable" intelligence.

Improvements in the current system of dissemination and distribution, however, might have led to uncovering the plot sooner, if other pieces from the CIA and FBI had been put together.

NSA director Michael Hayden was questioned about the lapse during closed-door hearings in June 2002 of a joint House-Senate intelligence committee. His response was that NSA gathers huge volumes of intercepts every day and that it is nearly impossible to translate and disseminate it all in a timely manner. The exchange highlighted the key failing of U.S. technical spying agencies as it related to the September 11 attacks.

■ ■ ■

An al Qaeda terrorist who was picked up after the 1998 embassy bombings in East Africa disclosed that he had been given a contact telephone number to call in an emergency. The phone number was traced to an al Qaeda safe house in Nairobi, Kenya, which was run by a senior al Qaeda terrorist. Investigators managed to monitor the phone calls that were made to the house, including a series of calls from bin Laden's Inmarsat phone in Afghanistan. The same number was linked to another al Qaeda operations center in Yemen that the terrorists used for logistics and support in carrying out the October 2000 bombing of the USS *Cole* in Aden harbor.

After September 11, the NSA and FBI found out that the Nairobi safehouse telephone also was called by Ahmad al-Hada, father-in-law of Khalid al-Midhar, a lead hijacker on American Airlines Flight 77 that crashed into the Pentagon.

What the NSA did not detect was that al Qaeda terrorists were living only minutes away from its headquarters. At least six of the al Qaeda terrorists who carried out the attacks on September 11 were living and working in northern Prince George's County, Maryland, in the towns of Laurel, Bowie, and Greenbelt. They included the five hijackers who commandeered American Airlines Flight 77 from Dulles International Airport: Nawaq Alhazmi, Salem Alhazmi, Hani Hanjour, Khalid al-Midhar, and Majed Moqed. A sixth terrorist, Ziad Jarrah, was on United Airlines Flight 93, the plane that crashed in Pennsylvania after passengers on board fought off the hijackers. Several of the suspects had moved into the Valencia Motel and the Pin-Del Motel, seedy rest houses located on U.S. Route 1, the main road that passes through Laurel.

Restricted by federal guidelines limiting counterterrorism investigations, the FBI would not zero in on Laurel until after September 11. The reason their investigation led them there was simple: Laurel is home to Moataz al-Hallak, a fundraiser and grant writer at a College Park Muslim school. Al-Hallak was linked to Wadih el-Hage, who was convicted in early 2001 for his role in the bombing of the U.S. embassies in Kenya and Tanzania.

Laurel has two Islamic mosques, and one is located four blocks from the Valencia Motel. Gail North, a resident and former employee at the Valencia Motel, saw the men in Room 343, but they never allowed her to change the sheets on their bed or completely open the door. "They'd just look right through you," said North.

Intelligence officials said the terrorists entered the United States "under the radar screen" of U.S. intelligence monitoring capabilities. The men were adept at not being detected, as if they had been trained by a professional foreign intelligence service. They entered the country alone or in pairs, used legal documents, and sometimes adopted false identities. None had criminal records. Once in the country, the terrorists obtained post office boxes, covert E-mail accounts, drivers' licenses, and automated teller machine cards. They avoided contact with strangers and communicated with each other using prepaid calling cards at pay phones or E-mail sent from local public libraries, assuming correctly that the library Internet computer terminals were not under electronic surveillance.

Neighbors at the Valencia Motel occasionally saw Alhamzi and four other Arab men sitting quietly on blankets on the floor. "You never heard the phone or the TV," said Toris Proctor, who lived in an adjoining room. Gail North recalled driving into the motel parking lot once and seeing the men huddled together in conversation. She honked the horn to get them to move, but they sullenly ignored her. Most mornings the men left the motel in a blue Toyota Corolla with California tags, taking their luggage with them. They would return with grocery bags in the evening. The Toyota was later found at Dulles Airport after the September 11 attack. The manager of a Beltsville pornographic video store identified one of the terrorists who came into the store two or three times but purchased nothing. The visits raised questions among investigators as to whether all the terrorists were devout Muslims, or merely the terrorist equivalent of a drug "mule"—someone involved in an operation that he knew very little about it.

But what all this after-the-fact testimony proved was that traditional law enforcement techniques would have been of more use in developing intelligence on these terrorists than NSA technical wizardry, which proved utterly useless. It is ironic that a traditional cop on the beat, with plenty of local contacts, would have been more effective. He would have noted legitimate suspicions about these men by local residents and could have alerted the FBI. But that, of course, requires a local cop on the beat, one trained to think in terms of counterterrorism, and an intelligence community open to "human intelligence" from police officers.

■ ■ ■

A short time after the 1998 U.S. bombing strikes on Afghanistan, Minihan announced he would step down as NSA director in March 1999, after serving three years as DIRNSA, the agency's acronym for director of the National Security Agency. In his E-mail to the agency's employees announcing his retirement, Minihan noted that the agency was struggling to keep pace with modern technology. Electronic eavesdropping was relatively easy when communications were carried by copper wire and microwave transmitter. But the advent of fiber-optic cable was a whole new ball game, and tapping into the microsized channels was much harder.

Under the Clinton administration, the NSA, like all the defense and national security agencies, was starved for funds and forced to make personnel cuts. Minihan, a three-star general who was well liked by his subordinates at the NSA, told his employees that the agency would have to continue to "do the undoable" while "serving in silence, despite technological challenges few agencies have ever faced.

"Looking back on the past 2½ years, we have accomplished much together," Minihan said. "As is our tradition, those successes remain known only to a few. We have also experienced the continuation of the largest drawdown in our history."

Minihan continued: "At the same time, we have been confronted with a tidal wave of new technologies and transnational threats which some believed threatened our very existence. Throughout, you have performed brilliantly, never hesitating to rise to meet an avalanche of challenges." The general said he would spend his remaining months pressing within the government to get "the investment our modernization demands."

A U.S. official close to the NSA said Minihan lost several bureaucratic battles with the Clinton administration over such issues as limiting exports of data-scrambling technology. The administration loosened the controls and by doing so made it easier for terrorists, criminals, and spies to harden their communications against NSA eavesdropping, and severely hampered the agency's ability to intercept foreign communications.

For the NSA, the biggest problem of the 1990s was the cutbacks in its research and development budget. With hundreds of millions of dollars cut from research, the NSA rapidly found itself losing ground as communications technology advanced at rapid paces.

The NSA has a network of listening posts around the world that on an average day are capable of intercepting two million electronic messages per hour. The messages can include all forms of electronic communications, from cellular telephones to the most heavily encrypted military communications, such as nuclear command and control messages sent by Russian Strategic Rocket Forces to missile control centers. Its satellites are so comprehensive that they can be maneuvered over almost any point in the globe to zero in on a particular communications link.

Former director of Central Intelligence R. James Woolsey told me that the technical intelligence agencies like the NSA and the

National Reconnaissance Office are "both highly relevant to military action.

"The question is," Woolsey said, "what can they do to overcome the difficulties that they face in this new world of heavy encryption and fiber optics in the case of NSA, and underground stuff for NRO, in dealing with terrorist preparations. And clearly I think there will be some things they will do; it will just be hard. And I think that an awful lot of what we need to do is human intelligence and particularly from friendly countries."

Among the U.S. intelligence agencies, the technical intelligence agencies of the U.S. government are the least to blame for the September 11 intelligence failure. However, they are in need of strengthening and restructuring to better address the threats of international terrorism in the decades to come.

President George H. W. Bush said in a speech in 1992 that the NSA's "signals intelligence is a prime factor in the decision-making process by which we chart the course of this nation's foreign affairs." It was one of the few public comments on the role played by electronic intelligence.

During the administration of George Bush senior, the NSA underwent its first post–Cold War reorganization. It abolished its A Group, which focused on the Soviet Union and East Europe. It was the largest of the NSA's collection operations divisions. The B Group, which focused on electronic spying on communist China, North Korea, and Vietnam, was downgraded and combined with the G Group, which is in charge of the rest of the world.

After September 11, the NSA was reorganized again. According to Larry Castro, the NSA's Homeland Security Support coordinator, the agency is playing an important role domestically and in the war on terrorism. Castro told a conference of intelligence officials that the NSA is improving its ability to share intelligence with other government agencies, specifically law enforcement. The NSA is also working on improving its threat assessment and warning processes, and finding ways to increase the flow of "actionable" electronic intelligence from directors of intelligence to soldiers in the field or cops on the street.

National Imagery and Mapping Agency (NIMA) director James Clapper told intelligence officials at the same conference held in the spring of 2002 that NIMA is seeking to improve its imagery capabilities for the continental United States. NIMA in the past has focused on overseas targets. The focus on the United States is part of the overall U.S. intelligence agency efforts to improve intelligence gathering at home.

As for the National Reconnaissance Office, it is even more secret than the NSA. The NRO is in charge of the array of electronic imagery satellites that can photograph from space objects as small as several centimeters. The heyday of NRO was the period when Soviet missile fields were sprouting like vegetation throughout the vast Soviet Union.

The NRO's technical wizardry came originally from the CIA and was spun off into a separate agency whose very existence was a secret. It operated in relative obscurity, except for a funding controversy in the early 1990s. The NRO's supreme embarrassment came on New Year's Day 2000. It was the only national security agency to have suffered a millennium computer rollover glitch, which temporarily deafened the spy service. The problem was revealed on January 2, 2000, by Deputy Defense Secretary John Hamre, who told reporters the problem with "a satellite-based intelligence system" was significant and had reduced the ability of the spy agency to monitor world events. The problem lasted several days. "For a period of several hours we were not able to process information from that system," Hamre said.

But the key player is the NSA, which has been reorganized under Air Force lieutenant general Michael V. Hayden[1] to modernize rapidly and keep pace with technological change. "Essentially, the problem for this agency is we downsized a third [over the past twelve years] while the larger world has undergone the most significant revolution in human communications since Gutenberg," Hayden says. "We have got to get the technology of the global telecommunications revolution inside this agency."

Hayden understands that his agency is struggling to come to grips with advances in telecommunications technology. "If you are asking, 'Are we so far behind the curve that we can't get there?' the answer is no," he says. "People understand this is still a work in progress."

Since September 11, however, the agency's budget has skyrocketed, and it is getting the biggest share of the budget increases for intelligence spending. Much of the money is being spent to buy new electronic intelligence capabilities at both NSA and NRO.

Before September 11, General Hayden had been especially eager to counter charges that the NSA illegally spied on E-mail and other communications of Americans. "I'm here to tell you that we don't get close to the Fourth Amendment," he said, referring to the constitutional provision prohibiting unreasonable search and seizure. "We, for better or worse, stay comfortably away from that line," he said in a television documentary on the NSA aired on the History Channel in January 2001.

But that is likely to change as the war on terrorism presents new demands for the NSA's eavesdropping capabilities.

8

NONSECURITY

RICK RESCORLA BEGAN THE day as he usually did. He got up at 4:30 A.M., kissed his wife goodbye, and took the 6:10 train to Manhattan. A combat veteran who fought in Vietnam's bloody Ia Drang Valley, Rescorla was at his desk in a corner office of the World Trade Center by 7:30. It was September 11, 2001, and outside the day was clear and bright. Rescorla was on the forty-fourth floor of the South Tower when the first hijacked airliner slammed into its nearby twin. Rescorla sprang into action. Grabbing a bullhorn, he went to work in the same calm fashion that he showed under intense combat fire in Vietnam.

Born Cyril Richard Rescorla in Hayle, Cornwall, England, Rick was vice president for security at Morgan Stanley Dean Witter, one of Wall Street's largest brokerage houses. The company had 3,700 employees in the World Trade Center—2,700 employees in the south tower on floors forty-four through seventy-four and 1,000 employees in Building Five across the plaza. There was no hesitation. He ordered everyone to evacuate the building immediately. A short time after the aircraft hit, an official of the Port Authority of New York and New Jersey, which owned the Trade Center towers, called. Everyone in the building should stay put because there was no danger, the Port Authority man said. Rescorla shot back: "Piss off, you son of a bitch. Everything above where that plane hit is going to collapse, and it's going to take the whole building with it. I'm getting my people the f— out of here." He recounted the exchange in a telephone call to his longtime friend Dan Hill, then ran off and began helping the evacuation.[1]

As a security professional, it was Rescorla's job to think like a terrorist. In 1990, he saw that the World Trade Center was a likely target for a terrorist attack because it was a symbol of American economic power. He did a security survey of the building and concluded, with Hill's help, that driving a truck bomb into the basement near a key supporting column would bring down the entire complex. On February 26, 1993, that exact scenario almost played out. Islamic terrorists set off a homemade chemical bomb packed inside a rental truck that was parked in the basement, in an attempt to make the towers collapse.

Rescorla knew the Islamic terrorists who failed the first time would try again. He thought the terrorists' next attempt would be to fly a plane, possibly filled with chemical or biological weapons, into the towers. He had advised Morgan Stanley executives that the company should move from the Twin Towers to a safer location. But the company's lease went until 2006. The next best thing, Rescorla thought, was to practice evacuation drills. He pressed the company to conduct regular drills even though some employees grumbled and joked about them. Every few months, all 2,700 employees in the South Tower would be marched, with Rescorla at the bullhorn, in an arduous trek down the long winding stairwell of one of the world's highest skyscrapers and out of the building, just for practice. Another 1,000 employees would be evacuated from the Morgan Stanley offices nearby.

On September 11, the evacuation was real. A fireball erupted in the nearby tower, and all of Morgan Stanley's employees were making their way down and out of the other tower. By the time the second hijacked airliner hit the south tower at 9:07 A.M., most of the company's employees were out. But Rescorla's work was not finished. Three employees were missing. Rescorla and two assistants went back to look for them. Rescorla was last seen on the tenth floor of the burning tower. He died when the building collapsed a short time later. But he had saved thousands of lives. Out of 3,700 employees, Morgan Stanley lost only six, including Rescorla. R. James Woolsey, former director of Central Intelligence, sees Rescorla as the kind of person urgently needed by U.S. intelligence. An iconoclast and strategic thinker who wasn't afraid to buck the system, Rescorla "is an example of somebody who should have probably been at the top of the intelligence community, but wasn't," Woolsey told me. "He's a perfect example of the kind of guy that the Germans say has *fingerspitzengefühl*—fingertip feel" or intuition, he said. "God, it would have been wonderful if he had been the head of the DO's [the CIA's Directorate of Operations] counterterrorist operations, but at least he saved 3,700 people."

Aside from his military experience, Rescorla, sixty-two, had worked for British intelligence, conducting special operations in some dangerous places. And while his specialty was corporate security, intelligence and security are symbiotic. On September 11, they were hopelessly divided.

■ ■ ■

On Monday, March 11, 2002, a letter arrived at Huffman Aviation International, a flight training school in Venice, Florida. The letter was from the U.S. Immigration and Naturalization Service. It stated that Mohamed Atta and Marwan al-Shehhi had been approved for student visas to study flying. There was only one problem: Six months earlier Atta and al-Shehhi were at the controls of the two hijacked commercial airliners that hit the World Trade Center towers. The embarrassing incident highlighted that the Immigration and Naturalization Service (INS) has been unable to keep track of foreigners in the United States—even the most notorious mass murderers in American history.

In typical bureaucratic fashion, the INS sought to blame the gaffe on a subcontractor. "We certainly regret that our contractor was not notified after September 11," said INS spokesman Russ Bergeron. "It was our responsibility to notify the contractor that the notifications were not needed in this case." When the visas were approved, the agency noted, it was not known that the men were part of America's deadliest terrorist plot. Amazingly, this was true. The flight school had filed requests for M-1 student visas for the two men in August 2000, because their visa status had to be changed from nonimmigrant visitor to student if they were to take a year-long flying course. The INS didn't approve the requests until July 17, 2001, in the case of Atta, and August 9, 2001, for al-Shehhi. The final notification letter was not sent out until the week of March 6, 2002.

"This shows once again the complete incompetence of the immigration service to enforce our laws and protect our borders," said Congressman F. James Sensenbrenner Jr., a Wisconsin Republican, who has sought to disband the INS and start over with a new immigration security service. "If you look at the chronology of this, it shows why the INS has to be dismantled and put back together again."

Congress voted to do just that in late April 2002. One plan called for splitting the INS into two agencies, one for enforcement of immigration controls and a second agency to administer them. Members of Congress took to calling the agency the "Incompetent and Negligent Service" or saying INS stood for "Ignoring National Security." Another plan, which the House passed in late April 2002, split the INS into two parts. One would handle law enforcement issues and the other would be in charge of immigration services. The Bush administration opposed the legislation but was unable to stave off congressional action.

The terrorists probably understood that the U.S. immigration system is so deeply flawed that their visas didn't matter. Under current regulations, schools are not required to keep foreign nationals from receiving instruction while awaiting an INS student visa. In 1996, Congress ordered the INS to update its computerized tracking system to better monitor foreign students, something the INS had failed to do by 2001, the deadline set by the legislation. The nation's colleges didn't help. They refused to cooperate with the INS, claiming that the tracking system would be unfair to foreign students, who are big business for the schools. A total of 547,867 foreign students are enrolled on visas in accredited U.S. colleges and universities.[2]

A report issued in 2000 by the congressionally established National Commission on Terrorism, warned that the large number of foreign students in the United States posed a risk. "The United States lacks the nationwide ability to monitor the immigration status of these students," the report stated, and some of these students could be exploited to "support terrorist activity." The report said that some two million people entered the United States on valid visas but remained illegally, including "thousands" from nations designated as state sponsors of terrorism. The report noted the danger of terrorists using student visas. "Seven years ago, investigators discovered that one of the terrorists involved in bombing the World Trade Center had entered the United States on a student visa, dropped out, and remained illegally. Today, there is still no mechanism for ensuring the same thing won't happen again," the report said. The report recommended that the president and Congress work together to create an effective system of monitoring foreign students. Nothing was done in response to the recommendations. Nearly a year after September 11, the U.S. government was still considering new controls on foreign students but had taken no decisive action.

The task of preventing terrorists from entering the United States and carrying out similar suicide attacks is daunting. The

United States has a 7,500-mile long land and air border shared with Canada and Mexico. Each year, more than 500 million people enter the United States, including 330 million non-U.S. citizens. On land, 11.2 million trucks and 2.2 million rail cars cross into the United States each year, and 7,500 foreign ships make 51,000 port calls every year.

Fifteen of the nineteen hijackers involved in the September 11 attacks obtained U.S. visas in Saudi Arabia, where Saudi nationals who want to come to the United States usually are approved without interviews, according to U.S. officials. The State Department determined that only 3 percent of the Saudi visa applicants were rejected in 2000 and 2001. Most Saudis obtain U.S. visas through travel services, and only a small number are questioned by U.S. consular officials.

The remaining four hijackers were from the United Arab Emirates, Lebanon, and Egypt, although officials have cautioned that their identities and nationalities are still being investigated. All obtained tourist or business visas at U.S. consulates abroad. Eleven of the terrorists obtained visas at the coastal Saudi city of Jeddah and four in Riyadh, the capital. Mohammad Atta and Zaid Samir Jarrah, a Lebanese national, obtained their U.S. visas in Berlin. Fayez Rashid Ahmed Hassan Al Qadi Banihammad and Marwan al-Shehhi claimed to be United Arab Emirates nationals and obtained their visas there.

Mary Ryan, assistant secretary of state for consular affairs, told Congress the names of all nineteen hijackers were put through a computerized database that is designed to check for suspected terrorists when they apply for visas. In the case of the nineteen hijackers, there was no information. Ryan has blamed a lack of intelligence and not the visa system, which the State Department runs, for the September 11 lapse. "What went wrong is we had no information on them whatsoever" from U.S. intelligence agencies, Ryan said.

The State Department adopted its border security and counterterrorism computer check system following the 1993 World Trade Center bombing. (The terrorist who drove the truck bomb beneath the World Trade Center had entered the United States on a visa to study engineering at Wichita State University.) The State Department's system is known as "TIPOFF," and it is intended to screen visa applicants who are suspected of terrorism, drug trafficking, and other criminal activities. Before September 11, some State Department officials complained that the security check system had become the "piss-off" system because it created problems for people entering the country.

The TIPOFF system was developed by the State Department's Bureau of Intelligence and Research (INR), one of the five main U.S. intelligence agencies that, unlike its non-policy-oriented companion agencies, is really a policy support arm for the secretary of state. TIPOFF is supposed to combine sensitive intelligence and law enforcement information related to terrorists from the CIA, National Security Agency, FBI, and State Department overseas posts. "TIPOFF's objective is to detect these individuals either as they apply for visas overseas, or as they attempt to pass through U.S., Canadian, and Australian border entry posts," Ryan said. Unfortunately, the system does not work because of the reluctance of the FBI and CIA, in particular, to share information.

The TIPOFF staff in the INR screens all intelligence reports, embassy cables, and other information sources for names of terrorists. Officials said the system is fraught with problems. One of the biggest challenges is getting uniform spellings of names. This is a major problem for the Middle East because of the variations in translating names from Arabic. A congressional staff member involved in intelligence issues said U.S. intelligence agencies, particularly the CIA, have resisted efforts to require standardized spellings. Even today the CIA spells bin Laden's first name as "Usama," while most of the world spells it "Osama."

The commissioner of the U.S. Immigration and Naturalization Service, James W. Ziglar, made this comment about the problems facing his agency in the war against terrorism: "It's very easy to come into this country and disappear and not be found."

Before September 11, neither Ziglar nor U.S. Customs Service commissioner Robert Bonner received any U.S. intelligence briefings. Now they are regularly briefed.

■ ■ ■

A State Department intelligence analyst who has studied terrorism for twenty-five years described al Qaeda as an extremely secretive group that is, and will be, very difficult to track and destroy.

"You must understand the enemy," the analyst told me. "They live a clandestine lifestyle. They rarely travel in groups of more than two. They travel with false documents and disguises. They blend into their surroundings. Their communications are short and cryptic. They practice pretty good internal security. They are dedicated and thus not prone to betray the group. Their attack plans are treated like the codeword that the president uses to launch a nuclear strike. They are extremely patient. Their whole reason for existence is to act secretively. They also read newspapers and journals to detect how much we know about them. They are willing to die for their cause. And lastly, they are small in numbers."

The analyst defended the U.S. government's failure to anticipate and prevent September 11 and said tracking al Qaeda requires more than putting pieces of the puzzle together. "That is fiction, here is the reality," he notes. "Imagine your boss coming to your desk, placing a lunch-size brown bag twisted at the top on your desk and asking you to tell him what the contents mean? Dutifully, you untwist the bag and spill the contents on your desk. The contents are some sixty pieces of a puzzle. As you look over the puzzle pieces you immediately notice that about one-third of the pieces are blank, and another third appear to have edges that have been cut off. As you look at the pieces that have some part of a picture on them, you sense that this is really a mixture of about four different puzzles. Now keep in mind that you have no boxtop to tell you what the puzzle should look like and you do not know how many pieces are in the puzzle. America, welcome to the art of terrorism analysis. We rarely see a majority of the pieces of a terrorist threat puzzle. When we do, action is taken."

The analyst believes that no blame should be put on intelligence agencies for missing September 11 or other terrorist attacks. "In my twenty-five years of analyzing terrorist threats, I guess I have looked at about nine thousand anti-American terrorist threats," he said. "I can only think of about two dozen reports which provided all the key pieces of a credible terrorist plot. I think it is crucial that the American people understand that the quest of detecting key pieces of a terrorist plot is extremely difficult."

Terrorist operations normally contain five elements: target selection, surveillance, operational planning, the attack, and escape and evasion. Target selection is built around a group's guiding ideology and goals. Often many targets are picked. Surveillance is then carried out to determine the vulnerabilities, and a plan is formulated. Methods include car bombs, rocket attacks, and hand grenades, or, as in the case of September 11, crashing hijacked airliners into buildings. Terrorist leaders then decide who should carry out the attack.

"From a target's macro perspective, it is extremely difficult to prevent a terrorist attack," the analyst said. "The only way to prevent a terrorist attack is to totally neutralize the group posing a threat. For the United States to prevent a terrorist attack by al Qaeda it would be necessary to eliminate the group in its entirety."

Only two ways exist for finding out if a terrorist group is planning a specific attack. First, governments need intelligence from a human agent with access to the plot information, or intercepts from conversations detailing the plot. "The nature and internal security measures of a group like al Qaeda are such that it is virtually impossible to obtain a human source who would be in the position to know all the details of the plot," the analyst said. "You might obtain some sources that know bits and pieces of the plot but not all of the pieces. One source might have overheard that something will happen soon in Europe. Another might hear that three operatives have been sent to Africa. Prior to 9/11, it was extremely rare to obtain threat information that provided one or two of the most important operational elements that you need to deflect an attack—the specific target and the exact time of the attack."

A second method is to obtain specific attack information by analysis of pieces of intelligence. But the analyst believes it is impossible to deduce the specific target and exact timing through analysis.

Related to September 11, the analyst says, "There was no specific intelligence to suggest that al Qaeda was planning simultaneous aerial suicide attacks against the World Trade Center, the Pentagon, or any other target in the United States."

"There is no smoking gun," he said. "Since the August 1998 attacks on the U.S. Embassies in East Africa which, from al Qaeda's perspective, only killed 12 Americans, I think most terrorism analysts strongly suspected that al Qaeda would try to develop operations in the United States where they were guaranteed to kill a lot of Americans. I do not think that bin Laden was particularly happy with the fact that his attacks in 1998 killed some 289 non-American Muslims. He was looking for a place where he would only kill Americans.

"Secondly, it was clear to many analysts that terrorists could use aircraft in suicide attacks," he said. "We watched intently as a South Asian terrorist group known as the Liberation Tigers of Tamil Eelam (LTTE) developed different methods of suicide operations from human bombs to trucks to high-speed boats to minisubmarines. We remembered a Palestinian terrorist group in the 1980s that tried to penetrate Israeli border security by using ultra-lights. We read the report that a Turkish Islamic terrorist group was supposedly planning to fly an aircraft into the tomb of the founder of the modern Turkish state Kemal Ataturk. We all followed the 1994 hijacking of an Air France plane by Algerian extremists and read the reports that the plan was to crash the plane into the Eiffel Tower in Paris. And we saw the movie *Executive Decision.*" The film depicts a terrorist group that hijacks a Boeing 747 and threatens to blow it up unless a terrorist is released from prison.

"We are not stupid," he said. "There were signs that certain terrorist groups could tactically evolve to using aircraft as human smart bombs, either to explode over a target or fly into a target."

"Prior to 9/11, I think that most U.S. government terrorism analysts believed that al Qaeda would carry out an attack in the United States sooner rather than later," he said. "On this next point, I can only speak for a few other analysts and myself. The use of aircraft in a terrorist attack was becoming a logical and attractive tactic for a group like al Qaeda. However, most of us felt that it would most likely involve small private aircraft rather than commercial jetliners. It is easier to learn to fly the private aircraft, and security is less stringent at smaller regional or municipal airports. However, even this option was a possibility and not a probability. A possibility means that something can happen because it can be imagined. A probability means that what we have imagined is likely."

According to the analyst, the threat from al Qaeda is a "dialectical process" that changes as U.S. defenses change. "The al Qaeda that we thought we knew when it had a secure base of operations in Afghanistan no longer exits," he said. "It has most likely undergone a metamorphosis into a new structure with different characteristics, tendencies, procedures, communication codes, travel methods, financial channels, and objectives. The only way we can be confident that we have reduced the odds and opportunities of another al Qaeda 9/11-type terrorist attack is to totally neutralize the organization. From my perspective in the midsection of the U.S. government, where I have served under the Carter, Reagan, Bush, and Clinton administrations, I strongly believe that this current administration is the one that can and will neutralize al Qaeda. I have watched four previous administrations react to the terrorist threat, and the current president, with help from [CIA director George] Tenet, [FBI director Robert] Mueller, [Vice President Dick] Cheney, [Defense Secretary Donald] Rumsfeld, and [Secretary of State Colin] Powell, has displayed an unparalleled patience, determination, and intelligence in its fight against terrorism. Al Qaeda will be neutralized within five years."

■ ■ ■

An important component of security is the transportation system, especially the airlines. Michelle Van Cleave, a former White House national security official during the Reagan administration, said September 11 marked a major shift in the purpose of terrorist air piracy. She noted that in the past terrorists were viewed as people who chose violence to gain attention for their cause. That led to a "social science approach" to combating terrorism, where officials would seek root causes and the psychological origins for the terrorist acts. "Previously, airline crews had explicit instructions on what to do in the event of hijacking, which were based on the assumption that hijackers would most likely act as rational people, who had certain grievances or demands," Van Cleave said. "The instructions were to go along, stay calm, don't resist, leave it up to law enforcement authorities to capture and prosecute the hijackers."

All that changed with September 11. "The new instructions are different," said Van Cleave. "If threatened, the crew will act. So will the passengers."

Van Cleave said the new strategy against terrorism will include taking offensive action before terrorists can strike. "Our strategic purpose must be to create conditions that make it impossible for the terrorists to succeed," she said. "That requires the full range of tools at our disposal—economic, diplomatic, informational, as well as military, aimed at disrupting the terrorist cells: their support, communications, logistics, etc., and especially safe harbor. What the terrorists rely upon as their strength—their amorphous nature, their changing cell populations, their reliance on internet communications for continuity and connectivity, their lack of a fixed location, their mobility across international borders—must be turned into vulnerabilities."

One nation has been at the forefront in the war against terrorism: Israel. America's closest ally in the Middle East has been battling terrorism for decades and has developed the world's best airline security. The example of El Al pilot Uri Bar-Lev shows how the Israelis have done it.

Bar-Lev was at the controls of an El Al Boeing 707 on September 6, 1970. It was on the tarmac at Amsterdam's international airport about to take off for New York. Security agents came on board and said there were four suspicious passengers. Two of them were seated in first class and carried Senegalese diplomatic passports that were numbered consecutively, an indication they might have been forged. After consulting with El Al security, Bar-Lev had the two men removed from the plane. The plane took off and as it reached cruising altitude a crew member notified Bar-Lev that the aircraft was being hijacked. Through the peephole, the flight engineer saw that there were two hijackers: a man, pointing a gun at the head of a flight attendant, and a woman holding two grenades. A steward jumped one of the male hijackers and was shot five times. The hijackers ordered the pilot to let them inside the cockpit.

"We then heard a voice, I don't remember who it was, who said that if we don't open the door they will shoot the stewardess," Bar-Lev, a former Israeli air force pilot, recounted. "My first reaction was, and I said it aloud to the cockpit crew, 'We are not going to be hijacked!' and I believe that this state of mind of the crew, that we are not going to be hijacked, is one of the most important factors in the war against hijacking."

Bar-Lev quickly hatched a plan. "After informing El Al in Israel and London air traffic control, I threw the airplane into negative G dive, and since all the passengers were strapped into their seats, the hijackers would be thrown off balance and the security officers would be able to overcome them," he said. "This, indeed, succeeded. The male hijacker was killed and the female was captured and disarmed." The woman turned out to be Leila Khaled, wanted for hijacking a TWA flight to Damascus as part of a plot to capture Israel's then ambassador to the United States, Yitzhak Rabin.

Remembering the incident in a speech before a meeting of the international airline pilots' association, Bar-Lev said, "Air terror and hijacking did not begin on September 11, 2001. It began long before. I believe the world's policy in coping with air terror in the last thirty years has a direct link to the disastrous events of September 11." He noted that between 1968 and March 2001 there were twenty-four successful aircraft hijackings, but only one was an El Al airliner. "Had the world *then* reacted to these horrific terrorist attacks, perhaps the events of this year could have been prevented," he said.

Bar-Lev told me he believes fighting terrorism in the air involves several factors. First, the crew is the last line of defense and should be counted on only when all other security measures have failed. Cockpit doors must be kept closed at all times. "As long as the door is closed, the commander of the flight is the captain, and the flight cannot be hijacked," he said. "In these days of suicide bombers, not only now in Israel, the airplane can become a lethal weapon, as we saw on September 11." Air marshals should be stationed on all flights and should be government employees so that commercial interests will not affect their action. Air crews need legal protection in order to be able to fight terrorism in the air.

"The most important weapon against hijacking is the state of mind—'We are not going to be hijacked!' Once you believe in this, you will always find a way to win this war," he said.

There were legal problems for the El Al crew in resisting the hijacking, but the problems were worked out when British authorities dropped charges against El Al after it was determined that the hijacker had been killed outside British airspace. Israel changed its law to give air crews the legal right to resist hijackings, and these procedures, along with tough airport security, are a key reason why no Israeli jet has been hijacked since 1968. Bar-Lev believes commercial air crews are still faced with prosecution and lawsuits for resisting a hijacking and that current treaties on civil aviation are not clear in outlining what responsibility pilots have for protecting passengers.

The United States, he said, needs to arm its pilots. Making doors more secure, as has been done, is not enough. "If American aviation wants to fight terror," Bar-Lev said, "first it has to be built into the crew, and they need legal tools to be able to fight. It's not enough to hire extra personnel and train them to look at people."

Passenger airliners aren't the only targets. The lack of security for cargo jets is a major terrorist vulnerability, according to John O'Brien, director of engineering and air safety for the Airline Pilots Association International. "It is important that cargo aircraft cockpit doors be strengthened for several reasons," O'Brien told Congress, "including: (1) cargo aircraft are subject to air piracy, just like passenger aircraft; (2) security protecting cargo aircraft is nearly always less stringent than for passenger aircraft; (3) cargo flight crews are often required by their companies to board additional, nonscreened employees or couriers, about whom the pilots may know little or nothing, in seats outside the cockpit door."

Another major security problem to be addressed is the use of commercial airlines to transport people who have been expelled from the United States by the INS. "Anyone who is required to leave the country involuntarily is a security risk," O'Brien says. "They are traveling against their wishes to a destination where they may face prison or other hardships." The deportees have a built-in incentive to try to escape or change their travel destination. And many have criminal records or medical problems.

The U.S. government also needs to do more to get information on security threats to airlines quicker. "Currently, many pilots receive no timely security information at all," O'Brien says. "Some airlines, which can legally provide information from security directives to pilots because of their 'need to know,' instead withhold that information." Threat information from government needs to be provided to pilots on a timely basis.

Former director of Central Intelligence R. James Woolsey blames the Federal Aviation Administration (FAA) for the airline security failure of September 11. "Going back some years, on an average of a couple of times a year, some crazy person would get into a commercial airliner cockpit," Woolsey said. "And pilots and flight attendants would all write to the FAA saying we've got to do something to strengthen the door. And apparently, year after year, these went into the round file"—the garbage can, Woolsey said.

The U.S. military also came up short on September 11 when it was called in by the president. After two jetliners hit the World

Trade Center Towers and a third crashed into the Pentagon, a fourth airliner was detected heading for Washington, D.C.

President George W. Bush ordered the Pentagon to send fighter interceptors to shoot down the airliner if it threatened a fourth attack.

"The president gave what I'm sure was a very difficult order to shoot it down," Woolsey said. But the U.S. Air Force, despite having Bolling Air Force Base just across the Anacostia River from downtown Washington, and Andrews Air Force Base close to the Washington Beltway, had no fighters it could muster.

The nearest interceptors that could be scrambled into action were located at Langley Air Force Base in southern Virginia, about one hundred miles away.

"Most people before that happened, if they'd been asked, 'Does the United States have any fighter interceptors anywhere near Washington, D.C.?' would have probably said, 'Well sure, they must,'" Woolsey said. The fact is the Air Force did not.

For months after the attacks, U.S. warplanes flew nonstop combat air patrols over several key cities, including Washington, D.C., and New York City. Up to the cutback in March 2002, Navy and Air Force fighter aircraft flew more than nineteen thousand combat air patrols over U.S. cities. The flights cost more than $500 million.

Another new security challenge is protecting the United States from terrorists operating aboard ships or using ships in attacks. Coast Guard commandant Admiral Jim Loy said in a keynote address to a secret gathering of intelligence officials in early 2002 that America remains vulnerable to coastal attack. Ports and waterways, Loy said, offer targets that are extremely valuable economically, involving 25 percent of the U.S. gross domestic product. At the same time, ports are highly vulnerable. Loy said the intelligence community in the past has focused on threats overseas—what he called, using a sports term, the "away game." Now, better intelligence is needed on foreign maritime threats to the United States. He called for creating a maritime domain awareness program for homeland defense if the United States is to deter attacks on ports and waterways. It is a new area for American intelligence. Loy wants the intelligence community to provide the Coast Guard with information on ships, people, and cargo that is "actionable" for Coast Guard inspectors and operators.

Loy specifically asked for U.S. intelligence to produce a "common operating picture" based on high-technology intelligence collection, data mining, and fusion of intelligence information.

If America is to be secure, it is clear that it needs an integrated system of security that covers our waterways, airways, immigration rules, and law enforcement, and that puts fighting terror first.

CONCLUSION

THE WAY AHEAD

THE MOOD AT THE DEFENSE Intelligence Analysis Center at Bolling Air Force Base was somber. It was March 12, 2002, and six months had passed since the devastating surprise terrorist attacks had taken place in New York City and Washington, D.C. The meeting was a national intelligence symposium sponsored by the National Military Intelligence Association, a private group. The two days of meetings were classified at the secret security level—only people with U.S. government security clearances for access to classified information were permitted to attend. About 350 intelligence and security officials had gathered to take stock of the role of intelligence in the war on terrorism.

For many participants, the conference revealed that U.S. intelligence is losing the war on terrorism, despite the best efforts of the military to track down and find Islamic terrorists around the world. The main problem identified by intelligence officials at the conference is the failure to share intelligence information among agencies of the U.S. government. The most discouraging news was supplied by Linda Flohr, the deputy national coordinator on terrorism on the staff of the White House National Security

Council (NSC). Flohr, a former CIA official, said that President Bush was not sure structural changes in the intelligence community would lead to more "actionable" intelligence to prevent future terrorist attacks. It was a sign that career CIA officials intent on protecting the agency bureaucracy from needed reform were in key, influential positions within the U.S. government.

Flohr outlined the president's current strategy in the war on terrorism. She said there are "four Ds." They are Defending the United States; Diminishing the cause of terrorism; Denying sanctuary to terrorists; and Defeating terrorism. The major challenge for intelligence agencies is to learn how to convert intelligence on terrorists collected overseas to domestic use. Flohr believes this will require vast improvements in the way intelligence is shared across "the federal family" of security agencies. The administration has adopted the term "federal family" because it better characterizes what in the past was called "the U.S. intelligence community." The new members of "the federal family" include agencies like the Immigration and Naturalization Service and U.S. Customs Service. The president is also considering whether to expand the federal intelligence bureaucracy to include a National Threat Assessment Center, another bureaucratic "center" designed to augment a failed intelligence structure.

Flohr was a veteran of a public relations firm known as the Rendon Group, headed by John W. Rendon. According to an in-depth report in *The New Republic*, the Rendon Group was paid some $7.5 million to conduct propaganda operations—something normally carried out by the CIA. The group adopted the classic political spin techniques used so effectively during the Clinton administration. The result was that while the United States was engaged in a war against terrorism around the world, it was losing the ideological war against Islamic terrorism. The CIA, which had done so much during the Cold War to undermine communism ideologically, was essentially out of the propaganda business before September 11. And using political public relations firms was no substitute.

The intelligence conference identified common themes for fixing intelligence community problems. They included better intelligence sharing among agencies; better data mining to fruitfully harvest the vast amounts of intelligence collected; the importance of persistent surveillance of terrorists; and the need to improve operations against new intelligence targets. The conference participants offered no radical solutions and preferred merely to tinker with the status quo.

Signs that radical change was needed in the U.S. intelligence community began to show by mid-2002, even from within the community. Two intelligence officials, Aris A. Pappas and James M. Simon, Jr., wrote a critique of the entire U.S. intelligence system in the CIA's journal, *Studies in Intelligence*. They stated that "commission upon commission" of experts had called for changes but the "implacable champions of the status quo" had stifled urgently needed reform. Pappas and Simon are senior officers on the Intelligence Community Management Staff under the director of Central Intelligence.

"Human and technical collection procedures as well as our analytic capabilities are all in need of repair or replacement," they stated. "Most of our systems and organizations were designed to observe a slowly evolving and enormous target, the Soviet Union."

The clandestine service, the CIA's espionage branch, was formed to recruit spies to work against the Soviet Union. It now needs to penetrate terrorist groups. "We must recruit in more places and against more targets," they said. "Terrorist groups, in particular, are small and physically dispersed, but have tight, almost family-like cohesion. These new realities all increase significantly our need for a larger, broadly deployed, and well supported clandestine service."

The intelligence community's technological edge has been lost to the private sector and to America's adversaries. "The technology used by the intelligence community has become antiquated," they said. U.S. intelligence capabilities that relied on advanced technology and ignorance on the part of the targets of those systems are well known. "Virtually all the technical capabilities developed over the last several decades are now public knowledge," they wrote. "What we can do, and how we do it, is effectively in the public domain. Traditional evolutionary improvements to our existing capabilities cannot provide the same relative advantage once provided by the deployment of a new system."

Satellite imagery is now available from private companies and communications intercepts are much more difficult to obtain because of fiber optics and public encryption. "The public availability of secure communications means that security is now affordable and accessible to terrorists, organized criminals, and others," they wrote.

Agent-based operations, those that are most likely to discern terrorist plans and intentions, also have been affected by the loss of intelligence technology. Available technology makes it harder for U.S. clandestine agents to maintain cover identities and disguises, and countermeasures and detection devices have limited special documents and secret communications. "The new emphasis on security to hinder the free movement of terrorists also complicates the government's clandestine activities," Pappas and Simon said.

The solution they offer is to better integrate intelligence and law enforcement data. "Specific information that could lead to the identification and apprehension of a terrorist must flow unimpeded from the most classified and integrated data bases to the patrolman making a routine traffic stop," they said.

The two intelligence officers hit hard at the U.S. intelligence community's bureaucratic stagnation and said agencies risk irrelevance unless they are reformed. "It is difficult to abandon the comfort of routine," they said. "But, intelligence must be shaped to reflect the world in which it lives. Success will not be measured by our ability to find marginally better ways to use our existing resources, but in our ability to seek out and employ whatever is needed to do the new job. Neither easy nor cheap, the costs and risks of doing anything else are simply unacceptable. When the world changes, the single most important requirement for intelligence is to change with it."

The reality is that unless the president of the United States undertakes a top-to-bottom restructuring of U.S. intelligence agencies, the war on terrorism will be lost.

The first step in the reform process should be admitting that our intelligence services failed, and failed in part because of what former director of Central Intelligence R. James Woolsey believes was an overall de-emphasis on national security during the 1990s, the decade of the Clinton administration. "We were on a national beach party," Woolsey says. "We'd won the Cold War. Everybody figured there were no more problems. The stock market boomed just the way it did in the 1920s and even as able a man as Daniel Patrick Moynihan said, 'Let's get rid of the CIA.'"

"The country wasn't any more ready for September 11 than it was for Pearl Harbor," Woolsey notes. "And for a lot of the same, underlying reasons. The tactics were different, the intelligence was different, but the country was asleep."

During the 1990s, says Woolsey, three main currents of terrorism were growing more dangerous every year. All emanated from the Middle East. The first strain included the extremist Shia elements, the mullahs who run Iran and their connected terrorist organizations such as Hezbollah, or the Party of God. The second strain of terrorism active during the 1990s was the Baathists in Iraq, led by Iraqi dictator Saddam Hussein. The Iraqis launched at least one known terrorist attack against the United

States, the failed plot to assassinate former president George Bush in 1993, during a visit to Kuwait. The main threat from Iraq is its drive to develop weapons of mass destruction and missile delivery systems for those weapons.

Iraq's role in September 11 is still a question mark. There are signs that Baghdad was involved. A key indicator was the meeting in Prague, Czech Republic, in April 2001, between al Qaeda terrorist Mohamed Atta, the key figure in the September 11 attacks, and Ahmed Khalil Ibrahim Samir al-Ani, the second secretary of the Iraqi consulate in Prague. Al-Ani also was working undercover as an officer in the Iraqi foreign intelligence service, known as the Mukhabarat. The meeting was monitored by the Czech counterintelligence service, known as BIS.

According to intelligence specialist and author Edward Jay Epstein, the Czech surveillance of al-Ani was the result of an earlier encounter in December 1998. At that time, Jabir Salim, a forty-three-year-old Iraqi intelligence officer serving as Iraq's consul in Prague, was compromised in a homosexual scandal. Salim defected to Britain and during debriefings disclosed that Iraq's government had provided him with $150,000 to organize a car bomb attack on the Prague headquarters of Radio Free Europe/Radio Liberty, the American facility in Prague that broadcasts into Iraq. Britain then informed the Czech government of the plot. The discovery led to criticism of the Czech security service for not monitoring Iraqi intelligence operations. The BIS chief was replaced, and the new BIS chief began conducting more aggressive surveillance of Iraqi intelligence in Prague, which led to the intelligence they developed on Salim's replacement, al-Ani, and his meeting with Atta.

Epstein believes the Czech surveillance was not limited to physical coverage of the Iraqis but included electronic monitoring as part of a "full court press" in the Czech capital. Like its communist antecedent, BIS likely conducted major communications monitoring of the Iraqis, including faxes, E-mail, and cell phones. The Czech Interior Ministry claims that it does not know the details of the specific conversation between Atta and al-Ani. After the meeting, the Czechs suspected another bombing plot aimed at the U.S. radio broadcasting facilities and expelled al-Ani from the country. The real question to be asked, though, is why was the CIA not monitoring Iraqi intelligence around the world? The reason is simple. Within the CIA there remains an aversion to counterintelligence. U.S. officials said the CIA conducted no surveillance of Iraqi intelligence. If it had done so in 2001, it might have identified Atta and his seventy-two-hour meeting in Prague. Even so, the CIA has denied the relevance of such meetings, dismissing all intelligence of an Iraqi connection to September 11. According to one senior U.S. intelligence official, since September 11 the CIA has focused all its efforts on al Qaeda and behaves as though state-sponsored terrorism has ceased to exist.

In early May, officials who spoke on condition of anonymity from within the U.S. intelligence community put out word through *Newsweek* magazine that there was nothing to the Iraqi connection. The magazine reported in its April 28, 2002, edition that the Czech government had backed away from initial conclusions about the meeting between Atta and al-Ani. "We looked at this real hard because, obviously, if it were true, it would be huge," a senior U.S. law enforcement official told *Newsweek*'s Michael Skiff. "But nothing has matched up."

After the article appeared, the Czech government responded. Czech interior minister Stan Slav Gross insisted the meeting took place. "I believe the counterintelligence services more than journalists," Gross was quoted as saying in the Prague newspaper *Lido Nominee*. "I draw on the Security Information Service and I see no reason why I should not believe it." The service had not received any new information indicating the meeting had not taken place. Gross stated bluntly: "I consider the matter closed and cannot make any further comment on it."

U.S. intelligence officials also confirmed to me that there is information indicating Iraq supported the terrorists linked to September 11, but they declined to provide details. The Shias and Iraq apart, Woolsey identifies the third strain of terrorism as Sunni Islam extremism, and its most visible practitioners, al Qaeda, Egyptian Islamic Jihad, and several others that are part of the confederation.

"They had been focused on what they call the 'near enemy,' until very recently," Woolsey notes. "And it was Osama bin Laden who persuaded the Sunni extremists groups to pull together. He more or less did a merger and acquisition of Egyptian Islamic Jihad. He also persuaded these various groups to contribute people to move against us, rather than the 'near enemy'—to turn it into a war, as they put it, between Islam, on the one hand, and the crusaders and Jews on the other."

The goal for bin Laden's terrorist attacks was to get the United States out of the Middle East, something that would lead to the weakening of numerous governments that these Islamicists had targeted for overthrow, among them Saudi Arabia, Egypt, and Jordan.

"So they decided not just to attack us overseas, as in the bombing of the *Cole*, but to bring it here." Woolsey believes there is some coordination among the three strains, including al Qaeda and the Iraqis.

"And since September 11, there are a lot of reports that not just the Iraqis are helping al Qaeda, but also the Iranians," Woolsey said. The key indicator of Iraqi intelligence support to al Qaeda, Woolsey notes, is the professionalism of the terrorist group—its sophisticated and difficult-to-detect communications, its ability to hide its planning through tight security, its use of forged documentation, and its overall success at operating clandestinely. "I think there's some reasonable possibility that the sophistication of al Qaeda is in part caused by their cooperative work over the years with the Iraqis."

The involvement of the Iraqis does not mean that other states, like Iran and even Saudi Arabia, may not also have assisted al Qaeda. "Nothing bugs me more than the...assumption, which a lot of people seem to have, that if one of these groups is involved, others are not, as if there's some sort of sole source contract requirement for terrorism," Woolsey says. "Joint ventures are perfectly fine." Iraq may assist on some al Qaeda operations in limited ways, such as providing training instructors in hijacking.

And as other intelligence officials have indicated, there are clear signs that Iran helped al Qaeda, including providing lodging for two key al Qaeda operatives at the Iranian Embassy in Kuala Lumpur, Malaysia, during a January 2000 meeting of al Qaeda terrorists there.

Richard Perle, a senior defense official during the Reagan administration, believes the weak response to terrorist attacks for at least a decade before September 11 made the World Trade Center and Pentagon attacks inevitable. "We failed again and again to respond adequately to acts of terror against the United States, against Americans abroad, and American installations abroad," Perle says. The response was ineffective, whether it was prosecuting terrorists and ignoring their state supporters, or ineffectively using cruise missiles. "So it is hardly surprising that the terrorists became emboldened by each success, or are more ambitious with each attack," Perle says. "And that's why I think September 11 was inevitable."

Retired Army lieutenant general Patrick M. Hughes, a former director of the Defense Intelligence Agency, said U.S. intelligence failed to act adequately in a key area. "We did not field a credible and effective human intelligence capability," he said. "We did not know what these terrorists were doing." To defeat terrorists will require "our human intelligence and counterintelligence organizations to engage in clever, risky, exceptional intelligence operations that may enable us to see inside the terrorists' cabal, to know in advance what their plans and intentions might be and to act to interdict or to preclude the terrorists from acting," Hughes said. The retired three-star general said the new task of defeating terrorists will not be easy and many within the U.S. intelligence, security, and law enforcement communities are working hard on the problem. "I was one of them," he said. "We had the intent to succeed but we did not succeed. Why? We did not have the collective will to do the right thing. That sort of failure can no longer be tolerated."

To win the war on terrorism requires an intelligence system redesigned for helping the United States to attack terrorists at the group and individual level through penetration and disruption. Under the current system, with the current management and restrictions, this is impossible.

Policymakers interested in creating an intelligence system worthy of America's superpower status and responsibilities need to effect change—and here's a blueprint for change that would reform and improve our intelligence capabilities. The following is based on consultations with intelligence professionals.

• **A New Clandestine Service:** The United States needs a new clandestine service to replace the CIA Directorate of Operations and the DIA Defense HUMINT Service. The focus of the new service would be to conduct much more extensive intelligence operations. It would rely on its own forces and break the over-reliance on liaison with foreign intelligence services. Liaison has become an excuse for not conducting unilateral intelligence operations by American spies. The new service would utilize America's natural diversity to recruit people as operations officers who can operate inside what are known as "hard targets." In the war on terrorism, that means Islamic terrorist groups. There can be no excuse for the CIA's failure to penetrate al Qaeda, when twenty-year-old Islamic convert John Walker Lindh gained access to al Qaeda and met Osama bin Laden in Afghanistan.

A new and more effective clandestine service would be the lynchpin for a restructured U.S. intelligence community. This new clandestine service will require new methods of recruiting and training officers. The human intelligence-gathering system now in place is not sized or trained to provide the secret intelligence required by the world's sole superpower. It is ultimately the reason why U.S. intelligence failed to detect and prevent the September 11 attacks. Ultimately, at its core, intelligence is secret information—getting it and using it, and we have not been getting it and using it effectively.

Currently, the Central Intelligence Agency, like the Pentagon, is a statist, welfare bureaucracy where rules are more important than getting the job done. The entire nature of the institution must be altered before it will be capable of winning the war against international terrorism. "The United States does not have a clandestine service with the size, mission, recruitment, and training to adequately address the problems facing the United States," a senior U.S. intelligence official in favor of radical reforms told me. The bureaucratic structure of U.S. intelligence agencies in general, and the CIA in particular, has evolved away from the kind of specialized service that is needed for the work of gathering secret intelligence. Although the director of Central Intelligence is given special hiring and firing authority under the 1947 National Security Act that created the CIA, that authority is rarely used and instead a parallel civil service has developed. One official described the CIA as "AFSCME in a trenchcoat," a reference to the American Federation of State, County, and Municipal Employees—the federal employees union.

The new clandestine service would also conduct peacetime covert action operations—semisecret operations designed to support U.S. goals internationally, usually involving political or paramilitary activities. War-time covert action would be transferred to U.S. military special operations commandos.

• **A Domestic Counterintelligence Service:** In the aftermath of September 11, the United States government needs to set up a constitutionally governed domestic intelligence service. This new service should be modeled after Britain's MI-5 domestic intelligence service, which does not have police or arrest powers. Like MI-5, which seeks assistance from the Special Branch of Scotland Yard to carry out arrests, the new service would work closely with the FBI and other law enforcement agencies.

In its over ninety-year career, the FBI has often had competing roles of collecting intelligence and enforcing laws. Under the new war on terrorism, the FBI is being reoriented toward preventing terrorist attacks before they occur, rather than investigating terrorism with the goal of bringing suspects and organizations to prosecution and trial. Under the current structure, the FBI is not capable of conducting the kind of domestic intelligence operations that are needed to meet the demands of terrorism prevention. Only the creation of a new service outside the FBI would resolve this conflict.

The mission of the new domestic service must be clear. It would be designed to discover, analyze, and—with the assistance of the FBI and military counterintelligence and security services—thwart clandestine foreign activities against the United States, including terrorism and intelligence activities. The main goal would be to stop terrorist attacks—and that could involve arrests with the help of the FBI. Under this reorganization, the FBI would retain a small counterintelligence unit that would be analogous to the Special Branch at Scotland Yard and would deal with counterintelligence law enforcement issues and prosecutions. But information and intelligence would be the province of the new domestic intelligence service.

- **Military Intelligence:** The Defense Intelligence Agency would be abolished. The DIA has done some things well in the past but has become superfluous and a hindrance to effective military intelligence operations. However, the DIA's J-2 function of coordinating and providing intelligence for the Joint Chiefs of Staff and for supporting the Office of the Secretary of Defense would be retained and even enhanced. The Defense HUMINT Agency would become part of the new clandestine service.

The remainder of DIA functions would be returned to the military services or to the unified combatant commands, which currently operate Joint Intelligence Centers, and in the case of the European Command, the Joint Analysis Center. The DIA's war-planning function also would be given to the commanders in chief of the war-fighting commands.

- **Central Analysis Agency:** The Central Intelligence Agency does the bulk of U.S. intelligence analysis within the intelligence community. Under the reorganized U.S. intelligence system, it would become the Central Analysis Agency, and its primary function would be to produce analysis and technology research. Moreover, its analytical function would be reoriented toward support for military activities overseas. The CIA's current analytical culture has atrophied to the point where the usefulness of its analysis is a question mark, and the agency serves more often as an unofficial check on the decisions of policymakers. The new agency's analyses would be balanced with a new system of "competitive analysis" conducted in a structured fashion by outside specialists. The outside analysis function would become an integral feature of all U.S. intelligence analysis—to keep it sharp.

The State Department's Bureau of Intelligence and Research would become part of the new analysis agency, and, because of its role in supporting secretary of state policies, it would be downgraded within the intelligence community. Its analysis would be weighted to reflect its parochial, bureaucratic interests.

• **Military Clandestine Operations Force:** A new and relatively small military clandestine operations service would be set up. Its primary mission would be to conduct covert and clandestine operations to prepare the battlefield for military operations. It would recruit, train, and equip military intelligence officers, and infiltrate foreign countries, conducting intelligence missions. In advance of a military operation, the service would send officers to establish a forward communications network and provide logistics support, and would have clandestine combat support capability, utilizing special operations commandos and intelligence officers to perform unique, military-related functions. The beginnings of this new service were demonstrated in late 2001 with the impressive activities of U.S. special operations forces in Afghanistan.

• **Technical Intelligence:** The new system would upgrade the capabilities of the two main technical intelligence-gathering agencies: the National Security Agency, for electronic eavesdropping and code breaking; and the National Reconnaissance Office and National Imagery and Mapping Agency, for the operation of reconnaissance, surveillance, and intelligence satellites, and the development of their products.

■ ■ ■

This new intelligence structure is urgently needed if we are going to avoid another tragedy like September 11, the Pearl Harbor of our generation. With it, we can achieve victory in the war on terror, as our own fathers defeated the Axis powers in World War II.

THE TRACE

THE FOLLOWING PAGES PRESENT various documents that highlight the systemic, structural, and cultural problems within U.S. intelligence agencies that contributed to the intelligence failures surrounding September 11. Most of the documents are classified. The publisher has agreed to withhold some material from publication at the request of the U.S. intelligence community in the interest of U.S. national security.

A top secret report by the CIA Counterterrorist Center on the role of Osama bin Laden in the 1996 terrorist attack on U.S. troops in Saudi Arabia.

TOP SECRET UMBRA
NOFORN ORCON

DCI
Counterterrorist
Center

COUNTERTERRORIST CENTER COMMENTARY

Central
Intelligence
Agency

Information Implicating Usama Bin Ladin in the Dhahran Bombing (S NF OC)

Summary (U)

MATERIAL RELATING TO COOPERATIVE INTELLIGENCE
EFFORTS WITHHELD AT THE REQUEST OF U.S. GOVERNMENT
INTELLIGENCE OFFICIALS.

★★★★★

The Report (U)

NOFORN ORCON
TOP SECRET UMBRA

TOP SECRET UMBRA
NOFORN ORCON

(S NF OC)

(S NF OC)

MATERIAL WITHHELD AT THE REQUEST
OF U.S. GOVERNMENT INTELLIGENCE OFFICIALS.

2

TOP SECRET UMBRA
NOFORN ORCON

(S NF OC)

MATERIAL WITHHELD AT THE REQUEST
OF U.S. GOVERNMENT INTELLIGENCE OFFICIALS.

NOFORN ORCON
TOP SECRET UMBRA

(TS U NF OC)

Difficulties in Verifying the Information (S)

MATERIAL WITHHELD AT THE REQUEST
OF U.S. GOVERNMENT INTELLIGENCE OFFICIALS.

Our capability to confirm   is extremely limited.

(TS U NF OC)

4

A top secret report from the National Security Agency Operations Center with a section on "Terrorism Around the World."

TOP SECRET UMBRA

NSA - NSOC
MORNING SUMMARY (U)

Information as of 0500L Wednesday 7 May 1997

RESOURCE EMPHASIS (U)

MATERIAL RELATING TO ELECTRONIC INTELLIGENCE GATHERING WITHHELD AT THE REQUEST OF U.S. GOVERNMENT INTELLIGENCE OFFICIALS.

TERRORISM AROUND THE WORLD (C)

HANDLE VIA TALENT KEYHOLE/COMINT CHANNELS JOINTLY
TOP SECRET UMBRA GAMMA ORCON US ONLY

A secret report on the arrest of a top aide to Osama bin Laden.

May 7, 1997

S E C R E T SPOKE ORCON US/UK EYES ONLY

SUBJ: U̶S̶A̶M̶A̶ ̶B̶I̶N̶ ̶L̶A̶D̶E̶N̶:̶ ̶S̶E̶N̶I̶O̶R̶ ̶B̶I̶N̶ ̶L̶A̶D̶E̶N̶ ̶F̶I̶N̶A̶N̶C̶I̶A̶L̶ ̶O̶F̶F̶I̶C̶I̶A̶L̶ ̶U̶N̶D̶E̶R̶
        ARREST IN UNSPECIFIED COUNTRY (SC-OC-US/UK EYES ONLY)
<TEXT>
REQS: 0R9011 2R1764 4R1765 2R1884 4R1795
TEXT: ((DISSEMINATION AND EXTRACTION OF INFORMATION CONTROLLED
        BY ORIGINATOR))

MATERIAL WITHHELD AT THE REQUEST
OF U.S. GOVERNMENT INTELLIGENCE OFFICIALS.

- - - - - - - - - - TEAR LINE - - - - - - - - - -
                    SECRET
                    REL UK

062100Z MAY 97
     "THIS INFORMATION IS PROVIDED FOR INTELLIGENCE PURPOSES IN AN
EFFORT TO DEVELOP POTENTIAL INVESTIGATIVE LEADS. IT CANNOT BE USED
IN AFFIDAVITS, COURT PROCEEDINGS, SUBPOENAS, OR FOR OTHER LEGAL OR
JUDICIAL PURPOSES."
SENIOR BIN LADEN FINANCIAL OFFICIAL UNDER ARREST IN UNSPECIFIED
COUNTRY (S-REL-UK)
     (S-REL-UK) ABU FADEL, A SENIOR OFFICIAL OF ISLAMIC EXTREMIST
FINANCIER USAMA BIN LADEN'S ORGANIZATION, IS UNDER ARREST IN AN
UNSPECIFIED COUNTRY, ACCORDING TO EARLY MAY INFORMATION. ABU FADEL
IS AN ALIAS USED BY A KEY BIN LADEN FINANCIAL OFFICIAL, SIDI
AL-MADANI AL-GHAZI MUSTAFA AL-TAYYIB.
                    SECRET
                    REL UK
- - - - - - - - - - TEAR LINE - - - - - - - - - -

S E C R E T SPOKE ORCON US/UK EYES ONLY

A secret report from a U.S. Embassy about a tip that an Islamic terrorist had been granted a visa to travel to the United States in the late 1990s.

```
PTP2901

                              SECRET         PTP2901

PAGE 01

@ACTION:  SCT(00)

@INFO:  A(00)    DSCC(00) G(00)    M(00)     P(00)
        PA(00)   PRS(00)  SSEX(00) WO(00)
====================

ACTION SCT-00
```

MATERIAL WITHHELD AT THE REQUEST OF
U.S. GOVERNMENT INTELLIGENCE OFFICIALS.

```
FM AMEMBASSY
TO SECSTATE WASHDC IMMEDIATE
AMEMBASSY
AMEMBASSY
AMEMBASSY

S E C R E T

TERREP

NOFORN




E.O.
TAGS:
SUBJECT:  REPORT THAT AN ALLEGED MEMBER OF
                        RECEIVED A VISA FOR TRAVEL
TO THE U.S.

REF:  (A) CAIRO 04443, (B) CAIRO 04477

1.  CLASSIFIED


2.  SUMMARY:              Consular Officer received a
call from an individual who identified himself as
                      claimed that              who
he identified as a member of
received a visa to travel to the United States.
          consular records checks revealed no issuance.
ROAL record check revealed no identifiable traces.  END
SUMMARY

3.               Consular Officer received a telephone
call from an individual who identified himself as
                      claimed to be a U.S. Citizen
residing in                 He stated that, at some
danger to himself, he was calling to warn U.S.
authorities that a member of
```

is attempting to travel to the United
States.

3.   identified the group member as
          is described as a 27-year old, white male (NFI).
According to   received a visa o/a
          Place of issuance unknown.
          allegedly told the issuing Consular Officer that
he intended to travel for business purposes to the
state of   is allegedly accompanied by his

4. A search of consular files at AmEmbassy
revealed no visa issuance for a   CLASS
checks revealed a hit on the name
                    and indicated a visa refusal in
          A hit on the name
                    indicated a visa refusal, also in
                    Additional CLASS hits were yielded by
the   none, however, matched the information
provided by the caller.

5. CLASS checks on the name   were
negative.

6.   record checks revealed no identifiable traces
on any of the above listed names.

SECRET

MATERIAL WITHHELD AT THE REQUEST OF
U.S. GOVERNMENT INTELLIGENCE OFFICIALS.

A top secret report from the director of the National Security Agency revealing that Iraq had been notified that a U.S. attack on Iraq was close.

TOP SECRET UMBRA

DATE: 2 February 1998
FROM: DIRNSA
TO: NSA/SPECIAL-HCO
          EXCLUSIVE FOR:

MATERIAL WITHHELD AT THE REQUEST OF U.S. GOVERNMENT INTELLIGENCE OFFICIALS.

INFO:

TOP SECRET UMBRA ORCON US ONLY

SERIAL:

TAGS:

SUBJ: Iraq/Crisis:

REQS:

TEXT: Dissemination and Extraction of Information Controlled by Originator
          (TSC-OC-UO)

DETAILS (U)
(TSC-OC-UO)

US ONLY
ORCON
TOP SECRET UMBRA

TOP SECRET UMBRA

Z-I3/OO/97-98
2 February 1998
Page 2 of 2

(TSC-OC-UO)

MATERIAL WITHHELD AT THE REQUEST
OF U.S. GOVERNMENT INTELLIGENCE OFFICIALS.

For dissemination/distribution questions, call P0213: NSTS: 963-3850; STU-III: 301-688-7383

Derived From:

Declassify On:

US ONLY
ORCON
TOP SECRET UMBRA

A portion of a U.S. government intelligence report indicating that Osama bin Laden may be seeking asylum in Iran.

(CONFIDENTIAL)

9. Iran/Terrorism: Bin Ladin Asylum?

A portion of the CIA's top secret daily intelligence summary reporting the director of Central Intelligence's list of potential hot spots around the world.

Top Secret
UMBRA

DCI Warning Committee Watchlist Summary

5 January 1998

Level of concern
(as compared to one week ago)

The following show the likelihood of a serious threat developing over the next six months. (C)

▼

Chances of occurring are as high as 5 in 10

→ **Confrontation between Iraq and US/coalition:** Additional standoffs likely when UN tries to conduct intrusive inspections.

→ **Major unrest in Nigeria:** Abacha foils 21 December coup; more arrests likely.

Chances of occurring are as high as 3 in 10

→ **Fighting in Bosnia:** Plavsic likely to form "government of experts" with Socialists and Muslims,

→ **Violence in Serbia-Kosovo:** More Kosovar demonstrations and terrorist attacks are likely and they will test Serb restraint.

→ **Conflict in the Aegean:** Announced Turkish training in the Aegean will increase tension.

→ **Loss of regime control in North Korea:** P'yongyang will need massive food aid this year.

→ **Direct fighting between Palestinian and Israeli forces:** Israel's redeployment proposal unlikely to meet Palestinian minimum requirements; Netanyahu's control of government increasingly tenuous.

→ **Instability in Haiti:** Political impasse remains as economic problems mount.

→ **Significant instability in Colombia:** Fighting among guerrillas, paramilitary elements, and the government continues.

→ **Breakdown of Angolan peace process:** If UN peacekeepers depart as scheduled on 1 February, security vacuum may spark fighting.

Secret *NOFORN*   361034PM6 1-98

Top Secret
5 January 1998

An article from the CIA's top secret daily intelligence summary highlighting the involvement of Osama bin Laden in illegal narcotics trafficking in Afghanistan in the late 1990s.

Afghanistan: Drugs and Terror Nexus (C/NF)

Afghanistan-based terrorism financier Usama bin Ladin recently may have agreed to a Taleban request to fund the repair of an irrigation canal in Helmand province, displacing a   NGO that had planned to rebuild the canal as part of a larger anti-narcotics crop-substitution program,

Reconstruction of the canal, which was destroyed during the war, was to cost the NGO $250,000 and, when completed, would irrigate 150,000 acres of land. (C)

Afghanistan is the world's second largest illicit opium producer and Helmand province is the country's top opium-producing region; last year it yielded an estimated 690 metric tons of opium on some 53,000 acres, (S/USO)

Comment: Repair of the canal will aid the cultivation of opium poppy, reportedly an important source of revenue for the Taleban. Bin Ladin, who does not have strong personal or ideological ties to the Taleban, probably believes he is buying insurance against US attempts to persuade the Taleban to expel him. The Taleban, in soliciting bin Ladin's funding for the irrigation scheme, are probably seeking to avoid the tough conditions of US-funding that require measurable reductions in opium cultivation. (S/USO)

(SECRET/US ONLY)

An article from the CIA's top secret daily intelligence summary on the terrorist targeting of the U.S. military headquarters in Riyadh, Saudi Arabia.

Top Secret
UMBRA

ᴀUDI ARABIA: Signs of Targeting US Compound in Riyadh (S)

— The Embassy and US military have taken steps to enhance security
- and relocate personnel stationed there. (S NF)

— In another, widely reported fax early last week, another group—the Islamic Movement for Change, had claimed responsibility for the Al Khubar Towers bombing and threatened an attack on the US, implying that the attack would be soon. This group had previously claimed responsibility for the bombing in November of the Saudi Arabian National Guard building in Riyadh.

— *Neither statement provides details to support its claims, and neither can be verified.* (S NF) -CIA, DIA-

Top Secret
24 July 1996

Top Secret
UMBRA

**Saudi Arabia: US Military Training Mission, Central Riyadh,
20 July 1996** (U)

AERIAL PHOTOGRAPH OF U.S. MILITARY HEADQUARTERS IN
SAUDI ARABIA WITHHELD AT THE REQUEST OF U.S. GOVERNMENT
INTELLIGENCE OFFICIALS.

Secret *NOFORN*

Top Secret
24 July 1996

A top secret CIA article on the involvement of Afghanistan's Taliban militia in the drug trade.

Top Secret
UMBRA

AFGHANISTAN: Taliban Drug Trade Connection (C NF)

Kabul has issued a statement defending its record on counternarcotics and accusing its opponents of involvement in the drug trade,
Kabul's statement singles out regions held by Taliban as particularly active in the drug trade. (C NF)

Because all major political factions in Afghanistan are involved in the drug trade to some degree, Kabul's claims appear self-serving. Nevertheless,   report Taliban complicity—if not direct involvement—with opium poppy cultivation and opiate trafficking.

—   indicates Taliban is facilitating drug trafficking in exchange for shipments of food and fuel.

—   indicates that most of the opium-producing areas in Afghanistan are in regions controlled by Taliban.

— Taliban collects a "religious tax" on poppy cultivation, according to

MATERIAL WITHHELD AT THE REQUEST OF U.S. GOVERNMENT INTELLIGENCE OFFICIALS.

Taliban has repeatedly stated that opiate production, trafficking, and use are forbidden under Islamic law.   however, state that Taliban officials realize the lack of economic alternatives makes stemming the drug trade difficult.

— Claims of direct Taliban involvement in the drug trade, and subsequent Taliban denial of such involvement, may continue as Afghanistan's opposing factions jockey for international political support and assistance. (S NF) -CIA, DIA-

Top Secret
17 June 1996

4

A top secret CIA article about Islamic terrorists in Egypt.

Top Secret
UMBRA

EGYPT: **Terrorists Divided but Still Dangerous (S NF)**

More than a month after the attack in Luxor, the Egyptian al-Gama'at al-Islamiyya is beset by growing divisiveness over its killing of 60 foreign tourists. The attack sparked public criticism by some of its leaders living abroad and leaders jailed in Egypt about the group's strategy and targets. (S NF)

— The group appears to have begun recruiting outside its traditional target population—three of the Luxor terrorists were advanced university students with no police record.

— The attackers may have been trained in Egypt rather than abroad. (S NF OC)

Role of Foreign Supporters (C)

say that foreign support has become increasingly important to al-Gama'at, however, and the group may have carried out the attack to impress them.

— operational leader Hamza resides in Afghanistan, possibly with bin Ladin, and indicates other Egyptian extremists are moving there.

— Iran is providing Egyptian extremist groups with training, logistic, and financial support,

Threats of More Attacks (S NF)

Hardline al-Gama'at elements are threatening more attacks if Cairo continues to crack down on them.

MATERIAL WITHHELD AT THE REQUEST OF U.S. GOVERNMENT INTELLIGENCE OFFICIALS.

Top Secret
5 January 1998

— A truck bomb attack there in late 1995 by the Egyptian al-Jihad group killed 17 people and nearly destroyed the building. (TS U NF OC)

Al-Gama'at's renewed willingness to challenge the Egyptian Government, its closer ties to ardent anti-US supporters, and its determination to appear strong in the midst of serious internal wrangling could lead it to conduct more spectacular attacks, including against a US target. The group still has skilled operatives in Egypt and abroad who are capable of such an operation. (S NF) -*CIA, DIA, NSA-*

A top secret National Security Agency report about a terrorist attack in Egypt.

TOP SECRET UMBRA

MORNING
SIGINT SELECTIONS

Information as of 0500 EST 05 January 1998

MATERIAL WITHHELD AT THE REQUEST
OF U.S. GOVERNMENT INTELLIGENCE OFFICIALS.

TOP SECRET UMBRA GAMMA ORCON NOFORN

A top secret National Security Agency report by the W Group of the National Security Operations Center.

TOP SECRET UMBRA ORCON NOFORN

TOP SECRET UMBRA ORCON US ONLY

****
****

W GROUP NSOC DAILY INTELLIGENCE SUMMARY

Wednesday   07 MAY 1997

****
****

* * * PROPOSED BRIEFING ITEMS * * *

Hamas Acquires Missiles for Attack

* * * SIGNIFICANT PRODUCT * * *

Senior Bin Laden Financial Official Under Arrest in Unspecified Country
(SC OC US/UK ONLY)

MATERIAL WITHHELD AT THE REQUEST
OF U.S. GOVERNMENT INTELLIGENCE OFFICIALS.

..... Narcotics Trafficking Kingpin   to Resume
Operations Following 3-Month Hiatus,   (TSC OC)

Iran's Chinese-Supplied Glass-Lined Equipment Factory to be Completed By
End of   Lack of Raw Materials May Delay Its Commissioning (TSC OC
US/AUS/CAN/UK ONLY)

    (TSC OC US/AUS/CAN/UK ONLY) Iran's Chinese-supplied glass-lined
equipment production plant will be complete by the end of June 1997,

A top secret report from the intelligence facility in Cheltenham, England.

```
FM DIRNSA
TO CIA // //
STATE/RCI // //
```

```
WHITE HOUSE



FBI
```

```
T O P  S E C R E T  UMBRA GAMMA ORCON
QQQQ
WARNING: THIS IS HIGHLY SENSITIVE GAMMA CONTROLLED COMINT
```

TAGS:

SUBJ:

REQS:

WARNING: Dissemination among U.S. customers of the information in
this report is subject to special control.

TEXT:

KEY POINTS

DETAILS

MATERIAL WITHHELD AT THE REQUEST
OF U.S. GOVERNMENT INTELLIGENCE OFFICIALS.

Footnotes:

DECL: OADR

NNNN

Excerpts of a letter from FBI special agent Coleen Rowley to FBI headquarters regarding the investigation of Zacarias Moussaoui. She alleges
FBI missteps and management failures, and charges that the FBI failed
to respond to September 11 warning signs.

May 21, 2002
FBI Director Robert Mueller
FBI Headquarters Washington, D.C.

Dear Director Mueller:

I feel at this point that I have to put my concerns in writing
concerning the important topic of the FBI's response to evidence of terrorist activity in the United States prior to
September 11th. The issues are fundamentally ones of
INTEGRITY and go to the heart of the FBI's law enforcement
mission and mandate. Moreover, at this critical juncture in
fashioning future policy to promote the most effective handling
of ongoing and future threats to United States citizens' security, it is of absolute importance that an unbiased, completely
accurate picture emerge of the FBI's current investigative and
management strengths and failures.

To get to the point, I have deep concerns that a delicate and
subtle shading/skewing of facts by you and others at the highest levels of FBI management has occurred and is occurring.
The term "cover up" would be too strong a characterization
which is why I am attempting to carefully (and perhaps over
laboriously) choose my words here. I base my concerns on my
relatively small, peripheral but unique role in the Moussaoui
investigation in the Minneapolis Division prior to, during and
after September 11th and my analysis of the comments I have
heard both inside the FBI (originating, I believe, from you and
other high levels of management) as well as your
Congressional testimony and public comments.

I feel that certain facts, including the following, have, up to now,
been omitted, downplayed, glossed over and/or mis-character-
ized in an effort to avoid or minimize personal and/or institutional embarrassment on the part of the FBI and/or perhaps
even for improper political reasons:

   1) The Minneapolis agents who responded to the call about
   Moussaoui's flight training identified him as a terrorist
   threat from a very early point. The decision to take him
   into custody on August 15, 2001, on the INS "overstay"
   charge was a deliberate one to counter that threat and was
   based on the agents' reasonable suspicions. While it can be
   said that Moussaoui's overstay status was fortuitous,
   because it allowed for him to be taken into immediate custody and prevented him receiving any more flight training,
   it was certainly not something the INS coincidentally undertook of their own volition. I base this on the conversation I
   had when the agents called me at home late on the evening
   Moussaoui was taken into custody to confer and ask for
   legal advice about their next course of action. The INS
   agents was assigned to the FBI's Joint Terrorism Task Force

and was therefore working in tandem with FBI agents.

2) As the Minneapolis agents' reasonable suspicions quickly ripened into probable cause, which, at the latest, occurred within days of Moussaoui's arrest when the French Intelligence Service confirmed his affiliations with radical fundamentalist Islamic groups and activities connected to Osama Bin Laden, they became desperate to search the computer lap top that had been taken from Moussaoui as well as conduct a more thorough search of his personal effects. The agents in particular believed that Moussaoui signaled he had something to hide in the way he refused to allow them to search his computer.

3) The Minneapolis agents' initial thought was to obtain a criminal search warrant, but in order to do so, they needed to get FBI Headquarters' (FBIHQ's) approval in order to ask for DOJ OIPR's approval to contact the United States Attorney's Office in Minnesota. Prior to and even after receipt of information provided by the French, FBIHQ personnel disputed with the Minneapolis agents the existence of probable cause to believe that a criminal violation had occurred/was occurring. As such, FBIHQ personnel refused to contact OIPR to attempt to get the authority. While reasonable minds may differ as to whether probable cause existed prior to receipt of the French intelligence information, it was certainly established after that point and became even greater with successive, more detailed information from the French and other intelligence sources. The two possible criminal violations initially identified by Minneapolis Agents were violations of Title 18 United States Code Section 2332b (Acts of terrorism transcending national boundaries, which, notably, includes "creating a substantial risk of serious bodily injury to any other person by destroying or damaging any structure, conveyance, or other real or personal property within the United States or by attempting or conspiring to destroy or damage any structure, conveyance, or other real or personal property within the United States") and Section 32 (Destruction of aircraft or aircraft facilities). It is important to note that the actual search warrant obtained on September 11th was based on probable cause of a violation of Section 32.[1] Notably also, the actual search warrant obtained on September 11th did not include the French intelligence information. Therefore, the only main difference between the information being submitted to FBIHQ from an early date which HQ personnel continued to deem insufficient and the actual criminal search warrant which a federal district judge signed and approved on September 11th, was the fact that, by the time the actual warrant was obtained, suspected terrorists were known to have highjacked planes which they then deliberately crashed into the World Trade Center and the Pentagon. To say then, as has been iterated numerous times, that probable cause did not exist until after the disasterous event occurred, is really to acknowledge that the missing piece of probable cause was only the FBI's (FBIHQ's) failure to appreciate that such an event could occur. The probable cause did not otherwise improve or change. When we went to the United States Attorney's Office that morning of

September 11th, in the first hour after the attack, we used a disk containing the same information that had already been provided to FBIHQ; then we quickly added Paragraph 19 which was the little we knew from news reports of the actual attacks that morning. The problem with chalking this all up to the "20-20 hindsight is perfect" problem, (which I, as all attorneys who have been involved in deadly force training or the defense of various lawsuits are fully appreciative of), is that this is not a case of everyone in the FBI failing to appreciate the potential consequences. It is obvious, from my firsthand knowledge of the events and the detailed documentation that exists, that the agents in Minneapolis who were closest to the action and in the best position to gauge the situation locally, did fully appreciate the terrorist risk/danger posed by Moussaoui and his possible co-conspirators even prior to September 11th. Even without knowledge of the Phoenix communication (and any number of other additional intelligence communications that FBIHQ personnel were privy to in their central coordination roles), the Minneapolis agents appreciated the risk. So I think it's very hard for the FBI to offer the "20-20 hindsight" justification for its failure to act! Also intertwined with my reluctance in this case to accept the "20-20 hindsight" rationale is first-hand knowledge that I have of statements made on September 11th, after the first attacks on the World Trade Center had already occurred, made telephonically by the FBI Supervisory Special Agent (SSA) who was the one most involved in the Moussaoui matter and who, up to that point, seemed to have been consistently, almost deliberately thwarting the Minneapolis FBI agents' efforts (see number 5). Even after the attacks had begun, the SSA in question was still attempting to block the search of Moussaoui's computer, characterizing the World Trade Center attacks as a mere coincidence with Misseapolis' prior suspicions about Moussaoui.[2]

4) In one of my peripheral roles on the Moussaoui matter, I answered an e-mail message on August 22, 2001, from an attorney at the National Security Law Unit (NSLU). Of course, with (ever important!) 20-20 hindsight, I now wish I had taken more time and care to compose my response. When asked by NSLU for my "assessment of (our) chances of getting a criminal warrant to search Moussaoui's computer", I answered, "Although I think there's a decent chance of being able to get a judge to sign a criminal search warrant, our USAO seems to have an even higher standard much of the time, so rather than risk it, I advised that they should try the other route." Leaked news accounts which said the Minneapolis Legal Counsel (referring to me) concurred with the FBIHQ that probable cause was lacking to search Moussaoui's computer are in error. (or possibly the leak was deliberately skewed in this fashion?) What I meant by this pithy e-mail response, was that although I thought probable cause existed ("probable cause" meaning that the proposition has to be more likely than not, or if quantified, a 51% likelihood), I thought our United States Attorney's Office, (for a lot of reasons including just to play it safe) in regularly requiring much more than probable cause before approving affidavits, (maybe, if quantified, 75%-80% proba-

bility and sometimes even higher), and depending on the actual AUSA who would be assigned, might turn us down. As a tactical choice, I therefore thought it would be better to pursue the "other route" (the FISA search warrant) first, the reason being that there is a common perception, which for lack of a better term, I'll call the "smell test" which has arisen that if the FBI can't do something through straight-up criminal methods, it will then resort to using less-demanding intelligence methods. Of course this isn't true, but I think the perception still exists. So, by this line of reasoning, I was afraid that if we first attempted to go criminal and failed to convinced an AUSA, we wouldn't pass the "smell test" in subsequently seeking a FISA. I thought our best chances therefore lay in first seeking the FISA. Both of the factors that influenced my thinking are areas arguably in need of improvement: requiring an excessively high standard of probable cause in terrorism cases and getting rid of the "smell test" perception. It could even be argued that FBI agents, especially in terrorism cases where time is of the essence, should be allowed ot go directly to federal judges to have their probable cause reviewed for arrests or searches without having to gain the USAO's approval.[4]

5) The fact is that key FBIHQ personnel whose jobs it was to assist and coordinate with field division agents on terrorism investigations and the obtaining and use of FISA searches (and who theoretically were privy to many more sources of intelligence information than field division agents), continued to, almost inexplicably,[5] throw up roadblocks and undermine Minneapolis' by-now desperate efforts to obtain a FISA search warrant, long after the French intelligence service provided its information and probable cause became clear. HQ personnel brought up almost ridiculous questions in their apparent efforts to undermine the probable cause.[6] In all of their conversations and correspondence, HQ personnel never disclosed to the Minneapolis agents that the Phoenix Division had, only approximately three weeks earlier, warned of Al Qaeda operatives in flight schools seeking flight training for terrorist purposes!Nor did FBIHQ personnel do much to disseminate the information about Moussaoui to other appropriate intelligence/law enforcement authorities. When, in a desperate 11th hour measure to bypass the FBIHQ roadblock, the Minneapolis Division undertook to directly notify the CIA's Counter Terrorist Center (CTC), FBIHQ personnel actually chastised the Minneapolis agents for making the direct notification without their approval!

6) Eventually on august 28, 2001, after a series of e-mails between Minneapolis and FBIHQ, which suggest that the FBIHQ SSA deliberately further undercut the FISA effort by not adding the further intelligence information which he had promised to add that supported Moussaoui's foreign power connection and making several changes in the wording of the information that had been provided by the Minneapolis Agent, the Minneapolis agents were notified that the NSLU Unit Chief did not think there was sufficient evidence of Moussaoui's connection to a foreign power. Minneapolis personnel are, to this date, unaware of the specifics of the ver-

bal presentations by the FBIHQ SSA to NSLU or whether
anyone in NSLU ever was afforded the opportunity to actually read for him/herself all of the information on Moussaoui
that had been gathered by the Minneapolis Division and the
French intelligence service. Obviously verbal presentations
are far more susceptible to mis-characterization and error.
The e-mail communications between Minneapolis and FBIHQ,
however, speak for themselves and there are far better wit-
nesses than me who can provide their first hand knowledge
of these events characterized in one Minneapolis agent's e-
mail as FBIHQ is "setting this up for failure." My only comment is that the process of allowing the FBI supervisors to
make changes in affidavits is itself fundamentally wrong,
just as, in the follow-up to FBI Laboratory Whistleblower
Frederic Whitehurst's allegations, this process was revealed
to be wrong in the context of writing up laboratory results.
With the Whitehurst allegations, this process of allowing
supervisors to re-write portions of laboratory reports, was
found to provide opportunities for over-zealous supervisors
to skew the results in favor of the prosecution. In the
Moussaoui case, it was the opposite — the process allowed
the Headquarters Supervisor to downplay the significance of
the information thus far collected in order to get out of the
work of having to see the FISA application through or possibly to avoid taking what he may have perceived as an
unnecessary career risk.[7] I understand that the failures of
the FBIHQ personnel involved in the Moussaoui matter are
also being officially excused because they were too busy
with other investigations, the Cole bombing and other important terrorism matters, but the Supervisor's taking of the
time to read each word of the information submitted by
Minneapolis and then substitute his own choice of wording
belies to some extent the notion that he was too busy. As an
FBI division legal advisor for 12 years (and an FBI agent
for over 21 years), I can state that an affidavit is better and
will tend to be more accurate when the affiant has first
hand information of all the information he/she must attest
to. Of necessity, agents must continually rely upon information from confidential sources, third parties and other law
enforcement officers in drafting affidavits, but the repeating
of information from others greatly adds to the opportunities
for factual discrepancies and errors to arise. To the extent
that we can minimize the opportunity for this type of error
to arise by simply not allowing unnecessary re-writes by
supervisory staff, it ought to be done. (I'm not talking, of
course, about mere grammatical corrections, but changes of
some substance as apparently occurred with the Moussaoui
information which had to be, for lack of a better term, "fil-
tered" through FBIHQ before any action, whether to seek a
criminal or a FISA warrant, could be taken.) Even after
September 11th, the fear was great on the part of
Minneapolis Division personnel that the same FBIHQ personnel would continue their "filtering" with respect to the
Moussaoui investigation, and now with the added incentive
of preventing their prior mistakes from coming to light. For
this reason, for weeks, Minneapolis prefaced all outgoing
communications (ECs) in the PENTTBOM investigation with
a summary of the information about Moussaoui. We just
wanted to make sure the information got to the proper pros-

ecutive authorities and was not further suppressed! This
fear was probably irrational but was nonetheless under-
standable in light of the Minneapolis agents' prior experiences and frustrations involving FBIHQ. (The redundant
preface information regarding Moussaoui on otherwise
unrelative PENTTBOM communications has ended up adding
to criminal discovery issues, but this is the reason it was
done.)

7) Although the last thing the FBI or the country needs now
is a witch hunt, I do find it odd that (to my knowledge) no
inquiry whatsoever was launched of the relevant FBIHQ personnel's actions a long time ago. Despite FBI leaders' full
knowledge of all the items mentioned herein (and probably
more that I'm unaware of), the SSA, his unit chief, and
other involved HQ personnel were allowed to stay in their
positions and, what's worse, occupy critical positions in the
FBI's SIOC Command Center post September 11th. (The SSA
in question actually received a promotion some months
afterward!) It's true we all make mistakes and I'm not sug-
gesting that HQ personnel in question ought to be burned at
the stake, but, we all need to be held accountable for serious
mistakes. I'm relatively certain that if it appeared that a
lowly field office agent had committed such errors of judgment, the FBI's OPR would have been notified to investigate
and the agent would have, at the least, been quickly reas-
signed. I'm afraid the FBI's failure to submit this matter to
OPR (and to the IOB) gives further impetus to the notion
(raised previously by many in the FBI) of a double standard
which results in those of lower rank being investigated
more aggressively and dealt with more harshly for misconduct while the misconduct of those at the top is often overlooked or results in minor disciplinary action. From all
appearances, this double standard may also apply between
those at FBIHQ and those in the field.

8) The last official "fact" that I take issue with is not really
a fact, but an opinion, and a completely unsupported opinion at that. In the day or two following September 11th,
you, Director Mueller, made the statement to the effect that
if the FBI had only had any advance warning of the
attacks, we (meaning the FBI), may have been able to take
some action to prevent the tragedy. Fearing that this statement could easily come back to haunt the FBI upon revelation of the information that had been developed pre-
September 11th about Moussaoui, I and others in the
Minneapolis Office, immediately sought to reach your office
through an assortment of higher level FBIHQ contacts, in
order to quickly make you aware of the background of the
Moussaoui investigation and forewarn you so that your public statements could be accordingly modified. When such
statements from you and other FBI officials continued, we
thought that somehow you had not received the message
and we made further efforts. Finally when similar comments were made weeks later, in Assistant Director Caruso's
congressional testimony in response to the first public leaks
about Moussaoui we faced the sad realization that the
remarks indicated someone, possibly with your approval,
had decided to circle the wagons at FBIHQ in an apparent

effort to protect the FBI from embarrassment and the relevant FBI officials from scrutiny. Everything I have seen and heard about the FBI's official stance and the FBI's internal preparations in anticipation of further congressional inquiry, had, unfortunately, confirmed my worst suspicions in this regard. After the details began to emerge concerning the pre-September 11th investigation of Moussaoui, and subsequently with the recent release of the information about the Phoenix EC, your statement has changed. The official statement is now to the effect that even if the FBI had followed up on the Phoenix lead to conduct checks of flight schools and the Minneapolis request to search Moussaoui's personal effects and laptop, nothing would have changed and such actions certainly could not have prevented the terrorist attacks and resulting loss of life. With all due respect, this statement is as bad as the first! It is also quite at odds with the earlier statement (which I'm surprised has not already been pointed out by those in the media!) I don't know how you or anyone at FBI Headquarters, no matter how much genius or prescience you may possess, could so blithely make this affirmation without anything to back the opinion up than your stature as FBI Director. The truth is, as with most predictions into the future, no one will ever know what impact, if any, the FBI's following up on those requests, would have had. Although I agree that it's very doubtful that the full scope of the tragedy could have been prevented, it's at least possible we could have gotten lucky and uncovered one or two more of the terrorists in flight training prior to September 11th, just as Moussaoui was discovered, after making contact with his flight instructors. If is certainly not beyond the realm of imagination to hypothesize that Moussaoui's fortuitous arrest alone, even if he merely was the 20th hijacker, allowed the hero passengers of Flight 93 to overcome their terrorist hijackers and thus spare more lives on the ground. And even greater casualties, possibly of our Nation's highest government officials, may have been prevented if Al Qaeda intended for Moussaoui to pilot an entirely different aircraft. There is, therefore at least some chance that discovery of other terrorist pilots prior to September 11th may have limited the September 11th attacks and resulting loss of life. Although your conclusion otherwise has to be very reassuring for some in the FBI to hear being repeated so often (as if saying it's so may make it so), I think your statements demonstrate a rush to judgment to protect the FBI at all costs. I think the only fair response to this type of question would be that no one can pretend to know one way or another.

Mr. Director, I hope my observations can be taken in a constructive vein. They are from the heart and intended to be completely apolitical. Hopefully, with our nation's security on the line, you and our nation's other elected and appointed officials can rise above the petty politics that often plague other discussions and do the right thing. You do have some good ideas for change in the FBI but I think you have also not been completely honest about some of the true reasons for the FBI's pre-September 11th failures. Until we come clean and deal with the root causes, the Department of Justice will continue to experience problems fighting terrorism and fighting crime in general.

I have used the "we" term repeatedly herin to indicate facts about others in the Minneapolis Office at critical times, but none of the opinions expressed herin can be attributed to anyone but myself. I know that those who know me would probably describe me as, by nature, overly opinionated and sometimes not as discreet as I should be. Certainly some of the above remarks may be interpreted as falling into that category, but I really do not intend anything as a personal criticism of you or anyone else in the FBI, to include the FBIHQ personnel who I believe were remiss and mishandled their duties with regard to the Moussaoui investigation. Truly my only purpose is to try to provide the facts within my purview so that an accurate assessment can be obtained and we can learn from our mistakes. I have pointed out a few of the things that I think should be looked at but there are many, many more.[8] An honest acknowledgment of the FBI's mistakes in this and other cases should not lead to increasing the Headquarters bureaucracy and approval levels of investigative actions as the answer. Most often, field office agents and field office management on the scene will be better suited to the timely and effective solution of crimes and, in some lucky instances, to the effective prevention of crimes, including terrorism incidents. The relatively quick solving of the recent mailbox pipe-bombing incidents which resulted in no serious injuries to anyone are a good example of effective field office work (actually several field offices working together) and there are hundreds of other examples. Although FBIHQ personnel have, no doubt, been of immeasurable assistance to the field over the years, I'm hard pressed to think of any case which has been solved by FBIHQ personnel and I can name several that have been screwed up! Decision-making is inherently more effective and timely when decentralized instead of concentrated.

Your plans for an FBI Headquarters' "Super Squad" simply fly in the face of an honest appraisal of the FBI's pre-September 11th failures. The Phoenix, Minneapolis and Paris Legal Attache Offices reacted remarkably exhibiting keen perception and prioritization skills regarding the terrorist threats they uncovered or were made aware of pre-September 11th. The same cannot be said for the FBI Headquarters' bureaucracy and you want to expand that?! Should we put the counterterrorism unit chief and SSA who previously handled the Moussaoui matter in charge of the new "Super Squad"?! You are also apparently disregarding the fact the Joint Terrorism Task Forces (JTTFs), operating out of field divisions for years, (the first and chief one being New York City's JTTF), have successfully handled numerous terrorism investigations and, in some instances, successfully prevented acts of terrorism. There's no denying the need for more and better intelligence and intelligence management, but you should think carefully about how much gate keeping power should be entrusted with any HQ entity. If we are indeed in a "war", shouldn't the Generals be on the battlefield instead of sitting in a spot removed from the action while still attempting to call the shots?

I have been an FBI agent for over 21 years and, for what it's worth, have never received any form of disciplinary action throughout my career. From the 5th grade, when I first wrote the FBI and received the "100 Facts about the FBI" pamphlet, this job has been my dream. I feel that my career in the FBI has been somewhat exemplary, having entered on duty at a time when there was only a small percentage of female Special Agents. I have also been lucky to have had four children during my time in the FBI and am the sole breadwinner of a family of six. Due to the frankness with which I have expressed myself and my deep feelings on these issues, (which is only because I feel I have a somewhat unique, inside perspective of the Moussaoui matter, the gravity of the events of September 11th and the current seriousness of the FBI's and United States' ongoing efforts in the "war against terrorism"), I hope my continued employment with the FBI is not somehow placed in jeopardy. I have never written to an FBI Director in my life before on any topic. Although I would hope it is not necessary, I would therefore wish to take advantage of the federal "Whistleblower Protection" provisions by so characterizing my remarks.

Sincerely

Coleen M. Rowley

Special Agent and Minneapolis Chief Division Counsel

NOTES

1 And both of the violations originally cited in vain by the Minneapolis agents disputing the issue with FBIHQ personnel are among those on which Moussaoui is currently indicted.

2 Just minutes after I saw the first news of the World Trade Center attack(s), I was standing outside the office of Minneapolis ASAC M. Chris Briesse waiting for him to finish with a phone call, when he received a call on another line from this SSA. Since I figured I knew what the call may be about and wanted to ask, in light of the unfolding events and the apparent urgency of the situation, if we should now immediately attempt to obtain a criminal search warrant for Moussaoui's laptop and personal property, I took the call. I said something to the effect that, in light of what had just happened in New York, it would have to be the "hugest coincidence" at this point if Moussaoui was not involved with the terrorists. The SSA stated something to the effect that I had used the right term, "coincidence" and that this was probably all just a coincidence and we were to do nothing in Minneapolis until we got their (HQ's) permission because we might "screw up" something else going on elsewhere in the country.

4 Certainly Rule 41 of the Federal Rules of Criminal Procedure which begins, "Upon the request of a federal law enforcement officer *or* an attorney for the government" does not contain this requirement. Although the practice that has evolved is that FBI agents must secure prior approval for any search or arrest from the United States Attorneys Office, the Federal Rule governing Search and Seizure clearly envisions law enforcement officers applying, on their own, for search warrants.

5 During the early aftermath of September 11th, when I happened to be recounting the pre-September 11th events concerning the Moussaoui investigation to other FBI personnel in other divisions or in FBIHQ, almost everyone's first question was "Why?—Why would an FBI agent(s) deliberately sabotage a case? (I know I shouldn't be flippant about this, but jokes were actually made that the key FBIHQ personnel had to be spies or moles, like Robert Hansen, who were actually working for Osama Bin Laden to have so undercut Minneapolis' effort.) Our best real guess, however, is that, in most cases avoidance of all "unnecessary" actions/decisions by FBIHQ managers (and maybe to some extent field managers as well) has, in recent years, been seen as the safest FBI career course. Numerous high-ranking FBI officials who have made decisions or have taken actions which, in hindsight, turned out to be mistaken or just turned out badly (i.e. Ruby Ridge, Waco, etc.) have seen their careers plummet and end. This has in turn resulted in a climate of fear which has chilled aggressive FBI law enforcement action/decisions. In a large hierarchal bureaucracy such as the FBI, with the requirement for numerous superiors approvals/oversight, the premium on career-enhancement, and interjecting a chilling factor brought on by recent extreme public and congressional criticism/oversight, and I think you will see at least the makings of the most likely explanation. Another factor not to be underestimated probably explains the SSA and other FBIHQ personnel's reluctance to act. And so far, I have heard no FBI official even allude to this problem— which is that FBI Headquarters is staffed with a number of short term careerists* who, like the SSA in question, must only serve an 18 month-just-time-to-get-your-ticket-punched minimum. It's no wonder why very little expertise can be acquired by a Headquarters unit! (And no wonder why FBIHQ is mired in mediocrity! — that maybe a little strong, but it would definitely be fair to say that there is unevenness in competency among Headquarters personnel.) (It's also a well known fact that the FBI Agents Association has complained for years about the disincentives facing those entering the FBI management career path which results in very few of the FBI's best and brightest choosing to go into management. Instead the ranks of FBI management are filled with many who were failures as street agents. Along these lines, let me ask the question, why has it suddenly become necessary for the Director to "handpick" the FBI management?) **It's quite conceivable that many of the HQ personnel who so vigorously disputed Moussaoui's ability/predisposition to fly a plane into a building were simply unaware of all the various incidents and reports worldwide of Al Qaeda terrorists attempting or plotting to do so.**

*By the way, just in the event you did not know, let me furnish you the Webster's definition of "careerism" - - the policy or practice of advancing one's career often at the cost of one's integrity". Maybe that sums up the whole problem!

6 For example, at one point, the Supervisory Special Agent at FBIHQ posited that the French information could be worthless because it only identified Zacarias Moussaoui by name and he, the SSA, didn't know how many people by that name existed in France. A Minneapolis agent attempted to surmount that problem by quickly phoning the FBI's legal Attache (Legat) in Paris, France, so that a check could be made of the French telephone directories. Although the Legat in France did not have access to all of the French telephone directories, he was able to quickly ascertain that there was only one listed in the Paris directory. It is not known if this sufficiently answered the question, for the SSA continued to find new reasons to stall.

7 Another factor that cannot be underestimated as to the HQ

Supervisor's apparent reluctance to do anything was/is the ever present risk of being "written up" for an Intelligence Oversight Board (IOB) "error." In the year(s) preceding the September 11th acts of terrorism, numerous alleged IOB violations on the part of FBI personnel had to be submitted to the FBI's Office of Professional Responsibility (OPR) as well as the IOB. I believe the chilling effect upon all levels of FBI agents assigned to intelligence matters and their manager hampered us from aggressive investigation of terrorists. Since one generally only runs the risk of IOB violations when one does something, the safer course is to do nothing. Ironically, in this case, a potentially huge IOB violation arguably occurred due to FBIHQ's failure to act, that is, FBIHQ's failure to inform the Department of Justice Criminal Division of Moussaoui's potential criminal violations (which, as I've already said, were quickly identified in Minneapolis as violations of Title 18 United States Code Section 2332b [Acts of terrorism transcending national boundaries] and Section 32 [Destruction of aircraft or aircraft facilities]). This failure would seem to run clearly afoul of the Attorney General directive contained in the "1995 Procedures for Contacts Between the FBI and the Criminal Division Concerning Foreign Intelligence and Foreign Counterintelligence Investigations" which mandatorily require the FBI to notify the Criminal Division when "facts or circumstances are developed" in an FI or FCI investigation "that reasonably indicate that a significant federal crime has been, is being, or may be committed." I believe that Minneapolis agents actually brought this point to FBIHQ's attention on August 22, 2001, but HQ personnel apparently ignored the directive, ostensibly due to their opinion of the lack of probably cause. But the issue of whether HQ personnel deliberately undercut the probable cause can be sidestepped at this point because the Directive does not require probable cause. It requires only a "reasonable indication" which is defined as "substantially lower than probable cause." Given that the Minneapolis Division had accumulated far more than "a mere hunch" (which the directive would deem as insufficient), the information ought to have, at least, been passed on to the "Core Group" created to assess whether the information needed to be further disseminated to the Criminal Division. However, (and I don't know for sure), but to date, I have never heard that any potential violation of this directive has been submitted to the IOB or to the FBI's OPR. It should also be noted that when making determinations of whether items need to be submitted to the IOB, it is my understanding that NSLU normally used/uses a broad approach, erring, when in doubt, on the side of submitting potential violations.

8 For starters, if prevention rather than prosecution is to be our new main goal, (an objective I totally agree with), we need more guidance on when we can apply the Quarles "public safety" exception to Miranda's 5 Amendment requirements. **We were prevented from even attempting to question Moussaoui on the day of the attacks when, in theory, he could have possessed further information about other co-conspirators.** (Apparently no government attorney believes there is a "public safety" exception in a situation like this?!)

A letter from CIA director George Tenet on the CIA's "diversity management" effort.

Intelligence Community Functional Diversity Strategic Plan

If, in the 21st Century, we are to continue to succeed in our global Mission, the men and women of US Intelligence are going to have to be smarter, bolder and more agile than ever before — and we are going to have to become a much more diverse Intelligence Community.

This is not a matter of political correctness. Just as the business community does, we in the Intelligence Community must see Diversity as a **corporate imperative** – a **strategic goal.** Our people are our most precious assets—not satellites, or light tables or high speed computers. To meet the world-wide challenges of coming decades, our Community will need to attract, train and retain talented employees who have a deep understanding of other societies, cultures and languages. And we must be able to compete with private industry for the best and brightest from all across America.

I challenge each and every one of you to join me in increasing and nurturing diversity within our ranks. Each and every one of us can find ways to ensure that our Intelligence Community is a vibrant place where gifted Americans from all ethnic backgrounds and fields of expertise want to work. A Community where diversity is welcome and a variety of views is sought and heard. A Community where equal opportunities for training and advancement are afforded to all. A Community where our people are valued for the content of their characters and the quality of their work. In short, a Community that embodies American excellence, American values, and American ideals.

I consider the advancement of Diversity to be a vital part of our Strategic Plan for the Intelligence Community. By employing Diversity as a powerful tool, together we can build a workforce that is strongly equipped to deal with a 21st Century world full of challenges and opportunities for our nation. I urge your active support of our Community's Diversity efforts.

Sincerely,

George J. Tenet

Portions of a classified Republic of the Philippines intelligence report reveal that, as early as 1995, terrorists linked to al Qaeda were planning to use aircraft packed with explosives for a "suicide bombing" of CIA headquarters.

Republic of the Philippines
Department of the Interior and Local Government
National Police Commission
National Headquarters Philippine National Police
INTELLIGENCE COMMAND
SPECIAL INVESTIGATION GROUP
Camp Crame, Quezon City

09 January 199

Seizure of Terrorist Documents and Material
in Malate, Metro Manila)

I.   BACKGROUND

Analysis of seized documents, materials and computer print-outs generated through the decoded Toshiba laptop computer was conducted in two (2) separate analysis sessions on 08 January 1995 by SIG-IC analysts assisted by CIG-IC researchers.

session was conducted from 08'400 - 0818O: Jar in, while the second session was conducted from 082300 - 09033(J 1995. These analysis sessions were conducted at the SIG-IC office, Crame, Quezon City.

The report seeks to present several highlights on the terrorist plans and related information and background information on three (3) terrorist conspirators. A brief discussion on the PAL plane explosion in Narita Airport is likewise presented in the report. Concluding the document

5. At Hongkong Airport, SAEED AKMAN will wait for the flight schedule of UA FL Nr 02 bound for Singapore. He will board the plane and plant the bomb following the pattern he had undertaken with UA FL NR 01.

6. The long-time detonating period of the bombs planted at the bathrooms of the UA FL NRS 01 and 02 is good for four (4) days. It is estimated that when the UA FL NR 01 return flight from LOS ANGELES is approaching HONGKONG and the UA FL NR 02 is on its return flight from SINGAPORE and is similarly approaching, the two (2) bombs will simultaneously explode in the air.

After the successful terrorist attacks, SAEED will rendezvous with ABDUL BASIT in Karachi, PAKISTAN sometime last week of January 1994.

A future bombing target to be executed by SAEED AKMAN is principally directed on the CIA Headquarters in Langley, VIRGINIA. The document specifically cited the charter service of a commercial type aircraft loaded with powerful bombs to be dived-crashed by SAEED AKMAN. This is apparently intended to demonstrate to the whole world that a Muslim martyr is ready and determined to die for the glorification of Islam. There are no other details on this specific suicide bombing plan.

VI. THE PAL PLANE EXPLOSION IN NARITA AIRPORT, JAPAN

Several entries on a document specifically cited the involvement of ABDUL BASIT MAMMOD ABDUL KARIM in the PAL plane explosion in Narita Airport, Japan. Information lifted from the document clearly indicates that ABDUL BASIT was responsible in the planting of the nitro glycerin bomb in the PAL plane with flight route Manila-Cebu-Narita.

ABDUL BASIT planted the bomb at a life jacket at a time when the airplane passengers were taking their snacks. It appeared that he transferred seat when he planted the bomb at the Mactan International Airport. ABDUL waited for the arrival of another domestic flight bound for Manila.

A classified Philippines government document based on debriefing of an al Qaeda terrorist shows that the group was planning attacks on U.S. nuclear power plants and CIA headquarters as early as 1994.

AFTER DEBR..

=============

Abdullah Hakim
HASHIM

1. The ;   .. :he information provided by *MURAD*
debriefing cons   **(0 April** 995:

        ε.   .:ile BASIT was staying with MUR:..   :·e..`
apartment, the.   ':e idea of conducting an attac.
Prime Minister b: ·.u. ıO.

        b. M.·R.·.:) denies knowledge on Munir IBRAHIM /·· ·· :. Abdul
MADANI and Kha.. ...LUCH but he provided the following data about Abdul
SHAKOOR nad \·ı..... /ıL-BAHAR:

                .. . Abdul SHAKOOR

Nationality:	Pakistani
Height:	5'5 (approx)
Weight:	65 Kils (app...
Age:	24 yrs old
Build:	Medium
Occupation:	None
Address:	Liari, Karachi, Pakistan

                '.:.:ect formerly resides in Kuwait   ·' ıc
Pakistan toge...   ·· :amily when the Gulf War broke ·   ·.·:.h
BASIT when ı.   ..: the six (6) months explosive training   ..:istan.
However, he was able to complete only two (2) weeks of said training.
Apparently, BAS.." .:.:liked him because of his being immatur.· '   :· c· often
disregard simple ::   ·:.ich the former asked him to accomplish

                Yagoob AL-BAHAR (not AL-BAKAR)

                Subject is a Saudia national. He foug.   .· Afghan
war for fourteen (14) years. He went to Tajakistan after the A:· · ·· war and
fought with the Tajiks against the Russian. He died thereat in 1994.

        c. Murad denies familiarity regarding Al-Majid Importers Exporters
Company. Nevertheless he disclosed that Sharafabad Chowrang is an apartment
located in Karachi wherein Abdul MAJID used to stay.

        d. In mid 1993, BASIT have had an accident while he was making
detonators from lead azide. MURAD did not know exactly why BASIT was
making said detonators, however, he has a feeling then that the BASIT is planning
to attack PM Benazir BHUTTO since it was during said period that they were
discussing the idea of attacking the PM. Said accident was the first one that

BASIT had expeienced. The second was when he provided explosive training to Murad. It almost come to explosion when he carelessly mixed several kinds of chemicals inside a container. The third was when he drunk the sulfuric acid that he had poured into a medicine bottle which he had mistaken as the softdrink that he poured into the same kind of bottle. His face was burned during the said accident.

e. In his plan to attak the US Consulate office in Karachi, he intends to use an improvised rocket that he learned to assemble during his training in Afghanistan. It was drawn in the notes of MURAD which was among the items confiscated during the raid of apartment 603.

f. The plan to attack US nuclear station was discussed in Quetta in October 1994 while the idea of attacking the CIA headquarters was discussed in the Philippines in December 1994 as conceptualized by MURAD.

g. BASIT sent money to MURAD in Dubai through a money changer company whose office in Dubai is located in a place called AL-KHOUR.

A secret Philippines intelligence report based on the debriefing of an al Qaeda terrorist reveals how homemade bombs were constructed.

SECRET

Republic of the Philippines
Deparment of the Interior and Local Government
NATIONAL HEADQUARTERS PHILIPPINE NATIONAL POLICE
I N T E L L I G E N C E   C O M M A N D
SPECIAL INVESTIGATION GROUP
Camp Crame, Quezon City

21 February 1995

MEMORANDUM FOR:

Case Director
Case Supervisor

SUBJECT: Debriefing Report

1. The following are the information obtained during the debriefing conducted to ABDUL HASHIM MURAD on 21 February 1995;

a. MURAD stressed that there was no bomb that he and BASIT had manufactured or completed prior to his arrest. However, he claims that during the raid of apartment 603, one policeman showed him one (1) pipe bomb which according to the latter was already completed. Nevertheless, he cannot ascertain the truthfulness of the policeman's claim for as far as he is concerned, there was no bomb that he and BASIT have had manufactured during his stay in said apartment.

b. Before his arrest, MURAD is supposed to make one (1) 320 ml and (1) 350 ml nitroglycerine bombs which he will be placing in (2) bottles of contact lenses cleaning liquid. Said bombs are the ones he supposedly use in the plot to bomb US air carriers. Likewise, he is supposed to bring with him some nitrocellulose which he will be placing inside the bottles of nitroglycerine after passing through the X-Ray machines. Said nitrocellulose is in a form of cotton balls dipped in a mixture of citric and nitric acids and is being use to increases the stability of nitroglycerine. BASIT is the one supposed to make said nitrocellulose.

Nevertheless, he was able to make two (2) sets of timing devices from the four (4) casio wristwatches that he and BASIT bought from Shangri-La Plaza. He disclosed that two (2) wristwatches is needed in making a set of timing device capable of a four (4) days delay of detonation.

On the other hand, BASIT is supposed to make three (3) to four (4) sets of acetone broxide pipe bombs intended for the bombing of the Pope. Likewise, he was expected to make a remote control device from a handheld Icom radio which he will be using in detonating said bombs.

SECRET

SECRET

c. MURAD further stressed that there was no bomb that they have completed prior to his arrest, hence, there wasn't any bomb that has been transferred or taken to another location.

d. MURAD was given an assurance that the nitroglycerine can easily pass through the airport's X-Ray machine and was advised to follow the normal procedure in boarding an aircraft.

e. MURAD is not aware whether BASIT or any of the latter's companions have contacts with any airport, travel agency, cargo company or any group of the tourism industry.

f. MURAD denies knowledge of any terrorist conducting surveillance of any airport.

g. In the plot to bomb US air carriers, MURAD is expected to use first class ticket which BASIT will provide.

h. MURAD had used first class ticket once during his travel from Pakistan to Dubai.

i. MURAD claimed that they prefer to use chemicals in making explosives since they can easily acquire same. Likewise, explosives made from chemicals can easily pass on through airports' X-Ray machines because of its low density characteristic. Thus, he denies knowledge of any terrorist groups or individuals who use SEMTEX, C4 and the likes.

j. MURAD claimed that he use to follow legitimate or normal procedure in making flight reservations and he is not aware whether BASIT and his companions are doing same. Hence, he denies knowledge on specific travel agency being used by the latter.

k. MURAD claimed that BASIT and AHMAD AJAJ purchased Scandinavian passports from Peshawar, Pakistan sometime in November 1992. The duo used said passports during their trip to New York. However, he do not know from whom did the duo purchased same and he has no knowledge on the names listed in the said passports.

l. The only commercial or recreational places known to MURAD wherein BASIT used to meet his companions is the Seven Eleven Store located at M. Adriatico Street in Malate and a Karaoke Bar located along A. Mabini Street in Manila.

m. MURAD claimed that he has no knowledge regarding the personalities of BASIT's contacts in Algeria and Egypt. He knew BASIT's contacts in said countries are his former classmates in the Mujaheedin training that the latter had undergone in Jalalabad, Afghanistan. Likewise, he has never seen or observed BASIT making phonecall any individual in said countries.

SECRET

SECRET

n. MURAD recalls that BASIT told him once that "Someday the Liberation Army will grow and become an independent and structured organization". Said statement made MURAD speculate that BASIT is planning to form his own terrorist organization.

o. BASIT had travelled in Asia specifically in Singapore, Hongkong and the Philippines looking for a place wherein the standard of living is considerably low. Thus, he had chosen the Philippines to be his base country in Asia because of the low standard of living. Likewise, it is the only country in Asia wherein he contacted and had a formal meeting with fellow Muslim extremists.

2. For information.

Case Officer

SECRET

THE EVIDENCE

THE FOLLOWING PAGES PRESENT two documents that outline the terrorist activities of al Qaeda. The first is a British government dossier, published by Prime Minister Tony Blair's office, laying out a summary of evidence against bin Laden and his responsibility for the September 11 attacks. The second is the U.S. District Court indictment against Zacarias Moussaoui—which is the most complete U.S. government account of the events leading up to September 11—detailing the conspiracy and the activities of the al Qaeda terrorists.

A report by the British prime minister's office on the terrorist activities of al Qaeda. This report outlines evidence that links Osama bin Laden and al Qaeda to the September 11 attacks.

10 Downing Street
Newsroom
London

4 October 2001

This document does not purport to provide a prosecutable case against Usama Bin Laden in a court of law. Intelligence often cannot be used evidentially, due both to the strict rules of admissibility and to the need to protect the safety of sources. But on the basis of all the information available HMG is confident of its conclusions as expressed in this document.

RESPONSIBILITY FOR THE TERRORIST ATROCITIES IN THE UNITED STATES, 11 SEPTEMBER 2001

INTRODUCTION
1. The clear conclusions reached by the government are:

• Usama Bin Laden and Al Qaida, the terrorist network which he heads, planned and carried out the atrocities on 11 September 2001;

• Usama Bin Laden and Al Qaida retain the will and resources to carry out further atrocities;

• the United Kingdom, and United Kingdom nationals are potential targets; and

• Usama Bin Laden and Al Qaida were able to commit these atrocities because of their close alliance with the Taleban regime, which allowed them to operate with impunity in pursuing their terrorist activity.

2. The material in respect of 1998 and the USS Cole comes from indictments and intelligence sources. The material in respect of 11 September comes from intelligence and the criminal investigation to date. The details of some aspects cannot be given, but the facts are clear from the intelligence.

3. The document does not contain the totality of the material known to HMG, given the continuing and absolute need to protect intelligence sources.

SUMMARY
4. The relevant facts show:

Background

• Al Qaida is a terrorist organisation with ties to a global network, which has been in existence for over 10 years. It was founded, and has been led at all times, by Usama Bin Laden.

• Usama Bin Laden and Al Qaida have been engaged in a

jihad against the United States, and its allies. One of their stated aims is the murder of US citizens, and attacks on America's allies.

• Usama Bin Laden and Al Qaida have been based in Afghanistan since 1996, but have a network of operations throughout the world. The network includes training camps, warehouses, communication facilities and commercial operations able to raise significant sums of money to support its activity. That activity includes substantial exploitation of the illegal drugs trade from Afghanistan.

• Usama Bin Laden's Al Qaida and the Taleban regime have a close and mutually dependent alliance. Usama Bin Laden and Al Qaida provide the Taleban regime with material, financial and military support. They jointly exploit the drugs trade. The Taleban regime allows Bin Laden to operate his terrorist training camps and activities from Afghanistan, protects him from attacks from outside, and protects the drugs stockpiles. Usama Bin Laden could not operate his terrorist activities without the alliance and support of the Taleban regime. The Taleban's strength would be seriously weakened without Usama Bin Laden's military and financial support.

• Usama Bin Laden and Al Qaida have the capability to execute major terrorist attacks.

• Usama Bin Laden has claimed credit for the attack on US soldiers in Somalia in October 1993, which killed 18; for the attack on the US Embassies in Kenya and Tanzania in August 1998 which killed 224 and injured nearly 5000; and were linked to the attack on the USS Cole on 12 October 2000, in which 17 crew members were killed and 40 others injured.

* They have sought to acquire nuclear and chemical materials for use as terrorist weapons.

In relation to the terrorist attacks on 11 September
5. After 11 September we learned that, not long before, Bin Laden had indicated he was about to launch a major attack on America. The detailed planning for the terrorist attacks of 11 September was carried out by one of UBL's close associates. Of the 19 hijackers involved in 11 September 2001, it has already been established that at least three had links with Al Qaida. The attacks on 11 September 2001 were similar in both their ambition and intended impact to previous attacks undertaken by Usama Bin laden and Al Qaida, and also had features in common. In particular:

• Suicide attackers

• Co-ordinated attacks on the same day

• The aim to cause maximum American casualties

• Total disregard for other casualties, including Muslim

• Meticulous long-term planning

• Absence of warning.

6. Al Qaida retains the capability and the will to make further attacks on the US and its allies, including the United Kingdom.

7. Al Qaida gives no warning of terrorist attack.

THE FACTS

Usama Bin Laden and Al Qaida

8. In 1989 Usama Bin Laden, and others, founded an international terrorist group known as "Al Qaida" (the Base). At all times he has been the leader of Al Qaida.

9. From 1989 until 1991 Usama Bin Laden was based in Afghanistan and Peshawar, Pakistan. In 1991 he moved to Sudan, where he stayed until 1996. In that year he returned to Afghanistan, where he remains.

The Taleban Regime

10. The Taleban emerged from the Afghan refugee camps in Pakistan in the early 1990s. By 1996 they had captured Kabul. They are still engaged in a bloody civil war to control the whole of Afghanistan. They are led by Mullah Omar.

11. In 1996 Usama Bin Laden moved back to Afghanistan. He established a close relationship with Mullah Omar, and threw his support behind the Taleban. Usama Bin Laden and the Taleban regime have a close alliance on which both depend for their continued existence. They also share the same religious values and vision.

12. Usama Bin Laden has provided the Taleban regime with troops, arms, and money to fight the Northern Alliance. He is closely involved with Taleban military training, planning and operations. He has representatives in the Taleban military command structure. He has also given infrastructure assistance and humanitarian aid. Forces under the control of Usama Bin Laden have fought alongside the Taleban in the civil war in Afghanistan.

13. Omar has provided Bin Laden with a safe haven in which to operate, and has allowed him to establish terrorist training camps in Afghanistan. They jointly exploit the Afghan drugs trade. In return for active Al Qaida support, the Taleban allow Al Qaida to operate freely, including planning, training and preparing for terrorist activity. In addition the Taleban provide security for the stockpiles of drugs.

14. Since 1996, when the Taleban captured Kabul, the United States government has consistently raised with them a whole range of issues, including humanitarian aid and terrorism. Well before 11 September 2001 they had provided evidence to the Taleban of the responsibility of Al Qaida for the terrorist attacks in East Africa. This evidence had been provided to senior leaders of the Taleban at their request.

15. The United States government had made it clear to the Taleban regime that Al Qaida had murdered US citizens, and planned to murder more. The US offered to work with the Taleban to expel the terrorists from Afghanistan. These talks, which have been continuing since 1996, have failed to produce any results.

16. In June 2001, in the face of mounting evidence of the Al Qaida threat, the United States warned the Taleban that it had the right to defend itself and that it would hold the regime responsible for attacks against US citizens by terrorists sheltered in Afghanistan.

17. In this, the United States had the support of the United Nations. The Security Council, in Resolution 1267, condemned Usama Bin Laden for sponsoring international terrorism and operating a network of terrorist camps, and demanded that the Taleban surrender Usama Bin Laden without further delay so that he could be brought to justice.

18. Despite the evidence provided by the US of the responsibility of Usama Bin Laden and Al Qaida for the 1998 East Africa bombings, despite the accurately perceived threats of further atrocities, and despite the demands of the United Nations, the Taleban regime responded by saying no evidence existed against Usama Bin Laden, and that neither he nor his network would be expelled.

19. A former Government official in Afghanistan has described the Taleban and Usama Bin Laden as "two sides of the same coin: Usama cannot exist in Afghanistan without the Taleban and the Taleban cannot exist without Usama."

Al Qaida

20. Al Qaida is dedicated to opposing 'un-Islamic' governments in Muslim countries with force and violence.

21. Al Qaida virulently opposes the United States. Usama Bin Laden has urged and incited his followers to kill American citizens, in the most unequivocal terms.

22. On 12 October 1996 he issued a declaration of jihad as follows:

"The people of Islam have suffered from aggression, iniquity and injustice imposed by the Zionist-Crusader alliance and their collaborators . . .

It is the duty now on every tribe in the Arabian peninsula to fight jihad and cleanse the land from these Crusader occupiers. Their wealth is booty to those who kill them.

My Muslim brothers: your brothers in Palestine and in the land of the two Holy Places [i.e. Saudi Arabia] are calling upon your help and asking you to take part in fighting against the enemy - the Americans and the Israelis. They are asking you to do whatever you can to expel the enemies out of the sanctities of Islam."

Later in the same year he said that

"terrorising the American occupiers [of Islamic Holy Places] is a religious and logical obligation."

In February 1998 he issued and signed a 'fatwa' which included a decree to all Muslims:

". . . the killing of Americans and their civilian and military allies is a religious duty for each and every Muslim to be carried out in whichever country they are until Al Aqsa mosque has been liberated from their grasp and until their armies have left Muslim lands."

In the same 'fatwa' he called on Muslim scholars and their leaders and their youths to

"launch an attack on the American soldiers of Satan."

and concluded:

"We - with God's help - call on every Muslim who believes in God and wishes to be rewarded to comply with God's order to kill Americans and plunder their money whenever and wherever they find it. We also call on Muslims . . . to launch the raid on Satan's US troops and the devil's supporters allying with them, and to displace those who are behind them."

When asked, in 1998, about obtaining chemical or nuclear weapons he said

"acquiring such weapons for the defence of Muslims [was] a religious duty."

In an interview aired on Al Jazira (Doha, Qatar) television he stated:

"Our enemy is every American male, whether he is directly fighting us or paying taxes."

In two interviews broadcast on US television in 1997 and 1998 he referred to the terrorists who carried out the earlier attack on the World Trade Center in 1993 as "role models". He went on to exhort his followers "to take the fighting to America."

23. From the early 1990s Usama Bin Laden has sought to obtain nuclear and chemical materials for use as weapons of terror.

24. Although US targets are Al Qaida's priority, it also explicitly threatens the United States' allies. References to "Zionist-Crusader alliance and their collaborators," and to "Satan's US troops and the devil's supporters allying with them" are references which unquestionably include the United Kingdom.

25. There is a continuing threat. Based on our experience of the way the network has operated in the past, other cells, like those that carried out the terrorist attacks on 11 September, must be assumed to exist.

26. Al Qaida functions both on its own and through a network of other terrorist organisations. These include Egyptian Islamic Jihad and other north African Islamic extremist terrorist groups, and a number of other jihadi groups in other countries including the Sudan, Yemen, Somalia, Pakistan and India. Al Qaida also maintains cells and personnel in a number of other countries to facilitate its activities.

27. Usama Bin Laden heads the Al Qaida network. Below him is a body known as the Shura, which includes representatives of other terrorist groups, such as Egyptian Islamic Jihad leader Ayman Zawahiri and prominent lieutenants of Bin Laden such as Abu Hafs Al-Masri. Egyptian Islamic Jihad has, in effect, merged with Al Qaida.

28. In addition to the Shura, Al Qaida has several groups dealing with military, media, financial and Islamic issues.

29. Mohamed Atef is a member of the group that deals with military and terrorist operations. His duties include principal responsibility for training Al Qaida members.

30. Members of Al Qaida must make a pledge of allegiance to follow the orders of Usama Bin Laden.

31. A great deal of evidence about Usama Bin Laden and Al Qaida has been made available in the US indictment for earlier crimes.

32. Since 1989, Usama Bin Laden has conducted substantial financial and business transactions on behalf of Al Qaida and in pursuit of its goals. These include purchasing land for training camps, purchasing warehouses for the storage of items, including explosives, purchasing communications and electronics equipment, and transporting currency and weapons to members of Al Qaida and associated terrorist groups in countries throughout the world.

33. Since 1989 Usama Bin Laden has provided training camps and guest houses in Afghanistan, Pakistan, the Sudan, Somalia and Kenya for the use of Al Qaida and associated terrorist groups. We know from intelligence that there are currently at least a dozen camps across Afghanistan, of which at least four are used for training terrorists.

34. Since 1989, Usama Bin Laden has established a series of businesses to provide income for Al Qaida, and to provide cover for the procurement of explosives, weapons and chemicals, and for the travel of Al Qaida operatives. The businesses have included a holding company known as 'Wadi Al Aqiq', a construction business known as 'Al Hijra', an agricultural business known as 'Al Themar Al Mubaraka', and investment companies known as 'Ladin International' and 'Taba Investments'.

Usama Bin Laden and previous attacks
35. In 1992 and 1993 Mohamed Atef travelled to Somalia on several occasions for the purpose of organising violence against United States and United Nations troops then stationed in Somalia. On each occasion he reported back to Usama Bin Laden, at his base in the Riyadh district of Khartoum.

36. In the spring of 1993 Atef, Saif al Adel, another senior member of Al Qaida, and other members began to provide military training to Somali tribes for the purpose of fighting the United Nations forces.

37. On 3 and 4 October 1993 operatives of Al Qaida participatedin the attack on US military personnel serving in Somalia as part of the operation 'Restore Hope.' Eighteen US military personnel were killed in the attack.

38. From 1993 members of Al Qaida began to live in Nairobi and set up businesses there, including Asma Ltd, and Tanzanite King. They were regularly visited there by senior members of Al Qaida, in particular by Atef and Abu Ubadiah al Banshiri.

39. Beginning in the latter part of 1993, members of Al Qaida in Kenya began to discuss the possibility of attacking the US Embassy in Nairobi in retaliation for US participation in Operation Restore Hope in Somalia. Ali Mohamed, a US citizen and admitted member of Al Qaida, surveyed the US Embassy as a possible target for a terrorist attack. He took photographs and made sketches, which he presented to Usama Bin Laden while Bin Laden was in Sudan. He also admitted that he had trained terrorists for Al Qaida in Afghanistan in the early 1990s, and that those whom he trained included many involved in the East African bombings in August 1998.

40. In June or July 1998, two Al Qaida operatives, Fahid Mohammed Ali Msalam and Sheik Ahmed Salim Swedan, purchased a Toyota truck and made various alterations to the back of the truck.

41. In early August 1998, operatives of Al Qaida gathered in 43, New Runda Estates, Nairobi to execute the bombing of the US Embassy in Nairobi.

42. On 7 August 1998, Assam, a Saudi national and Al Qaida operative, drove the Toyota truck to the US embassy. There was a large bomb in the back of the truck.

43. Also in the truck was Mohamed Rashed Daoud Al 'Owali, another Saudi. He, by his own confession, was an Al Qaida operative, who from about 1996 had been trained in Al Qaida camps in Afghanistan in explosives, hijacking, kidnapping, assassination and intelligence techniques. With Usama Bin Laden's express permission, he fought alongside the Taleban in Afghanistan. He had met Usama Bin Laden personally in 1996 and asked for another 'mission.' Usama Bin Laden sent him to East Africa after extensive specialised training at camps in Afghanistan.

44. As the truck approached the Embassy, Al 'Owali got out and threw a stun grenade at a security guard. Assam drove the truck up to the rear of the embassy. He got out and then detonated the bomb, which demolished a multi-storey secretarial college and severely damaged the US embassy, and the Co-operative bank building. The bomb killed 213 people and injured 4500. Assam was killed in the explosion.

45. Al 'Owali expected the mission to end in his death. He had been willing to die for Al Qaida. But at the last minute he ran away from the bomb truck and survived. He had no money, passport or plan to escape after the mission, because he had expected to die.

46. After a few days, he called a telephone number in Yemen to have money transferred to him in Kenya. The number he rang in Yemen was contacted by Usama Bin Laden's phone on the same day as Al 'Owali was arranging to get the money.

47. Another person arrested in connection with the Nairobi bombing was Mohamed Sadeek Odeh. He admitted to his involvement. He identified the principal participants in the bombing. He named three other persons, all of whom were Al Qaida or Egyptian Islamic Jihad members.

48. In Dar es Salaam the same day, at about the same time, operatives of Al Qaida detonated a bomb at the US embassy, killing 11 people. The Al Qaida operatives involved included Mustafa Mohamed Fadhil and Khaflan Khamis Mohamed. The bomb was carried in a Nissan Atlas truck, which Ahmed Khfaklan Ghailani and Sheikh Ahmed Salim Swedan, two Al Qaida operatives, had purchased in July 1998, in Dar es Salaam.

49. Khaflan Khamis Mohamed was arrested for the bombing. He admitted membership of Al Qaida, and implicated other members of Al Qaida in the bombing.

50. On 7 and 8 August 1998, two other members of Al Qaida disseminated claims of responsibility for the two bombings by sending faxes to media organisations in Paris, Doha in Qatar, and Dubai in the United Arab Emirates.

51. Additional evidence of the involvement of Al Qaida in the East African bombings came from a search conducted in London of several residences and businesses belonging to Al Qaida and Egyptian Islamic Jihad members. In those searches a number of documents were found including claims of responsibility for the East African bombings in the name of a fictitious group, 'the Islamic Army for the liberation of the Holy Places.'

52. Al 'Owali, the would-be suicide bomber, admitted he was told to make a videotape of himself using the name of the same fictitious group.

53. The faxed claims of responsibility were traced to a telephone number, which had been in contact with Usama Bin Laden's cell phone. The claims disseminated to the press were clearly written by someone familiar with the conspiracy. They stated that the bombings had been carried out by two Saudis in Kenya, and one Egyptian in Dar es Salaam. They were probably sent before the bombings had even taken place. They referred to two Saudis dying in the Nairobi attack. In fact, because Al 'Owali fled at the last minute, only one Saudi died.

54. On 22 December 1998 Usama Bin Laden was asked by Time magazine whether he was responsible for the August 1998 attacks. He replied:

"The International Islamic Jihad Front for the jihad against the US and Israel has, by the grace of God, issued a crystal clear fatwa calling on the Islamic nation to carry on Jihad aimed at liberating the holy sites. The nation of Mohammed has responded to this appeal. If instigation for jihad against the Jews and the Americans . . . is considered to be a crime, then let history be a witness that I am a criminal. Our job is to instigate and, by the grace of God, we did that, and certain people responded to this instigation."

He was asked if he knew the attackers:

". . . those who risked their lives to earn the pleasure of God are real men. They managed to rid the Islamic nation of disgrace. We hold them in the highest esteem."

And what the US could expect of him:

". . . any thief or criminal who enters another country to steal should expect to be exposed to murder at any time . . . The US knows that I have attacked it, by the grace of God, for more than ten years now . . . God knows that we have been pleased by the killing of American soldiers [in Somalia in 1993]. This was achieved by the grace of God and the efforts of the mujahideen . . . Hostility towards America is a religious duty and we hope to be rewarded for it by God. I am confident that Muslims will be able to end the legend of the so-called superpower that is America."

55. In December 1999 a terrorist cell linked to Al Qaida was discovered trying to carry out attacks inside the United States. An Algerian, Ahmed Ressam, was stopped at the US-Canadian border and over 100 lbs of bomb making material was found in his car. Ressam admitted he was planning to set off a large bomb at Los Angeles International airport on New Year's Day. He said that he had received terrorist training at Al Qaida camps in Afghanistan and then been instructed to go abroad and kill US civilians and military personnel.

56. On 3 January 2000, a group of Al Qaida members, and other terrorists who had trained in Al Qaida camps in Afghanistan, attempted to attack a US destroyer with a small boat loaded with explosives. Their boat sank, aborting the attack.

57. On 12 October 2000, however, the USS Cole was struck by an explosive-laden boat while refuelling in Aden harbour. Seventeen crew were killed, and 40 injured.

58. Several of the perpetrators of the Cole attack (mostly Yemenis and Saudis) were trained at Usama Bin Laden's camps in Afghanistan. Al 'Owali has identified the two commanders of the attack on the USS Cole as having participated in the planning and preparation for the East African embassy bombings.

59. In the months before the September 11 attacks, propaganda videos were distributed throughout the Middle East and Muslim world by Al Qaida, in which Usama Bin Laden and others were shown encouraging Muslims to attack American and Jewish targets.

60. Similar videos, extolling violence against the United States and other targets, were distributed before the East African embassy attacks in August 1998.

Usama Bin Laden and the 11 September attacks

61. Nineteen men have been identified as the hijackers from the passenger lists of the four planes hijacked on 11 September 2001. At least three of them have already been positively identified as associates of Al Qaida. One has been identified as playing key roles in both the East African embassy attacks and the USS Cole attack. Investigations continue into the backgrounds of all the hijackers.

62. From intelligence sources, the following facts have been established subsequent to 11 September; for intelligence reasons, the names of associates, though known, are not given.

• In the run-up to 11 September, Bin Laden was mounting a concerted propaganda campaign amongst like-minded groups of people - including videos and documentation - justifying attacks on Jewish and American targets; and claiming that those who died in the course of them were carrying out God's work.

• We have learned, subsequent to 11 September, that Bin Laden himself asserted shortly before 11 September that he was preparing a major attack on America.

• In August and early September close associates of Bin Laden were warned to return to Afghanistan from other parts of the world by 10 September.

• Immediately prior to 11 September some known associates of Bin Laden were naming the date for action as on or around 11 September.

• Since 11 September we have learned that one of Bin Laden's closest and most senior associates was responsible for the detailed planning of the attacks.

• There is evidence of a very specific nature relating to the guilt of Bin Laden and his associates that is too sensitive to release.

63. Usama Bin Laden remains in charge, and the mastermind, of Al Qaida. In Al Qaida, an operation on the scale of the 11 September attacks would have been approved by Usama Bin Laden himself.

64. The modus operandi of 11 September was entirely consistent with previous attacks. Al Qaida's record of atrocities is characterised by meticulous long term planning, a desire to inflict mass casualties, suicide bombers, and multiple simultaneous attacks.

65. The attacks of 11 September 2001 are entirely consistent with the scale and sophistication of the planning which went into the attacks on the East African Embassies and the USS Cole. No warnings were given for these three attacks, just as there was none on 11 September.

66. Al Qaida operatives, in evidence given in the East African Embassy bomb trials, have described how the group spends years preparing for an attack. They conduct repeated surveillance, patiently gather materials, and identify and vet operatives, who have the skills to participate in the attack and the willingness to die for their cause.

67. The operatives involved in the 11 September atrocities attended flight schools, used flight simulators to study the controls of larger aircraft and placed potential airports and routes under surveillance.

68. Al Qaida's attacks are characterised by total disregard for innocent lives, including Muslims. In an interview after the East African bombings, Usama Bin Laden insisted that the need to attack the United States excused the killing of other innocent civilians, Muslim and non-Muslim alike.

69. No other organisation has both the motivation and the capability to carry out attacks like those of the 11 September - only the Al Qaida network under Usama Bin Laden.

Conclusion

70. The attacks of the 11 September 2001 were planned and carried out by Al Qaida, an organisation whose head is Usama Bin Laden. That organisation has the will, and the resources, to execute further attacks of similar scale. Both the United States and its close allies are targets for such attacks. The attack could not have occurred without the alliance between the Taleban and Usama Bin Laden, which allowed Bin Laden to operate freely in Afghanistan, promoting, planning and executing terrorist activity.

Federal indictment of Zacarias Moussaoui, who has been identified as the twentieth hijacker of the September 11 plot. The indictment lays out the conspiracy in detail.

IN THE UNITED STATES DISTRICT COURT

FOR THE EASTERN DISTRICT OF VIRGINIA

ALEXANDRIA DIVISION

UNITED STATES OF AMERICA	)	CRIMINAL NO:
	)	
	)	Conspiracy to Commit Acts of Terrorism
-v-	)	Transcending National Boundaries
	)	(18 U.S.C. §§ 2332b(a)(2) & (c))
	)	(Count One)
ZACARIAS MOUSSAOUI,	)	
a/k/a "Shaqil,")	Conspiracy to Commit Aircraft Piracy
a/k/a "Abu Khalid al Sahrawi,"	)	(49 U.S.C. §§ 46502(a)(1)(A) and (a)(2)(B))
	)	(Count Two)
Defendant.	)	
	)	Conspiracy to Destroy Aircraft
	)	(18 U.S.C. §§ 32(a)(7) & 34)
	)	(Count Three)
	)	
	)	Conspiracy to Use Weapons of Mass
	)	Destruction
	)	(18 U.S.C. § 2332a(a))
	)	(Count Four)
	)	
	)	Conspiracy to Murder United States
	)	(18 U.S.C. §§ 1114 & 1117)
	)	(Count Five)
	)	
	)	Conspiracy to Destroy Property
	)	(18 U.S.C. §§ 844(f), (i), (n))
	)	(Count Six)

JUNE 2002 TERM - AT ALEXANDRIA

SUPERSEDING INDICTMENT

THE GRAND JURY CHARGES THAT:

COUNT ONE
(Conspiracy to Commit Acts of Terrorism Transcending National Boundaries)

Background: al Qaeda

1.　At all relevant times from in or about 1989 until the date of the filing of this

Indictment, an international terrorist group existed which was dedicated to opposing non-Islamic

governments with force and violence. This organization grew out of the "mekhtab al khidemat"

(the "Services Office") organization which had maintained offices in various parts of the world,

including Afghanistan, Pakistan (particularly in Peshawar), and the United States. The group

was founded by Usama Bin Laden and Muhammad Atef, a/k/a "Abu Hafs al Masry," together

with "Abu Ubaidah al Banshiri," and others. From in or about 1989 until the present, the group

called itself "al Qaeda" ("the Base"). From 1989 until in or about 1991, the group (hereafter

referred to as "al Qaeda") was headquartered in Afghanistan and Peshawar, Pakistan. In or about

1991, the leadership of al Qaeda, including its "emir" (or prince) Usama Bin Laden, relocated to

the Sudan. Al Qaeda was headquartered in the Sudan from approximately 1991 until

approximately 1996 but still maintained offices in various parts of the world. In 1996, Usama

Bin Laden and other members of al Qaeda relocated to Afghanistan. At all relevant times, al

Qaeda was led by its emir, Usama Bin Laden. Members of al Qaeda pledged an oath of

allegiance (called a "bayat") to Usama Bin Laden and al Qaeda. Those who were suspected of

collaborating against al Qaeda were to be identified and killed.

2.　Bin Laden and al Qaeda violently opposed the United States for several reasons.

First, the United States was regarded as an "infidel" because it was not governed in a manner

consistent with the group's extremist interpretation of Islam. Second, the United States was

viewed as providing essential support for other "infidel" governments and institutions,

particularly the governments of Saudi Arabia and Egypt, the nation of Israel, and the United

Nations organization, which were regarded as enemies of the group. Third, al Qaeda opposed the involvement of the United States armed forces in the Gulf War in 1991 and in Operation Restore Hope in Somalia in 1992 and 1993. In particular, al Qaeda opposed the continued presence of American military forces in Saudi Arabia (and elsewhere on the Saudi Arabian peninsula) following the Gulf War. Fourth, al Qaeda opposed the United States Government because of the arrest, conviction and imprisonment of persons belonging to al Qaeda or its affiliated terrorist groups or those with whom it worked. For these and other reasons, Bin Laden declared a jihad, or holy war, against the United States, which he has carried out through al Qaeda and its affiliated organizations.

3.   One of the principal goals of al Qaeda was to drive the United States armed forces out of Saudi Arabia (and elsewhere on the Saudi Arabian peninsula) and Somalia by violence. Members of al Qaeda issued fatwahs (rulings on Islamic law) indicating that such attacks were both proper and necessary.

4.   Al Qaeda functioned both on its own and through some of the terrorist organizations that operated under its umbrella, including: Egyptian Islamic Jihad, which was led by Ayman al-Zawahiri, and at times, the Islamic Group (also known as "el Gamaa Islamia" or simply "Gamaa't"), and a number of jihad groups in other countries, including the Sudan, Egypt, Saudi Arabia, Yemen, Somalia, Eritrea, Djibouti, Afghanistan, Pakistan, Bosnia, Croatia, Albania, Algeria, Tunisia, Lebanon, the Philippines, Tajikistan, Azerbaijan, Malaysia, Singapore, Indonesia, and the Kashmiri region of India and the Chechnyan region of Russia. Al Qaeda also maintained cells and personnel in a number of countries to facilitate its activities, including in Kenya, Tanzania, the United Kingdom, Germany, Canada, Malaysia, and the United States.

5.   Al Qaeda had a command and control structure which included a majlis al shura (or consultation council) which discussed and approved major undertakings, including terrorist operations. Al Qaeda also had a "military committee" which considered and approved "military" matters.

6.   Usama Bin Laden and al Qaeda also forged alliances with the National Islamic Front in the Sudan and with representatives of the government of Iran, and its associated terrorist group Hizballah, for the purpose of working together against their perceived common enemies in the West, particularly the United States.

7.   Since at least 1989, until the filing of this Indictment, Usama Bin Laden and the terrorist group al Qaeda sponsored, managed, and/or financially supported training camps in Afghanistan, which camps were used to instruct members and associates of al Qaeda and its affiliated terrorist groups in the use of firearms, explosives, chemical weapons, and other weapons of mass destruction. In addition to providing training in the use of various weapons, these camps were used to conduct operational planning against United States targets around the world and experiments in the use of chemical and biological weapons. These camps were also used to train others in security and counterintelligence methods, such as the use of codes and passwords, and to teach members and associates of al Qaeda about traveling to perform operations. For example, al Qaeda instructed its members and associates to dress in "Western" attire and to use other methods to avoid detection by security officials. The group also taught its members and associates to monitor media reporting of its operations to determine the effectiveness of their terrorist activities.

8.   Since in or about 1996, Usama Bin Laden and others operated al Qaeda from their headquarters in Afghanistan. During this time, Bin Laden and others forged close relations with

the Taliban in Afghanistan. To that end, Bin Laden informed other al Qaeda members and associates outside Afghanistan of their support of, and alliance with, the Taliban. Bin Laden also endorsed a declaration of jihad (holy war) issued by the "Ulema Union of Afghanistan."

The September 11 Hijackers

9.   On September 11, 2001, co-conspirators Mohamed Atta, Abdul Aziz Alomari, Wail al-Shehri, Waleed al-Shehri, and Satam al-Suqami hijacked American Airlines Flight 11, bound from Boston to Los Angeles, and crashed it into the North Tower of the World Trade Center in New York. (In this Indictment, each hijacker will be identified with the flight number of the plane he hijacked.)

10.   On September 11, 2001, co-conspirators Marwan al-Shehhi, Fayez Ahmed, a/k/a "Fayez Banihammad," Ahmed al-Ghamdi, Hamza al-Ghamdi, and Mohand al-Shehri hijacked United Airlines Flight 175, bound from Boston to Los Angeles, and crashed it into the South Tower of the World Trade Center in New York.

11.   On September 11, 2001, co-conspirators Khalid al-Midhar, Nawaf al-Hazmi, Hani Hanjour, Salem al-Hazmi, and Majed Moqed hijacked American Airlines Flight 77, bound from Virginia to Los Angeles, and crashed it into the Pentagon.

12.   On September 11, 2001, co-conspirators Ziad Jarrah, Ahmed al-Haznawi, Saeed al-Ghamdi, and Ahmed al-Nami hijacked United Airlines Flight 93, bound from Newark to San Francisco, and crashed it in Pennsylvania.

The Defendant

13.   ZACARIAS MOUSSAOUI, a/k/a "Shaqil," a/k/a "Abu Khalid al Sahrawi," was born in France of Moroccan descent on May 30, 1968. Before 2001 he was a resident of the

United Kingdom. MOUSSAOUI held a masters degree from Southbank University in the United Kingdom and traveled widely.

MOUSSAOUI's Supporting Conspirators

14.   Ramzi Bin al-Shibh, a/k/a "Ahad Sabet," a/k/a "Ramzi Mohamed Abdellah Omar," was born in Yemen on May 1, 1972. He entered Germany in or about 1995 and afterwards lived in Hamburg, where he shared an apartment with hijacker Mohammed Atta (#11) in 1998 and 1999. Bin al-Shibh also was employed with Atta as a warehouse worker at a computer company in Hamburg.

15.   Mustafa Ahmed al-Hawsawi, a/k/a "Mustafa Ahmed," was born in Jeddah, Saudi Arabia on August 5, 1968.

The Charge

16.   From in or about 1989 until the date of the filing of this Indictment, in the Eastern District of Virginia, the Southern District of New York, and elsewhere, the defendant, ZACARIAS MOUSSAOUI, a/k/a "Shaqil," a/k/a "Abu Khalid al Sahrawi," with other members and associates of al Qaeda and others known and unknown to the Grand Jury, unlawfully, wilfully and knowingly combined, conspired, confederated and agreed to kill and maim persons within the United States, and to create a substantial risk of serious bodily injury to other persons by destroying and damaging structures, conveyances, and other real and personal property within the United States, in violation of the laws of States and the United States, in circumstances involving conduct transcending national boundaries, and in which facilities of interstate and foreign commerce were used in furtherance of the offense, the offense obstructed, delayed, and affected interstate and foreign commerce, the victim was the United States Government, members of the uniformed services, and officials, officers, employees, and agents of the

governmental branches, departments, and agencies of the United States, and the structures, conveyances, and other real and personal property were, in whole or in part, owned, possessed, and leased to the United States and its departments and agencies, resulting in the deaths of thousands of persons on September 11, 2001.

Overt Acts

In furtherance of the conspiracy, and to effect its objects, the defendant, and others known and unknown to the Grand Jury, committed the following overt acts:

The Provision of Guesthouses and Training Camps

1.   At various times from at least as early as 1989, Usama Bin Laden, and others known and unknown, provided and supported training camps and guesthouses in Afghanistan, including camps known as al Farooq, Khalden, Derunta, Khost, Siddiq, and Jihad Wal, for the use of al Qaeda and its affiliated groups.

The Training

2.   At various times from at least as early as 1990, unindicted co-conspirators, known and unknown, provided military and intelligence training in various areas, including Afghanistan, Pakistan, and the Sudan, for the use of al Qaeda and its affiliated groups, including the Egyptian Islamic Jihad.

Financial and Business Dealings

3.   At various times from at least as early as 1989 until the date of the filing of this Indictment, Usama Bin Laden, and others known and unknown, engaged in financial and business transactions on behalf of al Qaeda, including, but not limited to: purchasing land for training camps; purchasing warehouses for storage of items, including explosives; purchasing communications and electronics equipment; transferring funds between corporate accounts; and

transporting currency and weapons to members of al Qaeda and its associated terrorist organizations in various countries throughout the world.

The Efforts to Obtain Nuclear Weapons and Their Components

4.   At various times from at least as early as 1992, Usama Bin Laden, and others known and unknown, made efforts to obtain the components of nuclear weapons.

The Fatwahs Against American Troops in Saudi Arabia and Yemen

5.   At various times from in or about 1992 until the date of the filing of this Indictment, Usama Bin Laden, working together with members of the fatwah committee of al Qaeda, disseminated fatwahs to other members and associates of al Qaeda that the United States forces stationed on the Saudi Arabian peninsula, including both Saudi Arabia and Yemen, should be attacked.

The Fatwah Against American Troops in Somalia

6.   At various times from in or about 1992 until in or about 1993, Usama Bin Laden, working together with members of the fatwah committee of al Qaeda, disseminated fatwahs to other members and associates of al Qaeda that the United States forces stationed in the Horn of Africa, including Somalia, should be attacked.

The Fatwah Regarding Deaths of Nonbelievers

7.   On various occasions, an unindicted co-conspirator advised other members of al Qaeda that it was Islamically proper to engage in violent actions against "infidels" (nonbelievers), even if others might be killed by such actions, because if the others were "innocent," they would go to paradise, and if they were not "innocent," then they deserved to die.

The August 1996 Declaration of War

8. On or about August 23, 1996, a Declaration of Jihad indicating that it was from the Hindu Kush mountains in Afghanistan entitled, "Message from Usamah Bin-Muhammad Bin-Laden to His Muslim Brothers in the Whole World and Especially in the Arabian Peninsula: Declaration of Jihad Against the Americans Occupying the Land of the Two Holy Mosques; Expel the Heretics from the Arabian Peninsula" was disseminated.

The February 1998 Fatwah Against American Civilians

9. In February 1998, Usama Bin Laden endorsed a fatwah under the banner of the "International Islamic Front for Jihad on the Jews and Crusaders." This fatwah, published in the publication Al-Quds al-`Arabi on February 23, 1998, stated that Muslims should kill Americans - including civilians - anywhere in the world where they can be found.

Bin Laden Endorses the Nuclear Bomb of Islam

10. On or about May 29, 1998, Usama Bin Laden issued a statement entitled "The Nuclear Bomb of Islam," under the banner of the "International Islamic Front for Fighting the Jews and the Crusaders," in which he stated that "it is the duty of the Muslims to prepare as much force as possible to terrorize the enemies of God."

Usama Bin Laden Issues Further Threats in June 1999

11. In or about June 1999, in an interview with an Arabic-language television station, Usama Bin Laden issued a further threat indicating that all American males should be killed.

Usama Bin Laden Calls for "Jihad" to Free Imprisoned Terrorists

12. In or about September 2000, in an interview with an Arabic-language television station, Usama Bin Laden called for a "jihad" to release the "brothers" in jail "everywhere."

MOUSSAOUI Trains at Al Qaeda Training Camp

13.   In or about April 1998, ZACARIAS MOUSSAOUI was present at the al Qaeda-affiliated Khalden Camp in Afghanistan.

The German Cell

14.   Beginning in and about 1998, Ramzi Bin al-Shibh, Mohammed Atta (#11), Marwan al-Shehhi (#175), and Ziad Jarrah (#93), and others, formed and maintained an al Qaeda terrorist cell in Germany.

Hijackers Travel to the United States

15.   On or about January 15, 2000, Khalid al-Midhar (#77) and Nawaf al-Hazmi (#77) traveled from Bangkok, Thailand, to Los Angeles, California.

Hijackers Receive Flight Training

16.   On or about June 3, 2000, Mohammed Atta (#11) traveled to the United States from Prague, Czech Republic.

17.   In or about early July 2000, Mohammed Atta (#11) and Marwan al-Shehhi (#175) visited the Airman Flight School in Norman, Oklahoma.

18.   Between in or about July 2000 and in or about December 2000, Mohammed Atta (#11) and Marwan al-Shehhi (#175) attended flight training classes at Huffman Aviation in Venice, Florida.

Money is Moved to the Hijackers

19.   On or about June 29, 2000, $5,000 was wired from the United Arab Emirates ("UAE") to Marwan al-Shehhi (#175) in Manhattan.

20.   On or about July 18, 2000, $10,000 was wired from UAE into a Florida SunTrust bank account in the names of Mohammed Atta (#11) and Marwan al-Shehhi (#175).

21.   On or about July 26, 2000, in Germany, Ramzi Bin al-Shibh wired money to Marwan al-Shehhi (#175) in Florida.

22.   On or about August 7, 2000, $9,500 was wired from UAE into a Florida SunTrust bank account in the names of Mohammed Atta (#11) and Marwan al-Shehhi (#175).

23.   On or about August 29, 2000, $20,000 was wired from UAE into a Florida SunTrust bank account in the names of Mohammed Atta (#11) and Marwan al-Shehhi (#175).

24.   On or about September 17, 2000, $70,000 was wired from UAE into a Florida SunTrust bank account in the names of Mohammed Atta (#11) and Marwan al-Shehhi (#175).

Jarrah (#93) Attempts to Enroll Bin al-Shibh in Flight Training Courses

25.   On or about May 17, 2000, in Germany, Ramzi Bin al-Shibh applied for a visa to travel to the United States, listing a German telephone number ("German Telephone #1".) This visa application was denied.

26.   On or about June 15, 2000, in Germany, Ramzi Bin al-Shibh applied for a visa to travel to the United States. This visa application was denied.

27.   In or about August 2000, Ziad Jarrah (#93) attempted to enroll Ramzi Bin al-Shibh in a flight school in Florida.

28.   On or about August 14, 2000, Ramzi Bin al-Shibh arranged to wire money from his account in Germany to the account of a flight training school in Florida.

29.   On or about September 15, 2000, in Yemen, Ramzi Bin al-Shibh applied for a visa to travel to the United States, listing a residence in Hamburg, Germany. This visa application was denied in September 2000.

30.   On or about October 25, 2000, in Germany, Ramzi Bin al-Shibh applied for a visa to travel to the United States. This visa application was denied.

Bin al-Shibh Sends Money to al-Shehhi (#175)

31.   On or about September 25, 2000, in Hamburg, Germany, Ramzi Bin al-Shibh sent money via wire transfer to Marwan al-Shehhi (#175) in Florida.

MOUSSAOUI Inquires About Flight Training

32.   On or about September 29, 2000, ZACARIAS MOUSSAOUI contacted Airman Flight School in Norman, Oklahoma using an e-mail account he set up on September 6 with an internet service provider in Malaysia.

33.   In or about October 2000, ZACARIAS MOUSSAOUI received letters from Infocus Tech, a Malaysian company, stating that MOUSSAOUI was appointed Infocus Tech's marketing consultant in the United States, the United Kingdom, and Europe, and that he would receive, among other things, an allowance of $2500 per month.

Atta (#11) Purchases Flight Training Equipment

34.   On or about November 5, 2000, Mohammed Atta (#11) purchased flight deck videos for the Boeing 747 Model 200, Boeing 757 Model 200, and other items from a pilot store in Ohio ("Ohio Pilot Store").

Bin al-Shibh Travels to London

35.   Between on or about December 2 and December 9, 2000, Ramzi Bin al-Shibh traveled from Hamburg, Germany, to London, England.

MOUSSAOUI Travels from London to Pakistan

36.   On or about December 9, 2000, ZACARIAS MOUSSAOUI flew from London, England, to Pakistan.

Atta (#11) Purchases More Flight Training Equipment

37.   On or about December 11, 2000, Mohammed Atta (#11) purchased flight deck videos for the Boeing 767 Model 300ER and the Airbus A320 Model 200 from the Ohio Pilot Store.

Flight Training and Exercise

38.   Between in or about January 2001 and March 2001, Hani Hanjour (#77) attended pilot training courses in Phoenix, Arizona, including at Pan Am International Flight Academy.

39.   Between on or about February 1, 2001, and on or about February 15, 2001, Mohammed Atta (#11) and Marwan al-Shehhi (#175) took a flight check ride around Decatur, Georgia.

40.   In or about February 2001, Mohammed Atta (#11) and Marwan al-Shehhi (#175) attended a health club in Decatur, Georgia.

MOUSSAOUI Comes to the United States

41.   On or about February 7, 2001, ZACARIAS MOUSSAOUI flew from Pakistan to London, England.

42.   On or about February 23, 2001, ZACARIAS MOUSSAOUI flew from London, England, to Chicago, Illinois, declaring at least $35,000 cash to U.S. Customs, and then from Chicago to Oklahoma City, Oklahoma.

43.   On or about February 26, 2001, ZACARIAS MOUSSAOUI opened a bank account in Norman, Oklahoma, depositing approximately $32,000 cash.

44.   Between on or about February 26, 2001, and on or about May 29, 2001, ZACARIAS MOUSSAOUI attended the Airman Flight School in Norman, Oklahoma, ending his classes early.

Nawaf al-Hazmi (#77) Purchases Flight Training Equipment

45.   On or about March 19, 2001, Nawaf al-Hazmi (#77) purchased flight deck videos for the Boeing 747 Model 400, the Boeing 747 Model 200 and the Boeing 777 Model 200, and another video from the Ohio Pilot Store.

MOUSSAOUI Joins a Gym

46.   In or about March 2001, ZACARIAS MOUSSAOUI joined a gym in Norman, Oklahoma.

Hijackers Travel to and Within the United States

47.   On or about April 1, 2001, Nawaf al-Hazmi (#77) was in Oklahoma.

48.   Between on or about April 23, 2001, and on or about July 19, 2001, Satam alSuqami (#11), Waleed al-Shehri (#11), Ahmed al-Ghamdi (#175), Majed Moqed (#77), Marwan al-Shehhi (#175), Mohammed Atta (#11), Ahmed al-Nami (#93), Hamza al-Ghamdi (#175), Mohald al-Shehri (#175), Wail al-Shehri (#11), Ahmed al-Haznawi (#93), Fayez Ahmed (#175), and Salem al-Hazmi (#77) traveled from various points in the world to the United States.

MOUSSAOUI Contacts a Commercial Flight School

49.   On or about May 23, 2001, ZACARIAS MOUSSAOUI contacted an office of the Pan Am International Flight Academy in Miami, Florida, via e-mail.

Hijackers Open Bank Accounts

50.   In Summer 2001, Fayez Ahmed (#175), Saeed al-Ghamdi (#93), Hamza al-Ghamdi (#175), Waleed al-Shehri (#11), Ziad Jarrah (#93), Satam al-Suqami (#11), Mohand al-Shehri (#175), Ahmed al-Nami (# 93), and Ahmed al-Haznawi (#93) each opened a Florida SunTrust bank account with a cash deposit.

Other Hijackers Attend Gym Training

51.   Between in or about May and in or about July 2001, in Florida, Ziad Jarrah (#93) joined a gym and took martial arts lessons, which included instruction in kickboxing and knife fighting.

52.   In or about June 2001, in Florida, Waleed al-Shehri (#11), Marwan al-Shehhi (#175) and Satam al-Suqami (#11) joined a gym.

MOUSSAOUI Purchases Flight Training Equipment

53.   On or about June 20, 2001, ZACARIAS MOUSSAOUI purchased flight deck videos for the Boeing 747 Model 400 and the Boeing 747 Model 200 from the Ohio Pilot Store.

Al-Hawsawi and Fayez Ahmed (#175) Open UAE Bank Accounts

54.   On or about June 23, 2001, Mustafa Ahmed al-Hawsawi used a cash deposit to open a checking account at a Standard Chartered Bank branch in Sharjah, UAE, and an ATM account in connection with the checking account.

55.   On or about June 25, 2001, at the same Standard Chartered Bank branch in Sharjah, UAE, Fayez Ahmed (#175) used a cash deposit to open a checking account and also opened a savings account. Fayez Ahmed also opened an ATM and a VISA card account in connection with the checking account.

56.   On or about June 25, 2001, Mustafa Ahmed al-Hawsawi opened a savings account at the Standard Chartered Bank and a VISA card account on the same account.

Atta (#11) Purchases a Knife

57.   On or about July 8, 2001, Mohammed Atta (#11) purchased a knife in Zurich, Switzerland.

MOUSSAOUI Pays for Flight Lessons

58.   On or about July 10 and July 11, 2001, ZACARIAS MOUSSAOUI made credit

card payments to the Pan Am International Flight Academy for a simulator course in

commercial flight training.

Fayez Ahmed (#175) Gives Al-Hawsawi Control Over UAE Account

59.   On or about July 18, 2001, Fayez Ahmed (#175) gave power of attorney to

Mustafa Ahmed al-Hawsawi for Fayez Ahmed's Standard Chartered Bank accounts in UAE.

60.   On or about July 18, 2001, using his power of attorney, Al-Hawsawi picked up

Fayez Ahmed's VISA and ATM cards in UAE.

61.   Between on or about July 18 and on or about August 1, 2001, Mustafa Ahmed al-

Hawsawi caused Fayez Ahmed's VISA card to be shipped from UAE to Fayez Ahmed in

Florida. (The VISA card was then used for the first time on August 1, 2001, in Florida.)

Jarrah (#93) Travels to Germany

62.   On or about July 25, 2001, Ziad Jarrah (#93) traveled from the United States to

Germany.

Bin al-Shibh Moves Money to MOUSSAOUI from UAE

63.   Between on or about July 29 and August 4, 2001, in Norman, Oklahoma,

ZACARIAS MOUSSAOUI made several telephone calls from public telephones to a number in

Duesseldorf, Germany ("German Telephone # 2").

64.   On or about July 30 and 31, 2001, in Hamburg, Germany, Ramzi Bin al-Shibh,

using the name "Ahad Sabet," received two wire transfers, totaling approximately $15,000, from

"Hashim Abdulrahman" in UAE.

65.   On or about August 1 and 3, 2001, Ramzi Bin al-Shibh, using the name "Ahad

Sabet," wired approximately $14,000 to ZACARIAS MOUSSAOUI in Oklahoma from train

stations in Duesseldorf and Hamburg, Germany.

MOUSSAOUI Purchases Knives

66.   On or about August 3, 2001, ZACARIAS MOUSSAOUI purchased two knives in

Oklahoma City, Oklahoma.

Jarrah (#93) Returns to the United States from Germany

67.   On or about August 4, 2001, Ziad Jarrah (#93) traveled from Germany to the

United States.

MOUSSAOUI Travels from Oklahoma to Minnesota

68.   On or about August 10 and August 11, 2001, ZACARIAS MOUSSAOUI was

driven from Oklahoma to Minnesota.

MOUSSAOUI Takes Commercial Flying Lessons in Minnesota

69.   On or about August 13, 2001, in Minneapolis, Minnesota, ZACARIAS

MOUSSAOUI paid approximately $6,800 in cash to the Pan Am International Flight Academy.

70.   Between on or about August 13 and on or about August 15, 2001, ZACARIAS

MOUSSAOUI attended the Pan Am International Flight Academy in Minneapolis, Minnesota,

for simulator training on the Boeing 747 Model 400.

MOUSSAOUI Possesses Knives and Other Items

71.   On or about August 16, 2001, ZACARIAS MOUSSAOUI possessed, among

other things:

-       two knives;

-       a pair of binoculars;

- flight manuals for the Boeing 747 Model 400;

- a flight simulator computer program;

- fighting gloves and shin guards;

- a piece of paper referring to a handheld Global Positioning System receiver and a camcorder;

- software that could be used to review pilot procedures for the Boeing 747 Model 400;

- a notebook listing German Telephone #1, German Telephone #2, and the name "Ahad Sabet;"

-letters indicating that MOUSSAOUI is a marketing consultant in the United States for Infocus Tech; and

- a hand-held aviation radio.

MOUSSAOUI Lies to Federal Agents

72. On or about August 17, 2001, ZACARIAS MOUSSAOUI, while being interviewed by federal agents in Minneapolis, attempted to explain his presence in the United States by falsely stating that he was simply interested in learning to fly.

Jarrah (#93) Undertakes "Check Ride" At Flight School

73. On or about August 17, 2001, Ziad Jarrah (#93) undertook a "check ride" at a flight school in Fort Lauderdale, Florida.

A Co-Conspirator Calls Fayez Ahmed From Germany

74. On or about August 18, 2001, a co-conspirator made a telephone call from Germany to Fayez Ahmed (#175) in Florida.

Final Preparations for the Coordinated Air Attack

75.   On or about August 22, 2001, Fayez Ahmed (#175) used his VISA card in Florida to obtain approximately $4,900 cash, which had been previously deposited into his Standard Chartered Bank account in UAE.

76.   On or about August 22, 2001, in Miami, Florida, Ziad Jarrah (#93) purchased a Global Positioning System ("GPS"), other GPS related equipment, and schematics for 757 cockpit instrument diagrams. (GPS allows an individual to navigate to a position using coordinates pre-programmed into the GPS unit.)

77.   On or about August 25, 2001, Khalid al-Midhar and Majed Moqed purchased with cash tickets for American Airlines Flight 77, from Virginia to Los Angeles, California, scheduled for September 11, 2001.

78.   On or about August 26, 2001, Waleed al-Shehri and Wail al-Shehri made reservations on American Airlines Flight 11, from Boston, Massachusetts, to Los Angeles, California, scheduled for September 11, 2001, listing a telephone number in Florida ("Florida Telephone #1") as a contact number.

79.   On or about August 27, 2001, reservations for electronic, one-way tickets were made for Fayez Ahmed and Mohand al-Shehri, for United Airlines Flight 175, from Boston, Massachusetts, to Los Angeles, California, scheduled for September 11, 2001, listing Florida Telephone Number #1 as a contact number.

80.   On or about August 27, 2001, Nawaf al-Hazmi and Salem al-Hazmi booked flights on American Airlines Flight 77.

81.   On or about August 28, 2001, Satam al-Suqami purchased a ticket with cash for American Airlines Flight 11.

82.   On or about August 28, 2001, Mohammed Atta and Abdulaziz Alomari reserved two seats on American Airlines Flight 11, listing Florida Telephone #1 as a contact number.

83.   On or about August 29, 2001, Ahmed al-Ghamdi and Hamza al-Ghamdi reserved electronic, one-way tickets for United Airlines Flight 175.

84.   On or about August 29, 2001, Ahmed al-Haznawi purchased a ticket on United Airlines Flight 93 from Newark, New Jersey, to San Francisco, California, scheduled for September 11, 2001.

85.   On or about September 3, 2001, in Hamburg, Germany, Ramzi Bin al-Shibh, using the name "Ahad Sabet," received approximately $1500 by wire transfer from "Hashim Ahmed" in UAE.

86.   On or about September 5, 2001, Ramzi Bin al-Shibh traveled from Dusseldorf, Germany, to Madrid, Spain, and did not return to Germany.

87.   On or about September 6, 2001, Satam al-Suqami (#11) and Abdulaziz Alomari (#11) flew from Florida to Boston.

The Hijackers Return Excess Money to Al-Hawsawi in UAE

88.   On or about September 4, 2001, Mohammed Atta (#11) sent a FedEx package from Florida to UAE.

89.   On or about September 5, 2001, Fayez Ahmed (#175) wired approximately $8,000 from his Florida SunTrust account to the Standard Chartered Bank account over which Al-Hawsawi had power of attorney.

90.   On or about September 8, 2001, an Arab male retrieved the package from Mohammed Atta (#11) at FedEx in Dubai, UAE.

91.   On September 8, 2001, Mohammed Atta (#11) wired $2,860 to "Mustafa Ahmed" in UAE.

92.   On September 8, 2001, Mohammed Atta (#11) wired $5,000 to "Mustafa Ahmed" in UAE.

93.   On September 9, 2001, Waleed M. al-Shehri (#11) wired $5,000 to "Ahamad Mustafa" in UAE.

94.   On September 10, 2001, Marwan al-Shehhi (#175) wired $5,400 to "Mustafa Ahmad" in UAE.

95.   On September 11, 2001, in UAE, approximately $16,348 was deposited into Al-Hawsawi's Standard Chartered Bank account.

96.   On September 11, 2001, in UAE, at about 9:22 a.m. local time (the early morning hours of Eastern Daylight Time), Mustafa Ahmed al-Hawsawi moved approximately $6,534 from the $8,000 in Fayez Ahmed's (#175) Standard Chartered Bank account into his own account, using a check dated September 10, 2001, and signed by Fayez Ahmed; Al-Hawsawi then withdrew approximately $1,361, nearly all the remaining balance in Ahmed's account, by ATM cash withdrawal.

97.   On September 11, 2001, in UAE, approximately $40,871 was prepaid to a VISA card connected to Al-Hawsawi's Standard Chartered Bank account.

The September 11, 2001 Terrorist Attacks

98.   On September 11, 2001, the hijackers possessed a handwritten set of final instructions for a martyrdom operation on an airplane using knives.

99.   On September 11, 2001, Mohammed Atta (#11) and Abdulaziz Alomari (#11) flew from Portland, Maine, to Boston, Massachusetts.

100.   On September 11, 2001, Mohammed Atta (#11) possessed operating manuals for the Boeing 757 and 767, pepper spray, knives, and German travel visas.

101.   On September 11, 2001, Ziad Jarrah (#93) possessed flight manuals for Boeing 757 and 767 aircraft.

102.   On September 11, 2001, Mohammed Atta, Abdul Aziz Alomari, Satam al-Suqami, Waleed al-Shehri, and Wail al-Shehri hijacked American Airlines Flight 11, a Boeing 767, which had departed Boston at approximately 7:55 a.m. They flew Flight 11 into the North Tower of the World Trade Center in Manhattan at approximately 8:45 a.m., causing the collapse of the tower and the deaths of thousands of persons.

103.   On September 11, 2001, Hamza al-Ghamdi, Fayez Ahmed, Mohand al-Shehri, Ahmed al-Ghamdi, and Marwan al-Shehhi hijacked United Airlines Flight 175, a Boeing 767, which had departed from Boston at approximately 8:15 a.m. They flew Flight 175 into the South Tower of the World Trade Center in Manhattan at approximately 9:05 a.m., causing the collapse of the tower and the deaths of thousands of persons.

104.   On September 11, 2001, Khalid al-Midhar, Majed Moqed, Nawaf al-Hazmi, Salem al-Hazmi, and Hani Hanjour hijacked American Airlines Flight 77, a Boeing 757, which had departed from Virginia bound for Los Angeles, at approximately 8:10 a.m. They flew Flight 77 into the Pentagon in Virginia at approximately 9:40 a.m., causing the deaths of 189 persons.

105.   On September 11, 2001, Saeed al-Ghamdi, Ahmed al-Nami, Ahmed al-Haznawi, and Ziad Jarrah hijacked United Airlines Flight 93, a Boeing 757, which had departed from Newark, New Jersey bound for San Francisco at approximately 8:00 a.m. After resistance by the passengers, Flight 93 crashed in Somerset County, Pennsylvania at approximately 10:03 a.m., killing all on board.

Al-Hawsawi Flees the U.A.E. for Pakistan

106.   On or about September 11, 2001, Mustafa Ahmed al-Hawsawi left the U.A.E. for Pakistan.

107.   On or about September 13, 2001, the supplemental VISA card connected to Al-Hawsawi's account was used to make six ATM withdrawals in Karachi, Pakistan.

A Co-Conspirator Calls On Muslims To Fight The United States

108.   On or about October 7, 2001, in Afghanistan, Ayman al-Zawahiri called on Muslims to join the battle against the United States.

Bin Laden Praises The September 11 Attack And Threatens More Attacks

109.   On or about October 7, 2001, in Afghanistan, Usama Bin Laden praised the September 11 attack, and vowed that the United States would not "enjoy security" before "infidel armies leave" the Saudi Gulf.

A Co-Conspirator Solicits Violence Against United States Nationals

110.   On or about October 10, 2001, Sulieman Abu Ghaith announced, on behalf of al Qaeda, that all Muslims had a duty to attack United States targets around the world.

(In violation of Title 18, United States Code, Sections 2332b(a)(2) and 2332b(c).)

COUNT TWO
(Conspiracy to Commit Aircraft Piracy)

1. The allegations contained in Count One are repeated.

2. From in or about 1989 until the date of the filing of this Indictment, in the Eastern District of Virginia, the Southern District of New York, and elsewhere, the defendant, ZACARIAS MOUSSAOUI, a/k/a "Shaqil," a/k/a "Abu Khalid al Sahrawi," and other members and associates of al Qaeda and others known and unknown to the Grand Jury, unlawfully, wilfully and knowingly combined, conspired, confederated and agreed to commit aircraft piracy, by seizing and exercising control of aircraft in the special aircraft jurisdiction of the United States by force, violence, threat of force and violence, and intimidation, and with wrongful intent, with the result that thousands of people died on September 11, 2001.

Overt Acts

3. In furtherance of the conspiracy, and to effect its illegal objects, the defendant, and others known and unknown to the Grand Jury, committed the overt acts set forth in Count One of this Indictment, which are fully incorporated by reference.

(In violation of Title 49, United States Code, Sections 46502(a)(1)(A) and (a)(2)(B).)

COUNT THREE
(Conspiracy to Destroy Aircraft)

1.   The allegations contained in Count One are repeated.

2.   From in or about 1989 until the date of the filing of this Indictment, in the Eastern District of Virginia, the Southern District of New York, and elsewhere, the defendant, ZACARIAS MOUSSAOUI, a/k/a "Shaqil," a/k/a "Abu Khalid al Sahrawi," and other members and associates of al Qaeda and others known and unknown to the Grand Jury, unlawfully, wilfully and knowingly combined, conspired, confederated and agreed to willfully destroy and wreck aircraft in the special aircraft jurisdiction of the United States, and to willfully perform acts of violence against and incapacitate individuals on such aircraft, so as likely to endanger the safety of such aircraft, resulting in the deaths of thousands of persons on September 11, 2001.

Overt Acts

3.   In furtherance of the conspiracy, and to effect its illegal objects, the defendant, and others known and unknown to the Grand Jury, committed the overt acts set forth in Count One of this Indictment, which are fully incorporated by reference.

(In violation of Title 18, United States Code, Sections 32(a)(7) and 34.)

COUNT FOUR
(Conspiracy to Use Weapons of Mass Destruction)

1. The allegations contained in Count One are repeated.

2. From in or about 1989 until the date of the filing of this Indictment, in the Eastern District of Virginia, the Southern District of New York, and elsewhere, the defendant, ZACARIAS MOUSSAOUI, a/k/a "Shaqil," a/k/a "Abu Khalid al Sahrawi," and other members and associates of al Qaeda and others known and unknown to the Grand Jury, unlawfully, wilfully and knowingly combined, conspired, confederated and agreed to use weapons of mass destruction, namely, airplanes intended for use as missiles, bombs, and similar devices, and other weapons of mass destruction, without lawful authority against persons within the United States, with the results of such use affecting interstate and foreign commerce, and against property that was owned, leased and used by the United States and by departments and agencies of the United States, with the result that thousands of people died on September 11, 2001.

Overt Acts

3. In furtherance of the conspiracy, and to effect its illegal objects, the defendant, and others known and unknown to the Grand Jury, committed the overt acts set forth in Count One of this Indictment, which are fully incorporated by reference.

(In violation of Title 18, United States Code, Section 2332a(a).)

COUNT FIVE
(Conspiracy to Murder United States Employees)

1.   The allegations contained in Count One are repeated.

2.   From in or about 1989 until the date of the filing of this Indictment, in the Eastern District of Virginia, the Southern District of New York, and elsewhere, the defendant, ZACARIAS MOUSSAOUI, a/k/a "Shaqil," a/k/a "Abu Khalid al Sahrawi," and other members and associates of al Qaeda and others known and unknown to the Grand Jury, unlawfully, wilfully and knowingly combined, conspired, confederated and agreed to kill officers and employees of the United States and agencies and branches thereof, while such officers and employees were engaged in, and on account of, the performance of their official duties, and persons assisting such employees in the performance of their duties, in violation of Section 1114 of Title 18, United States Code, including members of the Department of Defense stationed at the Pentagon.

Overt Acts

3.   In furtherance of the conspiracy, and to effect its illegal objects, the defendant, and others known and unknown to the Grand Jury, committed the overt acts set forth in Count One of this Indictment, which are fully incorporated by reference.

(In violation of Title 18, United States Code, Sections 1114 and 1117.)

COUNT SIX
(Conspiracy to Destroy Property of the United States)

1. The allegations contained in Count One are repeated.

2. From in or about 1989 until the date of the filing of this Indictment, in the Eastern District of Virginia, the Southern District of New York, and elsewhere, the defendant, ZACARIAS MOUSSAOUI, a/k/a "Shaqil," a/k/a "Abu Khalid al Sahrawi," and other members and associates of al Qaeda and others known and unknown to the Grand Jury, unlawfully, wilfully and knowingly combined, conspired, confederated and agreed to maliciously damage and destroy, by means of fire and explosives, buildings, vehicles, and other real and personal property used in interstate and foreign commerce and in activities affecting interstate and foreign commerce, and buildings, vehicles, and other personal and real property in whole and in part owned and possessed by, and leased to, the United States and its departments and agencies, and as a result of such conduct directly and proximately caused the deaths of thousands of persons on September 11, 2001, including hundreds of public safety officers performing duties as a direct and proximate result of the said damage and destruction.

Overt Acts

3. In furtherance of the conspiracy, and to effect its illegal objects, the defendant, and others known and unknown to the Grand Jury, committed the overt acts set forth in Count One of

this Indictment, which are fully incorporated by reference.

(In violation of Title 18, United States Code, Sections 844(f), (i), and (n).)

                                 _____

                                   FOREPERSON

_____
MICHAEL CHERTOFF
ASSISTANT ATTORNEY GENERAL

_____
PAUL J. McNULTY
UNITED STATES ATTORNEY
ROBERT A. SPENCER
DAVID J. NOVAK
ASSISTANT UNITED STATES ATTORNEYS
EASTERN DISTRICT OF VIRGINIA

_____
JAMES B. COMEY
UNITED STATES ATTORNEY
KENNETH M. KARAS
ASSISTANT UNITED STATES ATTORNEY
SOUTHERN DISTRICT OF NEW YORK

NOTES

Introduction Breakdown

1. McFarlane, in an E-mail, agreed to be quoted after making his displeasure known about the CIA's mishandling of Abdul Haq, in an op-ed article in the *Wall Street Journal* published November 2, 2001. A U.S. government official said CIA officials were very unhappy with the comments and made their feelings known to McFarlane.
2. Tenet testified as part of the annual world threat briefing before the Senate Select Committee on Intelligence on February 6, 2002. Only one senator, Senator Richard Shelby, Alabama Republican and vice chairman, challenged Tenet on the intelligence failure.

Chapter 1 The Osama File

1. After military operations were launched against al Qaeda in Afghanistan, a senior U.S. intelligence official said the CIA had no comprehensive intelligence on the various al Qaeda groups and offshoots.

Chapter 4 The PCIA—Politically Correct Intelligence Agency

1. Baer's book, *See No Evil: The True Story of a Ground Soldier in the CIA's War on Terrorism* (New York: Crown Publishers), came out in January 2002 and was a national bestseller.
2. The letter was an unprecedented step by active case officers. CIA public affairs took the unusual step of putting news reporters in touch with three case officers in an effort to counter the negative letter.
3. "Countering the Changing Threat of International Terrorism," Report of the National Commission on Terrorism, Pursuant to Public Law 277, 105th Congress, June 2000. The commission report was largely ignored by both the government and the public.
4. Wiley was appointed associate director of Central Intelligence for homeland security in May 2002.
5. "Politics of a Covert Action: The US, the *Mujahideen*, and the Stinger Missile," John F. Kennedy School of Government Case Program, by Kirsten Lundberg for Professors Philip Zelikow and Ernest May, Harvard Intelligence and Policy Project, C15-99-1546.0.

Chapter 5 The FBI: The Decline of Domestic Intelligence

1. The extraordinary story was revealed in a little-noticed book, *Operation Solo: The FBI's Man in the Kremlin*, by John Barron (Washington, D.C.: Regnery Publishing, 1996).
2. Daniel Franklin is a Washington writer whose work has appeared in *Time* and *The American Prospect*. From "Freeh's Reign: At Louis Freeh's FBI, with carte blanche from congressional Republicans, real cops didn't do intelligence and counterterrorism," by Daniel Franklin, *The American Prospect*, January 1 to January 14, 2002.

Chapter 6 Congress and Destructive Oversight

1. Angleton is most noted for leading the counterespionage hunt for a Soviet penetration agent inside the CIA. He was disliked by some CIA officers because of his methods, which required challenging the loyalties of case officers. After his departure, the CIA as an institution became vehemently opposed to vigorous counterintelligence, and that would set the stage for the agency's worst counterintelligence failure, the Soviet and Russian penetration of the CIA by CIA turncoat Aldrich Hazen Ames. One CIA operations officer captured the anticounterintelligence spirit of the agency when he remarked in 1994 to a group of like-minded officers, "The only thing worse than having a mole in the DO, is having a mole uncovered in the DO."
2. Goss declined to be interviewed.
3. Codevilla was so despised by the CIA that the agency engineered numerous plots to discredit him, alleging, falsely, that he had violated security by improperly disclosing classified information.
4. Snider wrote a mildly critical report when he left as CIA inspector general saying the agency lacked focus and risked becoming irrelevant.
5. Rumsfeld declined to be interviewed.
6. The review committee was not scheduled to release its final report on the intelligence failures of September 11 until December 2002.

Chapter 7 Technical Spying

1. Hayden and other senior NSA officials declined to be interviewed.

Chapter 8 Nonsecurity

1. For a full account of the heroic story of Rick Rescorla, see James B. Stewart, "The Real Heroes are Dead," *New Yorker*, 11 February 2002.
2. According to the 2001 annual "Open Doors" survey of higher-education statistics prepared by the Institute of International Education (IIE).

ACKNOWLEDGMENTS

WRITING ON INTELLIGENCE IS A difficult task. My job was complicated by the wartime conditions that began October 7, 2001, when U.S. military forces launched operations inside Afghanistan, beginning what is being called a global war on terrorism. My purpose in writing this book was not simply to point the finger of blame but to start a public debate on the failings and weaknesses of American intelligence. The ultimate objective is to see that much needed reforms in the U.S. intelligence community are carried out so that attacks like those of September 11 will never happen again.

A well-known newspaper reporter once remarked that reporters who cover intelligence issues are lucky to get 50 percent of their facts right because of the secretive, and sometimes duplicitous, nature of the business. I hope I've doubled that accuracy rate in this book.

Many friends and intelligence professionals contributed to this work. Most cannot be named because they prefer the anonymity that is so much a part of the netherworld of intelligence.

Special thanks go to my employer, the *Washington Times,* a great newspaper that gave me a start in the newspaper business and the privilege of covering defense and national security issues in Washington for nearly two decades. The *Times* celebrates its twentieth anniversary this year after its founding by the Reverend and Mrs. Sun Myung Moon. The newspaper has made a tremendous contribution to the often difficult task of keeping governments around the world honest. In so doing, the *Times* has helped advance the cause of liberty in a significant way.

Several *Times* editors deserve mention for their support, namely Editor-in-Chief Wesley Pruden, Managing Editor Francis B. Coombs Jr., and National Editor Kenneth Hanner. My *Times* colleagues Jerry Seper, who provided crucial assistance, Rowan Scarborough, and Robert Morton helped as well. Thanks also go to Marc Lerner, who helped from the Philippines. My brother, Steve Gertz, gave important advice. Finally, I want to thank my wife, Debra, for her patience and support.

INDEX

ACS. *See* Automated Case Support System

Aden, Yemen, 40, 43

Afghanistan: Taliban opposition in, 1–4; unity in, 2, 4

Africa, bombings in, 15–16, 39, 130

Agent 58. *See* Childs, Morris

Agriculture Department, 125

Airline Pilots Association International, 153

airliners. *See* commercial airliners

air marshals, 153

Al Adid, 57

Albright, Madeleine, 115

al-Ani, Ahmed Khalil Ibrahim Samir, 162, 163

Al-Haramayn, 15

Al-Hayat, 96

Alhazmi, Salem, 131, 132

al Qaeda: bin Laden and, 1, 10, 217–18; CIA covert operations and, 78; clandestine cells of, 17; documentation of activities of, 217–56; FBI and, 87–88; first World Trade Center bombing and, 92; intelligence on, 11, 27; Iran and, 42–46, 49–50, 165; in Malaysia, 44; NSA and, 128–30; in Philippines, 21–25; September 11 and, 1, 229–32; Taliban opposition and, 2; terrorist attacks of, 90–91; tracking, 146–50; USS *Cole* and, 92

Al Wafrah, Kuwait, 11

al-Zawahiri, Ayman, 9, 47

American Airlines Flight 77, 45

American Federation of State, County, and Municipal Employees, 167

The American Prospect, 100

Ames, Aldrich, 59, 98

Amsterdam, Holland, 151

Analyst's Notebook, 39

Andrews Air Force Base, 155

Angleton, James Jesus, 105–6

Animal and Plant Health
Inspection Service, 124
AOL, 72
Aqsa Mosque, 19
Arabian peninsula, 40
"ARCHLANE," 65
Armitage, Richard, 2
Asara, Afghanistan, 3
Ashcroft, John, 87
Asia, 22
Ataturk, Kemal, 149
Atef, Mohammed, 222, 223
Atta, Mohammed, 141, 144, 162, 163
Australian Thinking Skills
Institute, 36
Automated Case Support System
(ACS), 111–12

Baathists, 161
Bacon, Kenneth, 50
Baer, Robert: CIA failures and, 62;
investigation of, 54–55; postem-
ployment intelligence of, 56–58
Baghdad, Iraq, 12
Bahrain, 9
Banihammad, Fayez Rashid
Ahmed Hassan Al Qadi, 144
Bar-Lev, Uri, air terrorism and,
151–53
Beijing, China, 75
Beirut, Lebanon, 52, 56
Bellows, Randy, 30
Berger, Samuel, 29
Bergeron, Russ, 141
Berlin Wall, 89
"Big Five," 14, 47–48
bin Laden, Osama: aliases of, 17; al
Qaeda and, 1, 10, 217–18; CIA

and, 4, 10–19; documentation of
activities of, 217–56; first World
Trade Center bombing and, 27;
grand jury indictment of, 19;
Iran and, 12, 183; Iraq and, 12;
military operations against, 18;
narcotics trafficking and, 185;
NSA and, 11; Philippines and,
22; Qatari government and, 57;
September 11 and, 1, 58, 218,
225–26; Sudan and, 28–29;
Taliban and, 1, 219–20; terrorist
attacks of, 7–11, 90–91, 173–76;
videotape messages of, 39, 44,
47, 80
biological weapons, 33, 93
Blacke, Randy, 48
Blair, Tony, 215
Blitzer, Bob, 25–27
Boland, Edward, 71
Bolling Air Force Base, 39, 155, 157
Bonner, Robert, 146
Border Patrol, 123
Boren, David L., 58–59
Bosnia, 11, 42, 184
Bowie, Md., 131
Bremer, L. Paul, 67, 69
Bremer Commission, 67, 68–69
Britain, 162
"Brother Sharif," 17
Bryant, Robert B. "Bear," 98
Bucknam, Robert B., 97
bureaucracy: in CIA, 34–35, 54–72,
158; in DIA, 39–52; in FBI, 31, 72;
in intelligence agencies, 5, 53–81
Bureau of Intelligence and Research
(INR), 14, 47–48, 145, 169
Burns, Nicholas, 96

Bush, George H. W., 135
Bush, George W., 30, 76, 117; homeland security and, 123; intelligence failure and, 123–24;
September 11 and, 155; Taliban
and, 1; war on terrorism and,
9, 87

California, 25, 124
Camp David, 87
Canada, 144
Cannistraro, Vincent, 8
Carter, Jimmy, 62, 107
Caruso, J. T., 35
Casey, William J., 77
Castro, Larry, 135–36
CBS News, 120
Center for Security Policy, 118
Central Command, 3
Central Intelligence Agency (CIA):
agent recruitment and, 68–71;
"Big Five" and, 14; bin Laden
and, 4, 10–19; bombing of headquarters of, 5, 208–11; bombing
of pharmaceutical factory and,
19; bureaucracy in, 34–35, 54–72,
158; Clinton and, 73, 88;
Congress and, 90–95; congressional oversight of intelligence
and, 105–9, 113–16; covert operations and, 53–54, 76–81; CTC
of, 12, 31, 34–35, 59, 61; field
agents of, 63–66; foreign language training and, 13, 62;
Homeland Security department
and, 125; intelligence analysis
and, 73–76, 169; intelligence
gathering and, 11, 34; intelli-

gence sharing and, 25, 35; intel-
ligence warnings and, 47–48;
Justice Department regulations
and, 29; leadership and, 66–68;
Moussaoui investigation and,
31; politicization of, 88; reform
of, 166–68; scandals in, 54–81;
September 11 and, 5, 36, 58,
59–60; Taliban opposition and,
2–4; terrorism and, 10, 34; ter-
rorist hot spots and, 184; USS
Cole bombing and, 60; weak-
nesses of, 5, 59–81. *See also*
Defense Intelligence Agency;
Federal Bureau of Investigation
Central Security Control, 8
Cetron, Marvin J., 37
"CG-5824S*," 89
Chechnya, 33
Cheltenham, England, 193
chemical weapons, 33, 93, 140
Cheney, Dick, 87, 116–18
Cherkasky, Michael, 27
Childs, Morris, 88–90
China: CIA analysis and, 73–76;
NSA and, 135; United States
and, 76
Church, Frank, 90, 107, 108
Church committee, 94, 108, 110
Clarke, Richard, 19, 122
Clarridge, Duane "Dewey," 34
Clinton, Bill, 64, 92, 115; African
bombings and, 17–18; Baer
investigation and, 53–54; bin
Laden and, 13–14; CIA and, 73,
88; Deutch and, 72; intelligence
agencies and, 90; response to
terrorism of, 8, 17–19

Coast Guard, 123, 124

Codevilla, Angelo, 5, 112, 113

Cohen, David, 64, 65

Cohen, William, 18, 57

Colby, William, congressional oversight of intelligence and, 105–9

Colombia, 184

Commerce Department, 125

commercial airliners: hijacking of, 55; suicide missions and, 23; terrorist campaigns against, 22; training to fly, 23, 24, 30–31, 46, 83–86

Committee for the Defense of Legitimate Rights, 9

Congress: intelligence agencies and, 90–95; oversight of intelligence of, 105–25

Counterterrorism and Middle East Section, 25

Counter Terrorist Center (CTC), 12, 15, 31, 34–35, 59, 61

covert operations: capabilities in, 14; CIA and, 53–54, 76–81

crop-dusting airplanes, 33

Crowe, William, 15

CTC. See Counter Terrorist Center

Customs Service, 123, 124

Czech Republic, 56, 162

Damascus, Syria, 152

Dar es Salaam, Tanzania, 15

Daschle, Tom, 121, 122

Davis, Rob, 54–55

DEA. See Drug Enforcement Administration

Dean, Diane, 60

"Death Star," 40

Defense Department: Homeland Security department and, 125; Taliban opposition and, 2

Defense Intelligence Agency (DIA): abolition of, 169; "Big Five" and, 14; bureaucracy in, 39–52; intelligence failures of, 41–45; intelligence warnings and, 47–48; Persian Gulf division of, 39; September 11 and, 5

DeLay, Tom, 122

Delfin, Robert, 25

Dellums, Ron, 108

Democrats, 107–8

Department of Homeland Security, 123–24

Deutch, John, 64; CIA and, 66, 68–71; FBI investigation of, 72

Dhahran, Saudi Arabia, 8–9, 11

DIA. See Defense Intelligence Agency

Doha, Qatar, 56

Dole, Robert, 77

Dolphin, 40

domestic intelligence, FBI and, 83–103

domestic intelligence service (DST), 33

Downes, Larry, 110–11

Drinan, Robert, 110

Drug Enforcement Administration (DEA), 77

DST. See domestic intelligence service

Dubai, United Arab Emirates, 52

Dulles International Airport, 131

Durenberger, David, 112

Eagan, Minnesota, 30
East Africa. *See* Africa
Egypt, 144, 188–90, 191
Egyptian Islamic Jihad, 9, 12, 44, 47, 164
Egyptian Islamic Group, 44
El Al, 151
electronic surveillance, FISA and, 30
el-Hage, Wadih, 17, 131
Embry-Riddle Aeronautical University, 83
Energy Department, 124
England, 193
Epstein, Edward Jay, 162–63
Executive Decision, 149

FAA. *See* Federal Aviation Administration
Fallis, Kie, 46–47; DIA and, 39–40, 42–45; intelligence warnings and, 48; resignation of, 49–51
Farsical, Aida, 21
Fazul, Haroun, 17
FBI. *See* Federal Bureau of Investigation
Federal Aviation Administration (FAA), 154
Federal Bureau of Investigation (FBI): African bombings and, 15–16, 39; "Big Five" and, 14; bin Laden and, 15, 18; bureaucracy in, 31, 72; Clinton administration and, 95–103; committee investigations of, 90–91; congressional oversight of intelligence and, 90–95; counterterrorism and, 25, 100–102;

domestic intelligence and, 83–103, 168; first World Trade Center bombing and, 25–27; funding for, 14, 100; Homeland Security department and, 125; information sharing and, 25, 35; intelligence failures of, 83–103; intelligence gathering and, 11; intelligence warnings and, 17, 47–48; Justice Department and, 96; Justice Department regulations and, 29; Khobar Towers bombing and, 39; Moussaoui investigation and, 31, 32–33, 196–206; National Security Division of, 98; Office of Intelligence in, 102; Oklahoma City bombing and, 85; Phoenix memo and, 83–86; politicization of, 88; Qatari government and, 55–56; September 11 and, 5, 29, 36; weaknesses of, 25–26, 28. *See also* Central Intelligence Agency; Defense Intelligence Agency
Federal Computer Incident Response Center, 125
Federal Emergency Management Agency, 123, 124
Federal Protective Service, 124
FISA. *See* Foreign Intelligence Surveillance
Fitzgerald, Sean, 66
flight schools. *See* commercial airliners
Flohr, Linda, 157–58
Florida, 3, 141
Ford, Gerald, 107

foreign intelligence services, reliance on, 10, 11

Foreign Intelligence Surveillance Act (FISA), 30, 32

foreign language training, 28, 39, 62

Fourth Amendment, 137

Fox, James, 89

France, 33

Franklin, Daniel, 100–101

Franks, Tommy, 3

Freeh, Louis: Baer investigation and, 54; FBI and, 97–98, 100; Phoenix memo and, 84–85; Wen Ho Lee investigation and, 30

Gaffney, Frank, 118–19

Garcia, Rafael, 22, 24

General Services Administration, 124

Gephardt, Richard A., 121

Gerecht, Reuel Marc, 34, 73

Germany, 80

Gertz, Bill, 74–75

Ghostbusters, 35

Gordon, John, 72

Goss, Porter, 113

Gow, W. Douglas, 97

Graham, Bob, 118, 123

Greco, Gary, 48

Greenbelt, 131

Gregg, Donald, 109

Gross, Stan Slav, 163–64

Guatemala, 66

al-Hada, Ahmad, 131

Hadhramaut, 40

al-Hadi, Ashra, 9

Haines, Gerald K., 108

al-Hallak, Moataz, 131

Hamre, John, 136

Hanjour, Hani, 131

Hanssen, Robert Philip, 98, 112

Haq, Abdul, Taliban opposition and, 1–4

Haram Mosque, 19

Harlow, Bill, 72

Hatch, Orrin G., 129

al-Hawali, Safar, 9

Hayden, Michael, 130, 136–37

al-Hazmi, Nawaf, 45, 46

Health and Human Services Department, 124

Heathrow Airport, 31

Hersh, Seymour, 105, 106, 107

Hezbollah, 90, 161

hijacking, 150–56

Hill, Dan, 140

Hill, Eleanor, 122

Hitler, Adolf, 80

House Armed Services Committee, 51

House Intelligence Committee, 35

House Permanent Select Committee on Intelligence, 85

Huffman Aviation International, 141

Hughes, Patrick M., 165–66

human intelligence, 11

Hussein, Saddam, 12, 161; CIA operations against, 53–55, 77–78

Ijaz, Manzour, 28–29

Immigration and Naturalization Service (INS), 124; Homeland Security department and, 123;

Moussaoui investigation and, 31; weakness of, 141–45

INC. *See* Iraqi National Congress

Inderfurth, Karl F. "Rick," 114–15

India, 59, 115

Indian Ocean, 18

INR. *See* Bureau of Intelligence and Research

INS. *See* Immigration and Naturalization Service

"Inside the Ring," 74

Intelink, 52

intelligence: analysis of, 73–76, 169; changes in, 157–70; communications interception and, 10; compartmentalization of, 44; congressional oversight of, 105–25; domestic, 83–103; foreign languages and, 39; high-technology approach to, 11; human, 11; Justice Department and, 29–30; law enforcement and, 33–34, 160; leadership and, 43; military operations and, 4, 52, 65, 128, 135; missed, 21–37; no-fault, 15; September 11 and, 58; September 11 and failure of, 4–6; sharing of, 15–16, 25, 35, 46; warnings and, 17, 50–51; war on terrorism and, 157

intelligence agencies: bin Laden and, 11; bureaucracy in, 5, 53–81; Congress and, 90–95; documents regarding problems in, 173–214; language training and, 62; warnings and, 47–49. *See also* Central Intelligence Agency; Defense Intelligence Agency; Federal Bureau of Investigation

Intelligence Authorization Act, 69

Intelligence Oversight Board, 72

Interagency Intelligence Committee on Terrorism, 48

Internal Security Division, 29, 30

International Relations and Information Center, 22

Internet, 72

Inter-Services Intelligence (ISI), 2

Iran: al Qaeda and, 42–46, 49–50, 165; bin Laden and, 12, 183

Iranian Revolutionary Guards Corps (IRGC), 45–46

Iraq: bin Laden and, 12; CIA covert operations in, 54; Khobar Towers and, 8; September 11 and, 162–65; terrorist attacks of, 161–62; United States and, 181–82

Iraqi National Congress (INC), 78

IRGC. *See* Iranian Revolutionary Guards Corps

ISI. *See* Inter-Services Intelligence

Islam: martyrs and, 23; Wahhabi, 9

Islamabad, Pakistan, 63

Islambuli, Shawqi, 55

Israel, 151, 152, 153

J-2. *See* Wilson, Thomas

Jalalabad, Afghanistan, 3

Japan, 23

Jarrah, Ziad Samir, 131, 144

Jeddah, Saudi Arabia, 144

John F. Kennedy Airport, 31

John Paul II, 22, 92

Joint Chiefs of Staff, 18

Justice Department: Baer investigation and, 54–55; bin Laden and, 18; FBI and, 96; FISA and, 32; Homeland Security department and, 124; intelligence and, 29–30; Internal Security Section of, 29; Office of Intelligence Policy Review, 29; politicization of, 29–30, 88; restrictions on intelligence agencies and, 29, 68–71, 95, 96

Kahane, Mehir, 27, 47
Kennedy, John F., 89
Kenya, 15, 130, 131
KGB, 90
Khaled, Leila, 152
Khalifa, Mohammed Jamal, 22
Khamenei, Ali, 44
Khartoum, Sudan, 7, 9–10, 12
Khobar Towers, bombing of, 8–9, 39
Korea, 75
Kuala Lumpur, Malaysia, 165
Kuwait, 162
Kuwaiti Interior Ministry, 11

Lake, Anthony, Baer investigation and, 53–55
Langley, Va., 5, 23
Langley Air Force Base, 155
language specialists. *See* foreign language training
Latin America, 75
Laurel, Md., 131–32
law enforcement, intelligence and, 33–34, 160
Lawrence Livermore National Laboratory, 124

leadership: CIA and, 66–68; intelligence and, 43; need for, 14
Lebanon, 144
Lee, Wen Ho, 30
Lehman, Richard, 109
letter bombs, 96
Liberation Tigers of Tamil Eelam (LTTE), 149
Lido Nominee, 163
Lindh, John Walker, 62, 167
London, England, 9, 31, 152
Lott, Trent, 77
Loy, Jim, 155
LTTE. *See* Liberation Tigers of Tamil Eelam

MacRobbie, Randy, 48
Major, David, 97
Malaysia, 25, 42, 165
Manila, Philippines, 21, 36
Martin, John L., 29, 30, 32
martyrs, Islam and, 23
Maryland, 131
al-Masari, Mohammad, 9
Masoud, Ahmad Shah, 2
McDill Air Force Base, 3
McFarlane, Robert, Taliban opposition and, 2–4
McVeigh, Timothy, 85
Mecca, 9
Mexico, 144
Middle East, 48
al-Midhar, Khalid, 45, 46, 131
military operations: against bin Laden, 18; clandestine, 170; intelligence and, 4, 52, 65, 128, 135
Millennium attacks, 60

Minihan, Kenneth A., 128–29, 133–34

Ministry of Intelligence and Security (MOIS), 12, 45, 53, 65

Minnesota, 30

Mohamed, Ali, 223

Mohamed, Khaflan Khamis, 224

Mohammed, Khalid Shaikh, 36, 55, 56

MOIS. *See* Ministry of Intelligence and Security

Monk, Paul, 36

Moqed, Majed, 131

Morell, Michael J., 74–75

Morris, Jim, 66

Moscow, Russia, 90, 127

mosques, 19

Moussaoui, Zacarias: arrest of, 85; background of, 232–33; indictment of, 228–56; investigation of, 30–33, 196–206; September 11 and, 32, 33, 85

Moynihan, Daniel Patrick, 112, 161

Msalam, Fahid Mohammed Ali, 223

Mueller, Robert S., III, 31; ACS and, 111–12; FBI reform and, 101–3; Phoenix memo and, 84–86; Senate Judiciary Committee and, 35–36

Mugniyah, Imad, 90

al-Muhajiroun, 84

Mukhabarat, 162

Murad, Abdul Hakim, terrorist activities of, 21–25

Nafi, Nafi Ali, 10

Nairobi, Kenya, 15, 47

Nasir, Mustaf. *See* Muhammed, Khalid Shaykh

National Commission on Terrorism, 143

National Imagery and Mapping Agency (NIMA), 128, 136, 170

National Islamic Front, 10

National Military Intelligence Association, 157

National Reconnaissance Office, 128, 135, 136, 170

National Security Act (1947), 167

National Security Agency (NSA): "Big Five" and, 14; bin Laden and, 11; congressional oversight of intelligence and, 107; funding for, 129; global terrorism and, 177; intelligence warnings and, 47–48; reorganization of, 135–37; September 11 and, 5; technical intelligence and, 133–37, 170; USS *Cole* bombing and, 51–52

National Security Council (NSC), 19, 53, 87, 157–58

National Terrorism Commission, 67

National Threat Assessment Center, 158

Nedzi, Lucien N., 107, 108

nerve gas, 19

The New Republic, 158

Newsweek, 163

New York (state), 25, 31

New York City, 27, 157

New York Post, 120

New York Times, 105, 107

Nicholson, Harold James, 66

Nigeria, 184

NIMA. *See* National Imagery and
Mapping Agency
Noriega, Manuel, 116
North, Gail, 131–32
North Alliance, 2
North Carolina, 25
North Korea, 135, 184
Nosair, El Sayyid, 27
NSA. *See* National Security Agency
NSC. *See* National Security Council
nuclear weapons, 23–24, 93

O'Brien, John, 153
Odeh, Mohammed Sadeek, 224
Office of Domestic Preparedness,
124
Office of Intelligence Policy
Review, 29
Office of Special Operations and
Low Intensity Conflict, 37
Office of Strategic Services, 80
Office of the Program Manager, 7
Okinawa, Japan, 23
Oklahoma City, Okla., 35
Oklahoma City bombing, 85
O'Neill, John P., 96
O'Neill, Michael J., 71, 72
Operation Solo, 90
al-Owhali, Muhammed Hassen, 47

Pakistan, 2, 22, 24, 25, 115
Palestinian Islamic Jihad, 9
Panama, 116
Pan Am Flight Academy, 30
Pappas, Aris A., 159, 160
Party of God, 161
Pashtuns, Taliban opposition and,
1–4

Pavitt, James L., CIA covert opera-
tions and, 78–80
Pearl Harbor, 36, 68, 80, 111
Pearl Harbor: Warning and Decision
(Wohlstetter), 68
Pecha, Bob, 49
Pentagon, 37; Al Adid and, 57; DIA
and, 42; Office of Special
Operations and Low Intensity
Conflict of, 37; September 11
attack on, 1
PENTBOM, 112
Perle, Richard, 165
Persian Gulf, 12, 18, 42
Peshawar, Pakistan, 3
PFIAB. *See* President's Foreign
Intelligence Advisory Board
Philippine National Police, 21, 25
Philippines, 21; al Qaeda in, 21–25;
intelligence information from,
207–14; United States and, 27
Phoenix memo, air terrorism and,
46, 83–86
Pickard, Thomas J., Phoenix memo
and, 84–85
Pike, Otis, 94, 107, 108–9
Pike committee, 94, 108, 110
Plum Island Animal Disease
Center, 125
Poland, 12
Pope, Robert, 53, 54
Port Angeles, Wash., 60
Port Sudan, Sudan, 9
Powell, Colin, 87
Prague, Czech Republic, 56, 162,
163
President's Foreign Intelligence
Advisory Board, 72

Prewitt, Gregg, 48–49
Proctor, Toris, 132
Project Bojinka, 22, 24, 25, 27

Qatar, 12
Qatari government, terrorist support by, 55–58
Qetta, Pakistan, 24

Rabin, Yitzhak, 152
radical Shiism, 12
Rahman, Assadullah, 47
Rahman, Omar Abdel, 47, 121–22
Rapp, Dave, 31
Rassan, Ahmed, 60
Razon, Avelino, 24
Reagan, Ronald, 2, 95, 112, 127
Redmond, Paul, 65
Red Sea, 9
Rendon, John W., 158
Rendon Group, 158
Reno, Janet, 29–30, 33, 97
Rescorla, Rick, September 11 heroism of, 139–41
Ressam, Ahmed, 225
Revell, Oliver B. "Buck," 97; September 11 and, 90–95
Rice, Condoleezza, 87, 121–22
Rice, Susan, 29
Ridge, Tom, 125
Ritchie, Joseph, 2–3
Riyadh, Saudi Arabia, 7, 11, 92, 144, 186
Rockefeller, Nelson, 107
Rockefeller Commission, 107
Rowley, Coleen, 31, 111; Moussaoui investigation and, 196–206
Rumsfeld, Donald, 76, 87, 118

Russia. *See* Soviet Union
Ryan, Mary, 144

Salim, Jabir, 162
Saudi Arabia: Islamic extremists in, 57; royal family in, 8; terrorist attacks in, 7–8, 14–15, 92, 186–87; United States and, 8
Saudi Arabia National Guard, 7
Saunders, Jay, 39–40, 42
Schelling, Thomas C., 68
Scheunemann, Randy, CIA covert operations and, 77–79
Scruggs, Richard, 29–30
Secret Service, 123
Senate Judiciary Committee, 35–36, 85
Senate Select Committee on Intelligence, 58, 90, 109
Senate Select Committee to Study Government Operations with Respect to Intelligence Activities, 107
Sensenbrenner, F. James, Jr., 141
September 11: air piracy and, 150; al Qaeda and, 1, 229–32; bin Laden and, 1, 58, 218, 225–26; events leading up to, 228–56; hijackers of, 232; history leading to, 90–95; Iraq and, 162–65; military and, 154–55; Moussaoui and, 33; Moussaoui investigation and, 32; origins of, 36
Serbia-Kosovo, 184
Sessions, William, 88–89
Shapiro, Howard M., 97
al-Shehhi, Marwan, 141, 144
"the sheikh." *See* bin Laden, Osama

Shelby, Richard, 62–63, 75
Shelton, Hugh, 18
Shias, 161, 164
Shields, Vince, 66
ships, terrorism on, 155–56
shoe bombs, 23
SIG-IC. *See* Special Investigative
　Group-Intelligence Command
"Significant Revelation of Abdul
　Hakim Al Hashim Murad," 24
Simon, James M., Jr., 159, 160
Skiff, Michael, 163
Slatkin, Nora, 71, 72
Smith, I. C., 99
Snider, L. Britt, 114, 118–20
Soba, Sudan, 10
Somalia, 92, 222
Sorodi, Afghanistan, 3
Soviet Union, 2, 78, 135, 159
Special Investigative Group-
　Intelligence Command (SIG-IC),
　23
Specter, Arlen, 86
Stainbrook, Mike, 43
Star Wars, 40
State Department: African bomb-
　ings and, 15; border security
　and, 145; INR of, 14, 47–48, 145,
　169; Sudan pharmaceutical fac-
　tory bombing and, 19; Taliban
　opposition and, 2
Steele, Robert, 77
The Strategy Machine (Downes), 111
Studies in Intelligence, 159
Sudan, 7; bin Laden and, 28–29;
　intelligence from, 28; National
　Islamic Front in, 10; pharmaceu-
　tical factory bombing in, 19, 29

Sufaat, Yazi, 46
Sunni Islam extremism, 12, 164
Swedan, Ahmed Salim, 223
Switzerland, 57
Szady, David, 32, 90, 110

Taas, Nap, 22
Tajiks, 2
Taliban: bin Laden and, 1, 219–20;
　Clinton and, 14; drug trade and,
　188; opposition to, 1–4
Tampa, Fla., 3
Tanzania, 15, 131
technical spying, 127–37
Tehran, Iran, 12
Tenet, George: CIA failures and, 5,
　60–62, 72, 118, 207; CIA field
　agents and, 65; Deutch Rules
　and, 69, 71; September 11 and,
　58–59; Sudan pharmaceutical
　factory bombing and, 19; war on
　terrorism and, 87
"Terror 2000: The Future Face of
　Terrorism," 37
terrorism: air, 150–56; CIA and, 10,
　34; Clinton's response to, 8,
　17–19; global, 177; information
　sharing and, 15–16; penetration
　of organizations of, 61; preven-
　tion of acts of, 7–11, 43; sponsors
　of, 8, 28; Taliban and, 1; training
　and, 18, 46; training camps for,
　18; war on, 9, 157–58; watch list
　for, 46
"Terrorist Busters," 35
Texas, 25
Tilelli, John H., Jr., 75
Time magazine, 224

"TIPOFF," 145
Torricelli, Robert G., 66
Transportation Department, 124
transportation system, terrorism and, 150–56
Treasury Department, 124
Turabi, Hassan, 10, 28
Turco, Fred, 54
Turkey, 42, 48
Turner, Stansfield, 62
TWA, 152

United Airlines, 24
United Arab Emirates, 144
United States: China and, 76; Communist Party in, 89; Iraq and, 181–82; nuclear power station in, 23–24; Philippines and, 27; Saudi Arabia and, 8; Taliban and, 1; terrorist attacks on, 92–95
University of Oklahoma, 58
USA Patriot Act, 32, 88
USS *Cole*: al Qaeda and, 92; bombing of, 39–42; CIA and, 60; intelligence failure and, 50–51; NSA and, 51–52; warning about, 50–51
Uzbeks, 2

Van Cleave, Michelle, 150–51
Venice, Fla., 141
videotape messages, 39, 44, 47, 80
Vietnam, 109, 135
Virginia, 5, 23

Wahhabi Islam, 9
Wallop, Malcolm, 112, 114

Warsaw Pact, 78
Washington (state), 60
Washington, D.C., 157, 37
Washington Post, 33, 36, 129
Washington Times, 74
Watson, Dale, 30–31, 88
Webster, William, 99
Weldon, Curt, 51
W Group, 15
Wiley, Winston P., 74, 76
Williams, Kenneth, Phoenix memo and, 83–86
Wilson, Thomas, 19, 42, 49
Wiser, Leslie, 98
Wisner, Frank, 114–15
Wohlstetter, Roberta, 68
Woolsey, R. James: Deutch Rules and, 68; FAA and, 154; Islamic extremists and, 164; language specialists and, 28; national security and, 161; September 11 and, 155; technical spying and, 134–35; terrorism investigations and, 87–88; U. S. intelligence and, 141
World Trade Center: first attack on, 11, 22, 25–27; September 11 attack on, 1
Yemen, 40, 43, 57
Yousef, Ramzi, 55; first World Trade Center bombing and, 22, 26; Murad conspiracy with, 24; in Philippines, 22; shoe bombs and, 23; terrorist attacks and, 23

Ziglar, James W., 145
Zubaydah, Abu, 84